Silent Voices, Untold Stories

Women Domestic Workers in Pakistan and their Struggle for Empowerment

Silent Voices, Untold Stories

Women Domestic Workers in Pakistan and their Struggle for Empowerment

Ayesha Shahid

OXFORD
UNIVERSITY PRESS

OXFORD
UNIVERSITY PRESS

Great Clarendon Street, Oxford OX2 6DP

Oxford University Press is a department of the University of Oxford.
It furthers the University's objective of excellence in research, scholarship,
and education by publishing worldwide in

Oxford New York

Auckland Cape Town Dar es Salaam Hong Kong Karachi
Kuala Lumpur Madrid Melbourne Mexico City Nairobi
New Delhi Shanghai Taipei Toronto

with offices in

Argentina Austria Brazil Chile Czech Republic France Greece
Guatemala Hungary Italy Japan Poland Portugal Singapore
South Korea Switzerland Turkey Ukraine Vietnam

Oxford is a registered trade mark of Oxford University Press
in the UK and in certain other countries

First published 2010

ISBN 978-0-19-547730-6

Typeset in Adobe Garamond Pro
Printed in Pakistan by
Kagzi Printers, Karachi.
Published by
Ameena Saiyid, Oxford University Press
No. 38, Sector 15, Korangi Industrial Area, PO Box 8214
Karachi-74900, Pakistan.

Dedicated to my parents

Sarwat Mohsin and Mohsin Ehsan

Thank you

for your unconditional love,
unflinching encouragement,
and constant belief in me
that kept me going over the years.

I am honoured to have you as my parents.

Contents

List of Tables

Table of International Treaties and Conventions

Convention against Trans-national Organized Crime, supplemented by the Protocol to Prevent, Suppress and Punish Trafficking in Persons, especially Women and Children. GA res. 55/25, annex II, 55 UN GAOR Supp. (No. 49) at 60, UN Doc. A/45/49 (Vol. I) (2001)

Convention for the Elimination of All Forms of Discrimination Against Women, adopted 18 December 1979, 1249 UNTS 13 (entered into force 3 Sept. 1981)

ILO Declaration on Fundamental Principles and Rights at Work, 1998 adopted at 86th Session, Geneva, 19 June 1998

ILO Discrimination Convention, (Employment and Occupation) 1958 (Number 111) adopted at 42nd Session, Geneva, 25 June 1958

ILO Equal Remuneration Convention, 195 (Number 100) adopted at 34th Session, Geneva, 29 June 1951

ILO Maternity Protection Convention, 1919 (Number 3) adopted at 12th Session, Geneva, 28 June 1919

ILO Maternity Protection Convention, 2000 (Number 183) adopted at 88th Session, Geneva, 15 June 2000

ILO Night Work Convention, 1919 (Number 4) adopted at 12th Session 1919

ILO Right to Organise and Collective Bargaining Convention, 1949

ILO Workers with Family Responsibilities Convention, 1981 (Number 156) adopted at 67th Session, Geneva, 23 June 1981

International Convention on the Protection of the Rights of All Migrant Workers and Members of Their Families, 1990. GA Res. 45/158, UN GAOR, 45th Sess., Supp. No. 49A, at 261, UN Doc. A/45/49 (1990) (entered into force 1 July 2003)

Recommendation 1523 (2001) adopted by the Parliamentary Assembly Committee, European Commission of Human Rights on 26 April 2001

Recommendation No. 1663 (2004), adopted by the Parliamentary Assembly Committee, European Commission on Human Rights on 22 June 2004

Slavery, Servitude, Forced Labour and Similar Institutions and Practices Convention 1926 60 LNTS 253, entered into force, 9 March 1927

Supplementary Convention on the Abolition of Slavery, the Slave Trade, and Institutions and Practices, Similar to Slavery, adopted at a Conference of Plenipotentiaries convened by Economic and Social Council Resolution 608 (XXI) of 30 April 1956 and adopted at Geneva on 7 September 1956 (entered into force 30 April 1957) in accordance with article 13

The Universal Declaration of Human Rights, adopted and proclaimed by General Assembly Resolution 217 A (III) of 10 December 1948

Table of Statutes

Employees Old Age Benefits Act, 1976

Labour Protection Policy 2005 (First Draft) Ministry of Labour, Manpower and Overseas Pakistanis, Government of Pakistan

Offence of Qazfh (Enforcement of Hadd) (vii of 1979)

Offences against Property (Enforcement of Hudood) Ordinance (vi of 1979)

Prohibition (Enforcement of Hadd) Ordinance (viii of 1979)

Provincial Employees Social Security Ordinance, 1965

The Factories Act, 1938

The Industrial Relations Ordinance, 2002

The Mines (Amendment) Act, 1973

The Mines Maternity Benefit Act, 1941

The Pakistan Penal Code, 1860

The Payment of Wages Act, 1936

The Shops and Establishment Ordinance, 1961

The West Pakistan Family Courts Act, 1964

The West Pakistan Hazardous Occupation Rules, 1963

The West Pakistan Industrial and Commercial Employment (Standing Order) Ordinance, 1964

The West Pakistan Maternity Benefit Ordinance, 1958

The West Pakistan Maternity Benefit Rules, 1961

West Pakistan Industrial and Commercial Employment Ordinance, 1968

Workmen's Compensation Act, 1923

Table of Case Law

Jibendra Kishore vs. Province of East Pakistan, PLD 1957 SC 9

Naseem Firdous vs. Punjab Small Industries Corporation, PLD 1995 Lah. 584

Pakistan International Airlines Corporation through Chairman and others vs. Samina Masood and Others, PLD 2005 SC 831

Shirin Dokht vs. Government of Pakistan, 1995 PLC (C.S) 251

Shrin Munir vs. Government of Punjab, PLD 1990 SC 295

Preface

Domestic work around the globe is considered as an under-valued and underpaid activity performed by the disadvantaged social groups of society. It is perceived as work with low economic value and an extension of unpaid household duties that hardly gets any recognition for the work performed. Traditionally domestic work in others' households has remained a principal way of earning a living for poor women. The vast literature on domestic work demonstrates that across the north-south divide, it is mostly women who are involved in domestic service, and it is this gendered nature of the work, which underestimates domestic service as having any value.[1] It also illustrates the role of gender, class, race, and ethnicity in placing domestic service at the bottom of the employment ladder. Women domestic workers (who migrate to these countries in search of jobs and better living) are employed by not only affluent families in the developed world but are also found working in their home countries in great numbers, particularly in developing countries for the middle class and the upper echelons of society.

It is interesting to note that all studies, irrespective of the country of origin, point to the inadequacy of a simple legal response to address the situation of women domestic workers. This appears to be the case even in the countries where legal systems are much well developed. Hence it can be argued that the problem is socio-legal, therefore all solutions must look beyond black letter law.

Pakistan is amongst those developing countries where most households employ women domestic workers. Domestic service is an unregulated, unorganized, and undervalued form of employment. Domestic workers are not included in the definition of the 'worker' in labour legislation. There is no law to regulate the relationship between employer and the domestic worker in Pakistan, thus a domestic worker does not exist as a person in labour law. As a result, domestic workers have no legal rights to a weekly rest day, maternity leave, and public holidays. In theory, they can bring a civil/criminal action, but in the absence of adequate labour law, they do not engage with the law or with the state on a daily basis in their lives, nor can they think of accessing courts due to their socio-economic situation in the country. In the absence of any labour legislative framework, women domestic workers are not able to claim any rights against their employers. There is also no specific complaint procedure available under labour law through which a domestic worker facing abuse could lodge a complaint. Domestic workers do not enjoy the same rights as the industrial workers, technical workers, sales persons and others in the informal employment sector, who are given protection under the labour laws of the country. In the absence of any legal framework, there is hardly any case law available specifically on domestic workers in Pakistan. Only recently two cases of abuse of child domestic labour have been reported in the press.[2] In both the cases, two young girls became victims of abuse due to indebtedness of their families to landlords. Only one case has been filed in the Supreme Court of Pakistan with the support of a human rights organization, the other family has not even been able to register a case with the police. These cases highlight the limits of law as a tool for empowerment.

Due to the existence of class hierarchies in the Pakistani society it is extremely difficult to challenge any abuse, more so if both parties are not of the same socio economic status. As employers, in comparison to the women in domestic service, are in a privileged position, they easily flout the law by using their money and social status. This is thus a probable explanation for non-registration at the police station in one of the above cases. Such cases also draw attention to the need for support structures without which it is unlikely that the law alone will provide any protection against exploitative conditions of work.

There are only oral agreements and no written contractual arrangements between the employer and the employee. Domestic service in Pakistan is also associated with bonded labour.[3] Families who have debts to pay to landlords in rural areas are also engaged in domestic service, to pay off their family debts. In this form of service, workers not only surrender their labour but also all control over their lives. It is for the landlord to decide who is going to work for him and he may send the domestic worker to his relatives or to other members of the family. In such situations women domestic workers, especially young girls are in a dangerous situation as they often become victims of sexual abuse.

Jobs are mostly acquired through friends, community, or family members working as domestics in other households. In the case of global/ migrant domestic workers there is a network of employment agencies helping women find jobs, thus creating a labour market and some standardization of jobs with respect to wages, working hours, and tasks. In Pakistan any such network of employment agencies is almost non-existent, therefore domestic workers have to find jobs on their own or depend on friends and kin to find jobs for them.

Domestic service in Pakistan has also got the element of migration. Chronic poverty, landlessness, and natural disasters such as droughts and floods are compelling many rural residents to migrate to the urban areas to seek work. Other push factors include debts payments and a lack of viable livelihood options. When women from such poor households move to urban areas with their male family members they start working as domestic workers in other households as that is the only employment area for which they have some skills.

Women domestic workers are employed as full-time, part-time, and live-in domestic workers. The wage structure varies according to the localities where they work, the economic status of the employer and the nature of jobs they perform. Those who work for upper class families are slightly better paid as compared to those who work for middle-class families. In Pakistan, hiring of women domestic workers also represents the reinforcement and replication of gender inequalities: for instance women domestic workers are given less than half the wages that male workers in the same occupation receive. A male cook, cleaner, or a guard get a higher salary as compared to a woman domestic worker doing the same work. Similarly, a male domestic worker would not do any extra work whereas a woman though hired for a single job, would be expected to undertake additional chores.

As domestic work includes the traditional female roles, it is also not recognized as a 'job'. This gender bias and inequality of treatment has also been discussed by Rollins (1985, p. 23) who argues that 'the personal nature of this relationship partly develops from the fact that the work done by domestic is a work which could otherwise be done by the employer herself.' The responsibilities assigned to domestic workers are always seen as 'women's work' that is passed on from a woman to a waged worker. This relationship between the employers and their working class domestic workers shows how these privileged women exploit their domestic servants. It clearly demonstrates that women from the upper or middle classes turn a blind eye towards a system that creates class hierarchies and reinforces patriarchy. By shifting their responsibilities to other women, they reinforce gender stereotypes of housework and thus escape some of the challenges of patriarchy by using the labour of women who belong to the lowest rungs of society.

It is also interesting to note that domestic service stands at the boundary between the public and private sphere. The public sphere includes waged work, labour market and the institutions whereas the private consists of the home linked with kin and family. The domestic workers provide waged work but within the context of the household. For them the private territory of the employer counts as public domain. However, one of the reasons why some women prefer to work as domestic workers than in any other employment sector in the public sphere is that a household is considered a more secure place. Similarly, from the employer's point of view most of employers prefer to have women as their domestic workers because Pakistani society is a segregated society where it is not considered appropriate to allow a male outsider into the privacy of the home. This shows the concepts of women's honour, *purdah*, or segregation between men and women, and sanctity of home at play even at the level of running the day-to-day household chores.

As domestics work within the privacy of a home, it has also become an excuse for the state to not interfere in the so-called 'private sphere'. This division between the personal and the public adds to the vulnerability of women domestic workers because their work is a hidden form of employment performed within the four walls of other households, which leads to their isolation and invisibility. This dichotomy further leads to the devaluation of work performed within the private sphere.

In Pakistan there are various social classes and there is much disparity among these classes. The unequal treatment faced by women domestic workers is an outcome of class discrimination and an integral part of the patriarchal structures of the society. These women belong to the lower working class and are looked down upon in the society. They are expected to perform jobs that are considered menial. These workers are expected to work in a certain way and receive a certain type of treatment, which most people think is not wrong. Individually there may be many examples of charitable treatment, such as providing them with enough food or clothing, helping them send their children to schools, and financial help in case of sickness, emergency or mishap. However, when it comes to their well-being in an organized manner (either in the form of formal job contracts or under any law) people are usually sceptical. An obvious reason is that the upper class does not want their workers to be aware of their rights or to be protected by law, because they fear that awareness about their rights and legal cover might encourage their uprising against the rich and the powerful. Secondly, it is a matter of conflict of interest, because if this sector is regularized and legal protection is given to these workers, the upper classes will not be able to use their services by paying meagre salaries, nor would domestic workers be at the disposal of employers who could throw them out of jobs whenever they want.

Last but not the least there are no organizational support structures available for them and as a result their bargaining abilities are inadequate and they have a very limited or almost no choice but to work according to the terms and conditions laid down by the employers. To empower women domestic workers in Pakistan collective action and more concerted efforts in terms of networking and organizing them are needed. There are women's organizations and unions in other employment sectors including unions of industrial workers, women in fisheries etc, therefore setting up organizations for women in domestic service would not be an exception.[4]

My interest in women and employment issues stems from my experience of carrying out a survey on women in the industrial sector in NWFP.[5] While working in this area I realized that women domestic workers as a group in the informal sector have hardly received any scholarly, governmental or media attention.[6] Despite belonging to the largest employment category, these women continue to work at abysmally low salaries that bear little relation to the nature of their work. The long working hours, absence of off-days and exploitative working conditions of domestic workers have neither been highlighted nor attempts made to address key issues affecting their life and work.

On a more personal note, I want to share my experience with the readers which reflects the stories of thousands of women domestic workers in Pakistan who serve middle-class and upper-class households. Reliance on domestic workers is very much a part of the family setup in Pakistan as most of the families I know have domestic workers. Since my early childhood, our household has employed many domestic workers whose ages range from fifteen to sixty years. These women domestic workers have worked for my family, extended family, my neighbourhood and in my friends' households. They work in different capacities as live-in workers, who spend their entire lives serving their employers, as well as full-time and part-time workers.[7] My childhood memories are filled with the love and care given by our maid, Poshanae. The bond between us grew over the years and developed into an unconditional trust and confidence in each other. After my marriage and with two young children, I was finding it difficult to cope with my professional career as well as responsibilities at home. Poshanae again came to my rescue although she herself did not take up the job this time. It was her daughter and granddaughter who came to work for me as domestic workers, because on the one hand due to her age Poshanae could no longer undertake household chores, on the other, her daughter and granddaughter needed work to support their families.[8] I must confess here that, despite their valuable services they were not paid according to what would be the minimum wage. There was no formal job contract or fixed working hours. At the same time despite my claim to treat them as family members, both sides have not been able to remove the ever-present barriers of class and somehow these differences continue to exist creating a distance amongst us. By claiming them to be part of the family, we exploited their loyalty and emotional attachment in addition to the physical labour for which we paid them not what they actually deserved. Poshanae's case also shows that domestic work has become an intergenerational form of labour performed by different generations of women of the same family.

Drawing upon the findings of a socio-legal study about women, law and empowerment this monograph attempts to highlight the experiences of women domestic workers like Poshanae in Pakistan. The monograph fills the gap in existing literature by providing information about the profile, nature, working and living conditions of women domestic workers. It provides a starting point towards an understanding of the situation of women in domestic service by listening to their voices and lived experiences. By using feminist legal perspectives, Islamic perspectives on women's work and legal pluralism, the present study questions the efficacy of law as a tool for empowering women domestic workers in their struggle against exploitative treatment in the workplace. It advances the argument that women's lives are shaped by sharp gender and socio-economic disparities leading to unequal power relations vis-à-vis their employers, state and society. Access to justice through formal legal system is very often contingent upon the socio-economic position of the users. Women in domestic service have to negotiate the barriers of poverty and inequality before being able to employ the law as their ally. For an effective implementation of law, it is pertinent to look into non-legal strategies so that access to justice for women domestic workers in Pakistan could be made possible. As a critique of the impact of legality, it raises questions regarding the ways in which legislation can improve the position of women domestic workers. To what extent can formal legal mechanisms provide protection to women domestic workers in Pakistan? What factors are at play that may limit domestic workers' scope for legal action? Considering the law as a discourse, what could be a future strategy for bringing about a social change in the case of women domestic workers in

Pakistan? In light of these questions, the role of the law is re-examined by exploring the relationship between law, gender, and empowerment.

Grounded theory methodology is followed to collect empirical data on domestic service in Pakistan. Semi-structured group and individual interviews have been carried out at four sites in Karachi and Peshawar, Pakistan. A few case studies have also been included to substantiate some of the major themes arising during fieldwork. Listening to voices of women in domestic service has provided an opportunity to uncover the hidden lives of women domestic workers who work in the privacy of homes. It also explores the nature of domestic service, dynamics of employer-employee relations and complexities of class, gender and multiple identities affecting these relationships.

The monograph finally argues that in the presence of plural legal frameworks formal law alone cannot empower women in domestic service. Therefore, for an effective implementation of the law it is equally pertinent to look into non-legal strategies so that access to justice can be made possible for these women.

NOTES

1. Studies carried out in South Africa, India, Bangladesh, United States of America, United Kingdom, Thailand, Gulf countries to name a few suggest, that in developed and developing countries it is mostly women who are engaged as domestic workers. They work for extremely low wages and in unsafe, exploitative work conditions. Migration of domestic workers from developing countries to developed countries world has gained momentum in the past ten to fifteen years and compared to local workers these are comparatively educated women from urban areas. They are over-qualified as domestic workers.
2. *The News*, 10 November 2006, p. 4, and *Dawn*, 8 November 2006, p. 16.
3. 'Rapid Assessment Studies of Bonded Labour in Pakistan.' 2004. A study conducted by the Bonded Labour Research Forum in collaboration with the Ministry of Labour, Manpower and Overseas Pakistanis Government of Pakistan and International Labour organization.
4. These include All Karachi Labour and Hosiery Garments Labour Association, Working Women Forum and Fisher Folk Forum.
5. In 2001, I carried out a research study on women industrial workers in Peshawar district. The purpose of this study was to examine the extent to which existing employment legislation in Pakistan provides protection to women industrial workers and how far these women workers have been able to access justice. To assess the situation on ground interviews were carried out with women industrial workers, working in various industrial units at Hayatabad industrial estate.
6. For the first time in Pakistan the issue of domestic workers was raised by Ali, S.S. and Khattak, S. in their paper 'Domestic Servants and the Need for Legislation: The Case of the North-West Frontier Province' published in the report on 'The Workshop on Women and Employment Legislation in Pakistan 11-13 February 1993' organized by

the British Council in collaboration with the Ministry of Women Development, 1993. After that, there was a long gap and the issue was not addressed by activists and NGOs in Pakistan. Only recently in 2004 two small studies have been carried out one in Karachi by an NGO called Lawyers for Human Rights Association and another by Working Women Group a Lahore-based NGO.

7. There are three broad categories of women domestic workers (1) live-in workers, (2) full-time workers, i.e. women who work from morning till evening, and (3) part-time workers, i.e. women who work for few hours daily and perform only one or two chores like either dishwashing or cleaning or some of them work on alternate days or once or twice in a week like women who only do the laundry.
8. Domestic work as an intergenerational activity has been discussed in part three of this book.

Acknowledgements

To God, I thank for His blessings and for guiding me to bring this colossal task to fruition.

This academic ambition and the idea of publishing it in the form of a monograph could not have been achieved without the meticulous guidance of my supervisor and mentor Professor Shaheen Sardar Ali, who is an institution in herself. She has always been a role model and a source of inspiration to me. My association with her goes far beyond that of a supervisor and researcher. She has always inspired me as a person, as an academic scholar and as a colleague at the Faculty of Law, University of Peshawar, Pakistan. I express my deep gratitude to her for her valuable advice and critical analysis that helped in shaping this piece of work. Her maternal instincts and inexhaustible optimism never let me give up, even when the task seemed most daunting. For her, an acknowledgment cannot be a substitute for the endless support and confidence in me to achieve my goals over the years.

The monograph could not have been written without the generous support of women domestic workers in Pakistan. I owe an unlimited debt of gratitude to them for generously sharing their experiences and life stories with me. This study would not have been possible without their valuable input. I also ask forbearance of all other women in domestic service who have not been explicitly mentioned but have provided an important background to the study. This monograph is also a tribute to Poshanae Babo, my mother's domestic helper who served my family for thirty years with honesty, hard work, love, and care. She passed away in 2008 and will always be in our thoughts and prayers.

This monograph began as a doctoral thesis for the School of Law, University of Warwick, UK. I would like to take this opportunity to extend my thanks to the University of Warwick for awarding the Warwick Postgraduate Fellowship to me which led to the completion of this academic ambition. I would also like to express my thanks to Professor Lee Bridges (Former Dean, Warwick Law School and Chair Graduate Studies) and Dr Peter Byrd, Senior Tutor for providing funding for my fieldtrips. At Warwick, I am thankful to Professor Upendra Baxi, Professor

John McEldowney, Professor Abdul Paliwala, Professor Shirin Rai, Ann Stewart, Dr Reena Patel and Dr Helen Toner for their support and guidance. My particular thanks go to Dr George Meszaros, Ngeyi Kanyongolo, Celine Tan, Mamman Lawan and Zara Ali Khan for their valuable criticism and suggestions while I was writing the thesis.

I also want to express my sincere thanks to Professor Anne Hellum, Women's Law Institute, University of Oslo, Norway, Professor Javaid Rehman Cheema, School of Social Sciences and Law, Brunel University and Dr Siobhan Mullaly for sharing their ideas and expertise with me as well as for their support and encouragement. I am also thankful to all colleagues at the Law School, University of Hull in particular Professor Lindsay Moir, Professor Mike Feintuck, Professor Gerry Johnstone and Professor Patrick Birkinshaw for their support.

I appreciate the time that many organizations and individuals took to share their expertise with me. Many of the views expressed during discussions have been incorporated into this monograph. I am extremely thankful to Justice Majida Rizwi former chairperson National Commission on the Status of Women, Pakistan (NCSW) for sparing her precious time for an interview as well as for giving me the publications of NCSW. I would personally like to thank Barrister Nausheen Ahmad for her time and arranging my meetings with women domestic workers in Bhit Islands, Karachi. I am also thankful to Barrister Danish Zuberi for facilitating interviews with her colleagues from War Against Rape (WAR). Many thanks to Ayesha Khan, from Collective for Social Science and Research (CSSR) for sharing her views and findings of her study on bonded labour in Pakistan. I also owe a special thanks to Dr Fatima Hasan, Director Old Age Benefit Institute and to Mr Karamat Ali and his staff at Pakistan Institute for Education and Labour Research (PILER) for their time and for allowing me to use their library resources and for providing access to PILER's research projects. My special thanks to Rekha Narullah for sharing her reading materials and experiences with me. I am also thankful to Ameena Saiyid, Managing Director, Oxford University Press, Pakistan for publishing my monograph.

In Peshawar, individual and collective thanks are owed to Ms Rubina Khilji, Director, Gender Studies Centre, University of Peshawar, Mr Afrasiyab Khattak and Mr Kamran Arif from Human Rights Commission of Pakistan, Ms Rakshanda Naz and her staff at Aurat Foundation, Peshawar. I am also thankful in particular to Dr Saba Khattak, Director Sustainable Development Policy Institute Islamabad, Ms Mussarat Qadim Deputy Director, Women's Political Participation

Programme, Sadiya Hamdani, Programme Officer at ILO Liaison Office and Mr Hasan at Ministry of Labour, Manpower and Overseas Pakistanis, Islamabad for their time and support.

Family and friends are a source of emotional support. I feel fortunate that I always received it from both. First of all I am grateful to my parents Sarwat and Mohsin Ehsan who taught me to strive for knowledge than for monetary gains. I also owe them thanks for inculcating in me respect for dignity of labour. Throughout the writing process my loving brother Ali and his wife Saima encouraged me and extended their support to look after my children. I am also thankful to my cousins Zheela and Sana for extending their hospitality during my field visits to Pakistan. It is also a pleasure to express my wholehearted thanks to our friends Sardar Ali Sahib, Rubina and Javed and Leong and Fuleen for their thoughtfulness for my family.

Words fail to express my appreciation of my husband Shahid, who has been so supportive throughout the years. Without him I could not have even imagined completing this ambition in life. Thank you again for your love, dedication for the family and persistent confidence in me.

Finally, my adorable daughters deserve special mention. They are the greatest comforts of my life. Aiman and Roshanae thanks for your love and for being such cooperative and considerate daughters. I hope you will forgive your *Ami* for not giving you the quality time and attention during the past four years that you genuinely deserved.

Part I

The image of law, created by legal centralist approaches, is that formal codified law is the only tool for enforcing rights and protecting the vulnerable.[1] However, this portrayal of law contradicts the ground realities. Law does not appear only in the form of a set of codified rules but also as informal rules such as customary norms and religious traditions, which shape and influence the process of access to justice and implementation of formal laws.

Part I of this study provides the basis for initiating a discussion on the efficacy of law as an effective tool for empowerment of women in domestic service in Pakistan. Based on non-essentialist perspectives, Chapter 1 draws up a theoretical framework by following the arguments advanced by legal feminists, third world feminists, Islamic feminists and legal pluralists and by adopting these interdisciplinary views, this study takes a broader view of law as 'process' and a site for 'discursive struggle'. It attempts to expose the gendered nature of law and its limitations in terms of its effective implementation and access to justice. Insights from third world feminist perspectives draw attention to the fact that women have layered identities in the form of their ethnic, religious and class backgrounds which cannot be ignored. The discussion on 'woman's agency' seeks to dismiss the notion of considering women as always passive victims by emphasising women's strengths highlighted through their struggle and resistance to exploitative working conditions.

The section on Islamic feminist perspectives by using Quranic verses, Hadith literature and examples from early Islamic history reflect that equality, non-discrimination and dignity of labour are the main message of Islam. However, these principles are not followed in reality and despite the fact that countries like Pakistan have incorporated Islamic provisions in the constitution, in practice these are completely ignored. This chapter also seeks to engage in a discussion on legal pluralism as Pakistani society is legally pluralistic where different sets of norms co-exist and play a pivotal role in women's lives.

Chapter 2 highlights the nature and conditions of paid domestic work in some of the North and South countries. The literature reviewed has helped in drawing linkages between the situation of women in domestic service in Pakistan and those in other parts of the world. It also draws attention to the fact that in countries where laws have been framed for the protection of domestic workers, these laws remain largely ineffective, mainly due to the nature of the job itself, which is difficult to regulate, and the socio-economic position of women in domestic service.

1

Theoretical Perspectives on Women, Law, and Empowerment

INTRODUCTION

This chapter sets out the theoretical framework for research on women domestic workers in Pakistan. These workers are not given any protection under the labour laws of the country. To explore whether black letter law can be a tool for empowerment of women domestic workers, this chapter attempts to analyse the law as a discourse. It draws inspiration from non-essentialist perspectives including feminist theories relating to law as a 'process' and law as a 'site for discursive struggle'. Legal pluralism and Islamic feminist perspectives on women's work (in light of the principle sources of Islamic law and its interpretative techniques) are used to link these discussions to the main research hypothesis, i.e. to question the efficacy of the law as an effective measure in bringing empowerment to women domestic workers in Pakistan. The main objective is to deconstruct the role of the law in empowering women domestic workers by exploring the relationship between law, gender and empowerment in a plural legal framework.

WOMEN, LAW AND EMPOWERMENT: DEBATES WITHIN FEMINIST LEGAL SCHOLARSHIP

This section examines the relationship between women, law, and empowerment in light of feminist legal scholarship. Feminist legal scholarship benefits from the various waves of feminism, however it owes its existence to the second wave of feminism that started in the 1960s.[2] Like feminist theory in general, feminist legal theory has different strands—liberal, radical, and post-modernist.[3] The liberal perspective expects the law to become gender neutral if women's experiences and perspectives are included. Liberal feminists also promote the ideal of global sisterhood by ignoring the religious, racial, cultural, and ethnic diversities among women around the world.[4] The radical feminist strand on the other hand views the law as purely masculine, where legal institutions and the entire legal discourse reflect male concerns and priorities and can never incorporate the experiences of women.[5] Post-modernist feminists consider equality as a social construct that reflects patriarchal ideas and needs reconstruction.[6] This strand is anti-essentialist as it does not focus on the single category of a 'woman', rather it focuses on the situated realities of women and emphasises that there is no single theory of equality that will work for the benefit of all women.[7]

Feminist legal scholarship is critical of mainstream legal discourse which in its analysis of the law fails to take account of women's voices, experiences and practices, and questions whether formal/state/secular law situated within the patriarchal, capitalist, plural legal settings can provide remedy for the grievances and sufferings of women.[8] Can such law provide physical and economic security to women and can women use law as a strategy for social change? By raising such questions feminist legal scholarship engages with the law not as a set of formal rules but as a discourse to expose the gendered content of the law, which leaves women in a disadvantaged position. Feminist legal theory sets out to show how apparently gender neutral laws can treat men and women differently and the way the law constructs gender by invoking certain stereotype images of woman, which she must identify herself with.[9] Legal feminists within the western and non-western societies contest such images of women.[10] They consider such law as androcentric, based on male values and reflected in legal rules and legal institutions. This view of the law as 'male' suggests that it differentiates between men and women to such an extent that it works to the disadvantage of women by allocating them fewer resources, judging them through different standards and denying them equal opportunities. The law also fails to recognise the harm it does to women because it is more concerned with advancing the interests of men.

The idea of the law as male is strongly propagated by MacKinnon in her theory of sexual exploitation.[11] Focusing on women's sexuality in the area of rape, sexual harassment and pornography, she theorises the law as 'male' and 'sexist' not gender neutral and subconsciously addressing only the 'essential male'.[12] MacKinnon argues that all women experience oppression at the hands of patriarchal power and this power in law is expressed in the form of male laws and male systems of justice. MacKinnon further argues that the question of equality should be addressed by analysing male/female power relationship. In her view the unequal power relationship is due to the continuous existence of male supremacy.

The task of feminism is to unmask women's subordination and lack of power by challenging the male dominated structures of society. MacKinnon seeks to dismantle the dominance/subordinate relation through empowering women's voice with a view to achieve legal, social, and political equality.[13] An understanding of this unequal power relationship helps in reshaping laws and legal practices enabling women to use the law in their struggle against inequalities within the workplace. The present study also attempts to understand the patriarchal structures in order to find out how laws can be framed to provide protection to women in domestic service in Pakistan.

Smart disagrees with the view of law as being sexist and male.[14] For her such approaches could be dangerous as these presume law to be unitary and always representative of male values.[15] Smart views the law as gendered in its visions and practices. She critically examines how the law constitutes the gender and becomes a site in which gendered positions and identities are articulated.[16] Smart advices us to decentre the law by not according so much power to it as in her words:

> There are other power structures operating at the same time for which law alone is not sufficient. For example the issue of women's low pay cannot be resolved by achieving equality provisions for equal wages in law unless we address this issue in a wider context of segregation in job markets, racism, division of public/private and undervaluation of women's work.[17]

However she does not suggest a complete disengagement from the law but wants us to look into 'other non legal strategies and local struggles' rather than simply focusing on law reform.[18]

Dahl, a pioneer of Women's Law approach argues that women's actual lived realities and experiences in areas such as sexuality, birth, domestic work and care must be taken as a starting point to examine the relationship between women and law.[19] She further argues that although male domination in the society is the root cause of discrimination in law, yet law 'could also be a fertile soil for the cultivation of rules' that would help in improving the position of women and bringing changes in the relationship between the two sexes.[20] Dahl is of the view that a deeper understanding of the law from a feminist perspective must be applied in all existing legal areas as well as in developing new concepts for understanding issues in 'birth law', 'paid work law' etc.[21] She refers to it as 'the perspective of one looking upwards from below to see both law, reality and morality from women's point of view.'[22] By taking women's experience as the starting point of analysis, she also emphasizes the need to understand the impact of customary practices and public opinion.

Chunn and Lacombe tracing back the history of Canadian feminist approaches to law, analyse the diverse and contradictory ways in which law interacts with other institutions and constructs womanhood.[23] They argue that a social constructionist approach to feminist legal theory is needed that should take account of social context, structures and history.[24] The authors examine how gendered legal identities in Canada are negotiated by covering a wide-range of topics including culture, nationalism, pornography, prostitution, lesbian parenting, and corporate and tax law. In their view, law is a hegemonic process rather than a homogeneous force that coerces or determines human activity or subjectivity.[25]

Jhappan provides an insight into the merits and demerits of feminist engagements with law in the backdrop of constitutional litigation on the Canadian Charter of Rights and Freedoms 1982.[26] In her view, achieving justice should be the primary normative principle and discursive frame underpinning feminist litigation strategy hence she calls for winding up 'equality' in favour of 'justice'.[27]

Stewart states that in post-colonial societies state-based legal strategies have not been very effective.[28] In the presence of local cultural practices women have found it very difficult to claim their formal rights to 'equality' and 'non-discrimination'. This links to the main research question of the present study, whether a formal law would increase women's ability to access justice and claim their legal rights.

Kapur and Cossman, following Smart's line of argument, examine possibilities and limitations of the role of law in bringing social change for women in India.[29] In their work they look generally at the legal and constitutional implications of the Hindu Right in India and in particular, how it has affected the status of women in familial matters. By probing the role of familial ideology in law they argue how women can use the law to challenge the present patriarchal, traditional norms and alter their status in society for the better.[30] They critically examine how law constitutes gender by focusing on more localized and specific discourses in particular contexts. In their writings they address such tensions as to why law has failed to deliver gender justice and argue that law must not be viewed as an instrument of change or an instrument of oppression rather, a more sophisticated analysis must be developed to understand the complex and contradictory nature of law.[31] They are of the view that 'law needs to be revisioned as a site for discursive struggle where competing visions of the world and of women's place therein have been and continue to be fought out.'[32]

Agnes critiques demands for a uniform civil code in India arguing that statutory changes made in the Personal Laws of religious communities in India are half-hearted attempts towards gender equality.[33] She also warns that for a diverse religious and ethnic society like India, a uniform civil code may not be a workable solution. Her concerns are similar to those raised by Jhapann in the Canadian context who questions the effectiveness of the Canadian Charter of Rights and Freedoms as a progressive political and legal strategy for improving gender equality.

Similarly, Basu in her analysis of legal reforms under the Hindu Marriage Law in India observes that legal reforms have had very limited impact in improving the status of women in Hindu society as most of their problems persist and remain unresolved in the presence of social evils that could not be eradicated by law alone.[34] Laws could only be effective if they succeed in removing illiteracy, ignorance, creating awareness and changing social attitudes.[35] Basu also pinpoints the failure of the Widow Remarriage Act 1856 as most of the upper caste widows did not avail of the legislation regarding remarriage and secondly the Act did not improve women's economic position because upon their remarriage women were deprived of the right to retain their deceased husbands' property.[36]

Mukhopadhyay observes that the gap between formal rights and the actual status of disadvantaged groups has not decreased, and laws have not been able to serve their purpose of delivering gender justice or bringing any substantive improvements in the conditions on the ground.[37] The reason presented is that the apparent gender neutralization process of law does not take into consideration the lived experiences of women, nor does this process consider the existence of other norms and orders that control and govern women's lives in the private sphere of family or public domain.

Narasimhan too criticizes state policies and laws that have failed in alleviating the position of rural Indian women belonging to scheduled castes.[38] Criticizing state laws and policies, she draws attention to the non-political voluntary schemes and appreciates the performance of the 'Action for Welfare and Awakening in Rural Environment Scheme' initiative that not only helped improve health and education levels and increase in wages among women, but played a significant role in raising awareness among women.[39] Agnes argues that in India, laws on violence against women, rape, domestic violence, as well as dowry-related violence fail to provide any protection to women as they are structured to operate against the larger interests of women.[40] In her view oppression cannot be tackled by merely providing legislation. In all cases (of the above mentioned forms of violence) legislation remained ineffective because judicial decisions were influenced by patriarchal values. As a result legislation remained a token gesture by the government to provide protection to women.[41]

Ali, Jilani, Zia, Shaheed, and Jehangir have attempted to expose the limits of law in Pakistan.[42] They are of the view that neither litigation nor legal reforms have been able to deliver gender justice. Ali assesses the limits of law as an effective tool for empowering women by using the example of a legal literacy course run for women in Pakistan.[43] The course participants found the course to be useful in terms of raising awareness about laws, but at the same time they were conscious of the fact that despite having the knowledge and awareness of laws, women still have to follow the status quo and are unable to use it for their empowerment.[44] Ali is of the view that it could be gauged from the responses of the course participants that formal laws can only be effectively used for the advantage of women if a 'multi-pronged hybrid' approach is used. She further argues that the presence of religious and customary norms and the public/private dichotomy in a plural legal society like Pakistan hinders women's access to justice through courts, impairing the use of formal law as an effective mechanism for empowerment.[45]

Jilani maintains the law-making process and its implementation has been carried out through institutions that have always remained male dominated whether it is the legislature, police or judiciary.[46] These institutions have always served the interests of men and protected the patriarchal privilege; thus access to justice and implementation of laws has always been difficult for women in Pakistan.[47] The male face of law, Jilani insists, should not preclude women from using it and for the application of law social institutions need to be changed. She is of the view that if law is made to overcome injustice then social institutions should not be able to override it by appealing to social norms and values or religion.[48]

Zia is of the view that as most of the legislators have feudal, industrial, military, and bureaucratic backgrounds, they have the power to control and implement the law.[49] Any attempt to ensure minorities' rights is viewed by these powerful groups as a potential threat to the interests of the ruling elite.[50] This situation raises further doubts about the effectiveness of law as a tool for empowerment because any effort to protect women domestic workers' rights under the law would be considered in direct conflict with the interests of the powerful ruling elite. Zia also draws attention to the presence of religious parties and groups which along with the powerful elite play a pivotal role in the implementation of discriminatory laws in Pakistan. These laws have been misinterpreted in the name of Islam by religious ideologues and have always been detrimental to women.[51]

In her work, Shaheed discusses the use of religion in Muslim societies to justify male domination.[52] The law in these societies reflects the patriarchal ideologies and existing power structures that are embodied in the legally defined rights and relationships between different segments of society.[53] She also pinpoints the presence of other parallel legal systems which co-exist with the formal law. However, unfortunately when there is an option available between the two, the one that is more disadvantageous to women is implemented. For instance, in Pakistan the practice of giving a wife verbal divorce is prohibited under the Muslim Family Law Ordinance 1961, but it is socially accepted and practiced by referencing Islamic doctrine.[54] Similarly, in the case of rape and adultery the formal law, that is more discriminatory against women is followed.[55] These examples suggest the ineffectiveness of law, whether formal or informal, when it comes to providing protection and support to women.

Jehangir and Jilani examine the impact of the Hudood Ordinances on women in Pakistan and argue how its discriminatory nature serves as a powerful weapon in the hands of men to subjugate women.[56] These laws and their rigid interpretation in the name of Islam have not only facilitated oppression and sexual violence against women to an alarming degree, but also seriously impeded women's chances of obtaining justice. Women in Pakistan reacted strongly to changes in the Islamic law of rape in 1979, because it posed a direct challenge. This paved the way for a strong women's movement against discriminatory legislation in Pakistan.[57] It also helped in creating awareness about the plight of women and in mobilizing women to evolve their own strategies to build resistance against discrimination.[58] At the same time, implementation of discriminatory laws has made women suspicious of the law as a mechanism for attaining justice.

Aubert in his study of the Norwegian Housemaid Law of 1948, raises the issue that in cases of housemaids in particular, it is important to study the variables that influence compliance or non-compliance with the law.[59]

In his view some of the main reasons for non-compliance were that this piece of legislation was concerned with a group of individuals who hardly had any connexion with law and public authorities.[60] The law was also interfering in an area which is traditionally considered to be in private domain and where the worker was apparently regarded as part of the family. Aubert also argues that implementation of law became more difficult as the language of law was beyond the comprehension of domestic workers and there were no inter-mediatory agencies which could help them in accessing justice. He further argued that those rules, which were fairly well known, happened to be those where the law corresponded to existing customs. The less known rules were those where the law on housemaids had a reformatory function and lacked sanction in custom.[61]

A more recent study by Sverdrup of the same Norwegian Domestic Servant Act with reference to *au pairs* in Norway draws our attention to the interpersonal nature of this form of work and suggests a complete revision of law in light of concrete lived realities of the work experience of *au pairs*.[62] In her study, Sverdrup argues that due to the interpersonal nature of domestic work, the application of this Act can be more harmful than providing any relief to *au pairs*. Legal limitations can conflict with the personal adjustments that are made between the employer and employee. For instance, law may not be able to protect an *au pair* from a continual extension of duties; insistence on exact provisions of law might therefore not work in favour of the *au pair* as the employer can become more inflexible in exercising control over them.[63] In such situations it is better for *au pairs* to depend on the employer showing consideration in some other way or compensating those extra hours of work because an exact counter balance of services is not possible in a job that is both interpersonal and contractual in nature at the same time.[64]

The issues raised by Aubert and Sverdrup are a matter of concern for this study as it questions the efficacy to provide an effective remedy for improving the condition of domestic workers in Pakistan. By raising these issues the study does not suggest that law is not required at all. It actually suggests that the black letter law can serve as a standard setting norm whose presence would provide legislative cover to domestic workers by recognising them as 'workers' and for improving their working conditions including working hours, wages, paid leave etc. However, for an effective implementation of such a law and for making access to justice possible for a vulnerable group of women in domestic service, certain other avenues need to be explored as reliance on law alone will not serve the purpose.

ENHANCING ACCESS TO JUSTICE THROUGH LAW REFORM: A CRITICAL OVERVIEW

Prashar in her work on family law reform in India argues that

> Law has a symbolic value: symbolic legislation can be of liberating value as it can provide a focus around which forces of change can mobilize....instead of dismissing law reforms as a means of achieving equality for women, it is more productive to realize the limitations of law and have appropriate expectations that law reform by itself will be insufficient to change society and symbolic value.[65]

Several instances can be cited to suggest that all over the world during the struggle for women's rights, legislation was enacted to respond to the demands of equality and justice for women. Married Women's Property Acts were introduced in America and Europe in the latter part of the nineteenth and early twentieth century. Similarly the efforts of vociferous activists before the Second World War who challenged the social and legal order of that time cannot be ignored, especially those who were involved in the suffragette movement and demanded the right to franchise for women. It was due to the efforts of feminists like Mary Wollstonecraft and Elizabeth Candy Stanton that women were granted the right to vote, education and property rights.[66] These measures are seen as an achievement for women and as a step towards their emancipation and empowerment.

In the South Asian context the demand for legal reforms has also been on the agenda of the women's movement since the nineteenth century, when it initially started as a social reform movement in the Indian subcontinent and after the partition in Pakistan. The Child Marriages Restraints Act (CMRA) of 1929 aimed to ban the practice of early-age marriage by changing the definition of 'child' to any female under sixteen years of age and any male eighteen years of age. It also prescribed punishment for any male above age eighteen who contracts a child into marriage.

The Dissolution of Muslim Marriages Act (DMMA) of 1939 is another important law which recognized certain grounds on the basis of which a woman could seek dissolution of marriage. When first established, its dual purpose was to clearly lay out the provisions of Muslim law pertaining to the dissolution of marriages by women who were married under Muslim law, and to specify the effect that a married Muslim woman's renunciation of Islam has on her marriage tie. A particularly important provision of the DMMA (in section 5) was the protection of the wife's right to dower in spite of dissolution of the marriage. Section 2 (vii) of the DMMA also granted to a Muslim girl the option of puberty available to repudiate her marriage (contracted for her by her father, grandfather or any other relative) if it occurred while she was a minor.

The Muslim Personal Law (Shariat Application) Act 1937 in its statement of object clearly lays down that customary law has been disgraceful to women and it has been the desire of Muslims in India that this law should not take the place of the Muslim Personal Law.[67] The Act excluded women's right to inherit agricultural land, and it also failed to apply the new law to those who had obtained inheritance interests under customary law prior to 1937. Mehdi is of the view that exclusion of agricultural land reduced the impact of the provision and the law was therefore widely criticized by those who supported women's rights to property.[68]

After the creation of Pakistan the first legal reform was in the area of inheritance. The West Punjab Muslim Personal Law (Shariat) Application Act (ix of 1948) was passed. It now gave women the right to inherit agricultural land. Efforts were also made to incorporate protections for women and girls into marriage law.[69] The most important piece of legislation in this respect was The Muslim Family Law Ordinance (herein after referred as MFLO) of 1961 which emphasized the importance of the marriage contract (*nikahnama*). MFLO was a response to recommendations made by the Family Law Commission set up in 1955 due to the pressure exerted by the women's movement in Pakistan for improving the status of women through law reform.[70] According to this Ordinance, registration of marriages was mandatory, provisions were made for orphaned grandchildren to inherit from their grandparents, polygamy was restricted and only one form of divorce was recognized.[71] A protectionist approach was also followed in labour laws where women were debarred from working in night shifts and maternity provisions were included for women factory workers.[72] The perusal of legislation from the Indian subcontinent and then Pakistan shows that despite laws made over the years little has changed regarding the socio, political, and economic position of women. Most changes in laws in Pakistan are in the area of criminal law and family law. These laws have proved to be highly discriminatory for women and miserably failed to serve their purpose of providing protection to women.[73] Such discriminatory laws as well as repressive policies are detrimental to women's position in society. Hardly any substantive move has been made towards women's empowerment by giving them more civil or political rights or improving their mobility and freedom of choice.[74] Moreover, only a handful of women have been able to access courts whereas for a majority of women due to low literacy rate, poverty, customs and cultural pressures and the complicated litigation process, access to courts is not an easy route to secure their rights.[75] Very few women come into direct contact with the legal system, as most of them neither have an awareness of their rights, nor do they have sufficient resources in terms of finances and time to invest in the existing legal system. The discussion thus far suggests that law reform was done to provide protection to women, but in terms of its effectiveness it remains limited. Laws and policies on their own are not sufficient as legislation can be easily evaded by the powerful. Similarly, the apparently neutral legislation may have gendered implications. Law is present in theory, but when it comes to law in practice we see that either it discriminates against women or is simply ignored and not implemented. The presence of equality provisions in the Constitution of Pakistan and Principles of Policy are a few examples.[76] The law generally covers direct discrimination, however, indirect discrimination also exists in the form of imposing such conditions that may appear to be gender neutral but could be discriminatory for one sex if applied.[77] Any proposal for law reform therefore must move beyond the idea of merely incorporating equality provisions and focus on law as a discourse in conjunction with other socio-economic and political interventions so that the implementation of laws and access to justice is made possible for women domestic workers in Pakistan. Law itself cannot displace dominant discourses of patriarchy and class positions therefore its ability to bring about social change on its own is questionable. In Kapur's words:

> Law has been a useful discourse in the struggle for women's human rights but the extent of its power to bring about social change must be measured against the very real constraints of particular and material contexts.[78]

The law on its own cannot bring empowerment to women in domestic service in Pakistan because of their vulnerable position in the society. This study analyses the circumstances due to which very few women access courts, while the majority of them remain silenced. Traditionally women have little connection with the public sphere and courts, being in the public domain, are beyond reach in their normal day-to-day lives. Being illiterate, the language of law is also incomprehensible and compliance with the requirements of the law is far more complicated for them. Another reason for laws being ineffective would be due to the nature of their workplace, i.e. domestic service being carried out in the privacy of homes it would be extremely difficult in the private homes to interfere or inspect and keep a check and control.[79]

THIRD WORLD FEMINISM AND MULTIPLE IDENTITIES OF WOMEN

This study on women domestic workers mainly draws inspiration from feminist legal perspectives, yet it is conscious of the 'woman centred' focus of the feminist legal viewpoint. Therefore it also looks into the Third World feminist perspectives which consider 'woman centeredness' as oppressive and essentialist as any male dominating discourse because it ignores women's multiple identities.[80]

Mohanty writes that an essentialist approach assumes that women have a coherent group identity within different cultures.[81] A further implication of such essentialism is that it has created a divide between 'First World women' and the 'Third World women'–the former being white western, middle-class, heterosexual women.[82] Such an approach is colonialist in its tone and based on a generalized notion of women's subordination, which considers women as passive victims of oppressive traditions, religious fundamentalism, and male oppression. She further argues that instead of considering women, as a socio-economic political group within particular local contexts, this approach defines women as a monolithic group merely on the basis of gender.[83] Ladner appreciates Mohanty's views and acknowledges the fact that western feminists have created an 'us' and 'them' scenario, where the former represents the educated and developed First World women and the latter the backward, illiterate Third World women.[84] However, Ladner's disagreement with Mohanty arises on the point that in his view Mohanty over emphasizes the role of particular structures and circumstances responsible for the oppression of women. In Ladner's opinion, without the recognition of a common goal and solidified voice on the global level the oppression of women cannot be effectively addressed.[85] Ladner argues that, the fact that patriarchy is the root cause of women's subordination in the Third world cannot be ignored and therefore it should be the starting point for First and Third World feminists to work together on the international level and from there to move on to particular structures and local context which Mohanty has pointed out in her work.[86] Third World feminists oppose the idea of homogeneity and sisterhood, propounded by the middle-class white feminists, by emphasizing multiple identities of women. Mohanty in her recent book while propagating feminist solidarity, moves beyond the idea of 'global sisterhood' and argues for building up feminist solidarities across national, racial, class, and sexual divides.[87] By comparing the situations of workers in diverse locations, including lace makers in Nasrapur, electronic workers in the Silicon Valley, and migrant women workers in Britain, she demonstrates how similar ideological patterns exist within different class dynamics.[88] She suggests that a way forward is to understand and theorize how the lives of both privileged and marginalized women are interconnected.[89] Listening to their experiences further suggests that despite belonging to different cultures they share certain commonalities with women belonging to similar classes in other cultures.[90] She thus enables us to think about common struggles without universalizing women workers across the world. Conaghan, in her overview of feminist theoretical project in law argues that the critique of essentialism was a call for more inclusive feminist politics, which recognizes and seeks to engage with diversity among women.[91] She is of the view that anti-essentialism does not preclude woman centeredness because just as there are risks involved in talking of 'women' as a category, similarly there are serious risks in excluding the category 'women or women centred approach' altogether.[92] Whilst recognizing diversities, she believes that there are commonalities of subordination and oppression which women suffer from and in this way the category 'woman' remains constitutive of women's identity. She therefore suggests that it would be useful for the feminist legal project if legal feminists revisit women's disadvantage, re-engage with feminism's normative aspirations and reinstate women-centeredness as a feminist political strategy.[93] The above literature highlights two important points: (i) women's experiences and their lived realities must be taken into account and (ii) women do not have a monolithic identity, rather they have multiple identities with regard to race, ethnic background, class, and religion.[94] This study is informed by both legal feminist and Third World feminist literature. It emphasizes the point that to assess the efficacy of formal law as a tool for empowerment it is essential to look into women's lived realities and to recognize their multiple identities. Therefore, the study acknowledges the differences on the basis of their multiple identities as well as recognizes those experiences that they have in common in their role as women domestic workers. By so doing this study attempts to avoid falling into the trap of an essentialist perspective.

WOMEN AS AGENTS OF CHANGE

Feminist legal theorists and Third World feminists, in addition to their critique of law, emphasize the concept of 'woman's agency', which is similar to the concept of autonomy in liberal theory.[95] Feminist legal scholars consider women's voices, practices, and experiences crucial for analysis of law. Littleton in her work argues that 'Feminist jurisprudence must take women's experience as central, and legal categories or doctrines as merely raw material—to cut and paste, stretch, arrange, and sew together to fit that experience.'[96] Similarly, Cain, while defining feminist legal theory emphasizes the importance of women's experiences and argues that 'legal scholarship is not feminist unless it is grounded in women's experience.'[97] The understanding of women's experiences helps in developing a critical consciousness of women's situations and the way in which women are excluded from the processes of law. Listening to women's experiences on the one hand provides an opportunity to men and women to understand sex discrimination, while on the other, it removes the misconception that women are not intelligent or perceptive enough to understand their situations. Women's experiences help in identifying 'women's agency' which focuses on women's strengths, their resistance and how they strategize in order to cope with their own situations. This concept of woman's agency stresses upon the capacity of women to direct their own lives through individual action and choice.[98] Nafinne is of the view that:

> ...Agency is a capacity or ability to make meaning within a given set of cultural practices which fail to offer a clear and consistent formula for life, but are marked by contradictions. Not surprisingly, these contradictions tend to be most apparent to those-who bear the full force of them and who benefit from them least. Agency, then is to be founding the ability to weave together the different parts of one's inherently communal life into a coherent and consistent story, the story of oneself...Agency or autonomy is not the legally preserved freedom to live outside our cultural practices, which is a thing without meaning. Agency is the ongoing endeavour to make sense these often-contradictory practices to render them coherent without going mad, and without being struck dumb.[99]

Naffine considers the legal subject 'Woman' as an agency struggling against gender inequality and negotiating women's social relations and identities.

Harris discusses the concept of women's agency by highlighting the struggle of black women against racist oppression. She is of the view that black women have succeeded in building their own identity not by sharing their experiences of victimization but through creative action.[100] In the South Asian context, women are often portrayed as passive victims, an image strongly contested by Third World feminists (discussed in the previous section). In contrast to that image, women in South Asia have been involved actively in social and political movements as well as in the struggle for improving women's status against male oppression.[101] Women's resistance against oppression also appears in their day to day lives, for instance, Gardner in the case of the Bangladeshi community of Talakpur, and Raheja and Gold in their study of North Indian women observe that songs and rituals of women in these communities depict 'poetic resistance' which show women with a positive self image, are a means of subverting dominant discourses of gender and kinship and reveal the agency and power of women.[102] However, by suggesting women's agency, one should not undermine the sufferings of women or completely ignore the fact that women are the victims of violence and male oppression. Chandra's account of Rukhambai's struggle in male dominated Hindu society shows how a woman can be an agent for legal and social change.[103] Rukhambai's refusal to accept the traditions and colonial law that bound her in a child marriage contract reflects her courage and strength to fight for her rights over her personhood. However, her decision to don the Hindu widow garb on the death of her husband shows the power of socio-cultural pressures, which (despite her resistance) forced her to follow the custom. Kapur in her study of violence against women in India suggests that we must first recognize the peripheral subject and her multiple identities then focus on the moments of resistance so that women are not always seen as victim subjects. Finally, there is a need to examine the implications of non-state actors emerging as contenders to state power.[104] By taking the example of dowry murders in India, Kapur objects to the way violence against women is portrayed as a result of an ancient Hindu cultural practice by the western feminists and some Indian scholars, thus holding culture responsible for violence against women.[105] She argues that, the problem with such an essentialist position is that it leads to the denial of the concept of 'woman's agency' by presenting her only as a victim subject. To see women as passive victims and to treat women as weak, vulnerable, and incapable of taking decisions is to deny them a voice. Such an approach underestimates the strengths of those women who struggle hard and make every possible effort within their limited resources to provide for their families and children. These women must be respected and understood if they are to be made participants in their own destiny. Shaheed argues that women's responses and survival strategies in the Muslim world are as diverse as their identities.[106] Strategies used by these women to cope with their situations vary from theological interpretations to a radical rejection of religion, from individual strategies of personal development to armed struggle.[107] An example is the Women Living under Muslim Laws network (hereinafter referred as WLUML), which provides support and attempts to build linkages between Muslim women with multiple identities, struggling against patriarchy and discrimination.[108] Hirsch's study of Swahili Muslim women in two coastal cities in Kenya shows how these women have used legal processes to transform the religious and customary norms that discriminate against them.[109] Griffiths observes that Hirsch's study provides a nuanced analyses of the ways in which Swahili Muslim women are both constrained and empowered in a setting where plural legal norms concerning male and female speech intersect and interact.[110] It also shows how language itself becomes a legal power, the way interactions take place on a daily basis in local courts, as well as between men and women while negotiating their legal claims in marriage. This study is also important as it challenges the stereotypical image of Third World Muslim women portrayed in Western feminist scholarship as victims of their religion and culture. Instead, it highlights their role as active agents in negotiating their relations with men under their marriage contracts.[111] The concept of 'woman's agency' is also relevant from the point of view of women domestic workers in Pakistan who struggle against and resist oppression that appears in the form of male domination, gender, and class differences.[112]

The present study makes the connection between the theoretical concept of 'woman's agency' with the issue of women's lived experiences in the form of struggle and resistance against the dominant oppressive structures of patriarchy, gender, and class. Women domestic workers' strength and ability is demonstrated, when they in their own way negotiate with the employers. The study shows how women domestic workers take a stand for the sake of their families and children in a male-dominated society where it is still not openly acceptable for women to come out of their homes.[113] Their strength also appears in the form of their resistance against any abusive relationship. The struggles or the coping strategies remove the image of women domestic workers as passive victims, but this does not mean that we can ignore the harsh realities of their lives. Women's inability to take a stand or to make decisions is not because of some innate inferiority rather it is due to the socio-economic structure of the society in which women encounter many hurdles while accessing justice. Nevertheless, listening to their lived experiences, their perceptions about themselves and what they believe their rights to be, is needed to dismantle the passive victim image and to recognize their strengths as agents of social change.

ISLAMIC FEMINIST PERSPECTIVES ON WOMEN'S WORK

Although much of the theoretical framework of this research is informed by feminist legal scholarship, it would remain incomplete without taking into consideration the phenomenon of feminism within the Islamic socio-economic, political, and cultural framework.[114] First, this study is based in a Muslim country where the state derives its legitimacy from Islam.[115] Constitutions adopted in Pakistan over the last five decades were cast within the framework of the Objectives Resolution, creating a legal hierarchy with Islam as the overarching norm. Previously a preamble, the Resolution became a substantive part of the existing constitution as article 2A in 1985.[116] It is therefore pertinent to explore the extent to which a legal framework constructed in the name of Islam upholds and implements Islamic notions of dignity of labour, equity, and justice with regard to women in domestic service. A look at Islamic feminism is also useful in demystifying the position of Muslim women in a Muslim jurisdiction because women's status in the Muslim world is not determined purely on the basis of religion as race, ethnicity, and class equally influence their status. Islamic feminism takes a conscious approach of looking at women not as uni-dimensional entities defined by their sex or religion only, but as individuals possessing multiple identities. Kandiyoti, Ahmad, and Shaheed have expressed their discontent on the use of the term 'Muslim women'.[117] They argue that use of this term implies a universality and uniformity, which simply does not exist in the Muslim world. Women in Muslim communities differ from each other on the basis of their ethnicity, class, race and socio-economic position. Furthermore, it is important to see how Islamic feminists are making a case for reinterpretation of the Quran and Shari'a by emphasising the egalitarian and non-discriminatory teachings of Islam as well as the concept of dignity of labour and duties/responsibilities of both employer and employee.[118] Finally, the study discusses how women's work is viewed in the Quran and interpreted by Islamic feminists in their writings.[119]

Islamic feminism derives its basis from the Quranic text and not from the interpretations of the early religious scholars. The basic argument of Islamic feminism is to consult Islam's fundamental and central text, the Quran, to understand and implement its egalitarian message. Islamic feminist discourse transcends all binaries of East and West, Muslim and non-Muslim.[120] It is being articulated, produced, and used by those who may or may not accept the Islamic feminist label or identity. They also include religious Muslims (by which is typically meant the religiously observant), secular Muslims (whose ways of being Muslim may be less publicly evident), and non-Muslims. Badran classifies Muslim Islamic feminists into three groups.[121] One group of women scholars focus exclusively on the Quran (Riffat Hassan, Saudi Arabian Fatima Naseef); the second group emphasizes the reinterpretation of the Quran to examine the various formulations of the Shari'a (Pakistani Shaheen Sardar Ali, Lebanese Aziza Al-Hibri); while the third group advocates the re-examining of the Hadith (Moroccan Fatima Mernissi, Turkish Hidayet Tuksal).[122] However, despite diverse point of views, the distinctive character of all Islamic feminists is that they do not place themselves within the Islamic framework alone, rather they articulate Islamic feminism within nationalist, humanitarian/human rights, and democratic discourses. Islamic feminism thus gains strength from the diversity of voices that contribute to the debate of women's rights within the Islamic paradigm. One common theme that runs across all views is in Yamani's words 'empowerment of Muslim women within a rethought Islam.'[123] However to achieve women's empowerment the socio-economic and political conditions in which Islam was revealed needs to be borne in mind. An analysis of the historical and cultural context of that time is imperative to reinterpret the Quranic texts and *Fiqh*[124] with a fresh eye. At the same time a Quranic verse should not be interpreted in isolation rather a holistic approach is required through which all other verses on the same subject matter should be taken into consideration before interpreting any single verse of the Quran.

Tohidi notes that Islamic feminists undermine the clerical agenda both within and outside the Islamist framework in a number of ways:

> ...by subtly circumventing the dictated rules (e.g., re-appropriating the veil as a means to facilitate social presence rather than seclusion, or minimizing and diversifying the compulsory *hijab* and dress code into fashionable styles), engaging in a feministic *ijtehad*, emphasizing the egalitarian ethics of Islam, reinterpreting the Quran, and deconstructing Shari'a-related rules in a women-friendly egalitarian fashion (e.g., in terms of birth control, personal status law,

and family code to the extent of legalizing a demand for 'wages for housework.[125]

Islamic feminists further argue that the term feminism, though originating in the West, is actually a movement for the emancipation of women, and a struggle against discriminatory practices that have existed in all cultures and in all countries, whether in the East or West, developing or the developed world.[126] In Badran's view, 'a feminist discourse exists within the Islamic paradigm, which derives its understanding and mandate from the Quran and the Sunnah of the Prophet and seeks rights and justice for women and men.'[127] Islamic feminists position themselves as revivalists and argue that Islam as a religion has always accommodated women's needs and women can benefit if they return to Islamic sources. Hussain argues that the issues raised by Islamic feminists are not directed at God's word as revealed in the Quran, rather Islamic feminists object to the religious scholar's interpretation of the Quran, and their reliance on inauthentic traditions, which either do not reflect what the Prophet [PBUH] said or 'represent fallible variations of his Hadith.'[128] A reading of the Quran reveals that its main message is equality of mankind and non-discrimination between the sexes. The Islamic concept of equality regards man and woman as complimentary to each other.[129] The Quran states: 'O' Mankind! Lo! We have created you male and female and have made you nations and tribes that ye may know one another. Lo! The noblest of you in the sight of Allah is the most God fearing of you. Lo! Allah is Knower and Aware.'[130] Similarly, the Quranic message, that all human beings spring from one single source, promulgates the doctrine of equality and negates the inequalities due to sex, race, colour, caste, or tribe.[131] As far as the relationship of man and woman is concerned in the Quran, no difference whatsoever is made between the sexes in relation to God, and the Quran mentions the fact that as regards the moral and spiritual development, men and women stand on an equal footing:

> For men who submit [to God] and for women who submit[to God], for believing men and believing women, for devout men and devout women, for truthful men and truthful women, for steadfast men and steadfast women, for humble men and humble women, for charitable men and charitable women, for men who fast and women who fast, for men who guard their chastity and women who guard, for men who remember God much and for women who remember—for them God has prepared forgiveness and a mighty reward.[132]

> Whoever performs good deeds, whether male or female and is a believer, we shall surely make him live a good life and we will certainly reward them for the best of what they did.[133]

In the verses mentioned above, God declares that He created men and women to be different, with unique roles, functions and skills.

As in society, where there is a division of labour, so too in a family, each member has different responsibilities. Generally, Islam upholds that women are entrusted with the nurturing role, and men, with the guardian role. Therefore, women are given the right of financial support. But having different roles does not mean that women are inferior or weaker in their position. It is only in relation to each other and society that a difference in their roles is created. The rights and responsibilities of a woman are equal to those of a man, but they are not necessarily identical. In the light of such verses of the Quran, Esposito suggests 'heirarchisation of Quranic values' to deal with women's human rights in Islam.[134] He divides the Quranic legislation into the ethico-religious, dealing with the spiritual and moral aspects of life, and the socio-economic sphere dealing with the social and economic status.[135] In the former category women are treated as equal to men in their creation as men and women, in their obligations and duties towards God, as well as for all the rewards that are bestowed upon both men and women for the fulfilment of their duties. In the latter category however he finds that women are differentiated from men in their social status, but such verses must be analysed in the socio-economic situation of the Arab society when the Quran was revealed to the Prophet Muhammad [PBUH]. Following Esposito's framework of women's human rights in Islam, Ali proposes to use a method of 'categorization of rights' by which she divides rights into protective/corrective, non discriminatory and discriminatory categories.[136] She argues that to achieve equality and non-discrimination, a strict implementation of the protective/corrective category is an imperative prerequisite, only then substantive equality would be possible as opposed to formal equality.[137] Besides, in the economic sphere Islam gives women the right to ownership of property and control of wealth. The Quran also clearly lays down their share in inheritance: 'Unto the men belongeth a share of that which parents and kindred leave, and unto the women share of that which parents and near kindred leave'.[138] The Quran and the Hadith do not prevent women from engaging in gainful employment. The Quran declares that women have every right over their earnings and over their possessions: 'And in no wise covet those things in which Allah hath bestowed His gifts more freely on some of you than on others; to men is allotted what they earn, and to women, what they earn; but ask Allah of His bounty for Allah hath full knowledge of all things.'[139] This verse gives women the right to earn and whatever she earns belongs to her. She can keep the fruits of her labour and is free to invest or spend it in any way she wishes. The idea behind this verse is that women and men should be compensated for the work they perform regardless of gender. Similarly, a woman can even charge her husband for nursing her own infants. The Quran says: 'And the mothers may nurse their children for two whole years, if they wish to complete the period of nursing; and it is incumbent upon him who has begotten the child to provide in a fair manner for their sustenance and clothing.'[140] This verse reveals that the decision to wean the child for two years is an option for the mother not a command. It also indicates that the upbringing of a child is not just a mother's responsibility because if she does not want to feed the baby it is the father who has to make some alternate arrangement.

Hadith literature and recorded stories of the life of the Prophet Muhammad [PBUH] are replete with women leaders, jurists, scholars, and women who participated fully in public life.[141] Hazrat Khadija, the first wife of the Prophet and the first convert to Islam, was a successful trader who helped the poor, freed her slaves and spread the message of Islam. She first employed the Prophet as her representative to carry out her trade and then asked him to marry her. Her wealth and business property gave the Prophet ease of circumstances and freedom from the cares of daily life to accomplish his mission.[142] After her death, the Prophet married Ayesha Siddiqah, a formidable young woman who led a Muslim army into battle. She also contributed towards the collection of Ahahdith as many of the Hadith were reported by her. She also exerted her strong political influence to ensure that her father become the caliph after the death of the Prophet.[143] Other women including Al-Shifa bint Abdullah was the chief inspector of the Medina market and Umm Waraqa bint Naulal was appointed as an imam by the Prophet.[144] These examples reflect that the wives of the Prophet and other Muslim women were dynamic, influential, and enterprising members of the community, and fully involved in Muslim public affairs. They were vocal about their status and demanded equal economic and socio-political rights mainly in the areas of inheritance, participation in warfare and booty, and personal (marital) relations. It can thus be argued that these women from the Prophet's household set a precedent for the emancipation of the Muslim women.

Contrary to the Quranic verses, traditions of the Prophet and examples from early Islamic history, are the views of traditional ulema or religious scholars on the issue of women's employment. Sheikh BinBaz's views reflect the notion that women's participation in public sphere separates them from their *fitra* (innate natures), which eventually leads to women's misery and demise. He asserts that taking a woman out from her home, 'her kingdom', means taking her out from her innate nature and character which God has moulded her into. Although BinBaz supports the view that women can work in fields that are women's domain, such as female education, nursing and medical care, but this is to be done within a strict segregation between men and women. In his view, taking women away from their private domain would lead to moral decay as involvement of women in men's domains is not only a major crime on her but also a crime against the young generation, males, and females, who lose proper education, compassion, and kindness. His ideas are shared by other many other religious scholars in Saudi Arabia, including the late Sheikh Muhammad Otheimin and the current Grand Mufti of Saudi Arabia, Sheikh Abdul Aziz Al-Asheikh.

Muhammad Al-Ghazali (1917-1996) from amongst the nineteenth and twentieth century scholars, and as compared to BinBaz, is the most revolutionary in addressing women's concerns.[145] Al-Ghazali praised the worldwide women's movement aiming for social and political development and called on Muslim women to participate in the public sphere. He asserted that we should not only open the doors for political and labour participation for women but should also be willing to accept an environment, where a certain amount of mixing between the genders should be expected and accepted. After reviewing Quranic verses, traditions of the Prophet, examples from early Islamic history and views of both traditional scholars as well as modern Islamic scholars, the conclusion may be drawn that it is not religion that discriminates against women in terms of employment or their participation in the public sphere. In fact, it is the customary and cultural face of Muslim societies that leads to discrimination against women. The distinction drawn between public and private spheres is also artificial, as not a single verse could be found in the Quran which prohibits women from participating in public life. On the other hand, conservative religious scholars attempt to provide a religious justification for customary and cultural practices which results in restricting women's participation in the employment sector.

Haddad and Esposito believe that the word of God was interpreted and applied in a socio-historical context by early jurists who were influenced by their diverse geographical locations as well as the social customs of a patriarchal society.[146] Esposito in his analysis of law and women's lives in the Muslim societies shows how Muslim family law reflected the social mores of the time, traditional roles of men and women and functions of an extended family in a patriarchal society.[147] Similarly, Engineer while emphasizing the egalitarian basis of the Quran, further argues that 'Shari'a must be seen both in its cultural as well as a normative and transcendental spirit.'[148] Engineer is of the view that revising Shari'a formulations does not mean that the wisdom and intelligence of past jurists is being challenged, rather it is a reiteration of the fact that their works are a reflection of their own times. Further, they themselves were aware of the possibilities of error of inferences. In this context, Hassan reminds us of the incredible richness of the Arabic language in which virtually every word has multiple meanings and nuances.[149] She therefore argues that Quranic verses can be reinterpreted by not merely considering the literal meanings of the words but by looking deeper into the spirit and message behind the words.[150]

With regard to the Hadith literature used by early scholars it must also be noted that it may not always be authentic and reliable and sometimes may even have been used to propagate patriarchal ideas and practices.[151] Islamic feminists argue that such interpretations represent women as subordinate and dependent on men.[152] Such thinking also ignores Islamic perspectives of equality and the legal position of women and work. Ali argues that:

> What is not acknowledged by many Muslim today is that we have lapsed into an acceptance of status quo, a situation where social, economical and political disparity has taken over our capacity for independent thought. We feel that there is more security in treading familiar terrain rather than embarking on the challenging task of separating the egalitarian tradition of Islam from its cultural, elitist manifestation.[153]

In this regard, it is interesting to note how male scholars have interpreted the Quranic verse: 'Men are the maintainers of women because Allah has made some of them to excel others and because they spend of their wealth for the support of women.'[154] The word *Qawwamun* has been translated by conservatives/orthodox as 'managers, protectors and maintainers [of women] having pre-eminence [above women] and sovereigns or masters [over women]'.[155] Such translations of the word *Qawammun* give the impression that women are subordinate to men and have a secondary status. Men are considered in charge of women and women are marginalized both within and outside the home.

Interpretations of the early jurists on Islamic *Fiqh are* based on men's experiences, focusing on male-centred questions, and present women as totally dependent on men. Hassan argues that this verse actually conveys the Islamic concept of division of labour in an ideal family or community where women shoulder the heavy burden of childbearing and rearing and should not have additional obligation of providing for the family.[156] However, it does not mean that it's always men who provide, or that women are incapable of being the providers or maintainers of the family. Ali and Engineer have also given a similar interpretation in their respective works and argue that *Qawwam* is a function or a duty. It is not a biological term that determines superiority or inferiority of one sex over another, rather a woman can also be a *Qawwam* if she is earning and providing for the family needs.[157] This liberal interpretation also suggests that guardianship and greater financial responsibility given to men requires that they provide women with not only monetary support but also physical protection and to treat them with kindness and respect. Ali is of the view that the tone of these verses does not represent women in any derogatory manner: rather kindness and fairness of treatment is enjoined.[158]Afshar argues that if fundamentalism is about returning to this golden age of Islam then it should not be forgotten how influential women were at that time, the manner in which they were treated and how they participated in the public domain.[159]

The above discussion also raises questions such as why women in the present age are not given the same rights and why are they considered inferior to men using religious arguments? Why is there a wide gap between the egalitarian principles of Islam and the lived realities of women in Muslim societies and finally, despite clear and unequivocal support for male-female equity, why are Muslim women today denied some of the basic rights such as education, health, employment, participation in politics and public life? These questions could be addressed by following the principle of *Ijtihad* that seeks to promote freedom of thought (*hurriyah al-ra'y*) and independent thinking (*Ijtihad*) among Muslims everywhere and other juristic methods of interpretation developed and explored by Islamic feminists.[160] The Quran says: 'We explain the signs in detail for those who reflect'.[161] Islamic scholars argue for the use of other concepts or juristic methods of change and reformation within the Islamic law. *Islah* (reform), *Tajdid* (renewal), and *Sahwah* (awakening) are a few examples that are being used by the new Islamic movement.[162] *Takhayur* or eclecticism is another juristic technique which has been used both by individual scholars, as well as by the state, to fulfil the present needs of society if these are not directly covered by the primary sources of law.

Under the process of *Takhayyur* the person chooses between the opinions of different schools of Islamic law or chooses from the opinions of individual scholars within a single school or from amongst different schools.[163] Ali has also explored *Takhayyur*, along with some other juristic techniques such as *Ikhtalaf*, and *Talfiq* and argues for the revival of such techniques which reflect the tolerant and democratic nature of the Islamic legal tradition.[164] Engagement with such principles of interpretation would help in advancing analytical critical thought in Muslim communities and would set some ground rules for a tolerant, non-discriminatory, democratic polity.[165] Anderson, Pearl, and Menski consider *Takhayyur* to be the most significant in developing a number of women friendly codes of family laws in Muslim jurisdictions.[166] A more flexible approach towards personal law has been adopted by applying the juristic concept of *Takhayyur*, for instance cruelty has been considered grounds for dissolution of marriage and stipulating conditions in the marriage contract is considered acceptable under the Hanbali school.[167]

In the light of these discussions, there is need to study Islamic law by going back to the Qura'nic texts and Sunnah from a fresh perspective in light of the juristic concepts of *Ijtihad*, *Ikhtilaf*, *Talfiq* and *Takkyyaur*. Islamic feminists need to make an effort to remove the misconceptions that exist regarding Islamic teachings about women as they prepare the ground for revisiting the Quran and reform of the Islamic law.[168] If Islam is to be considered a religion for all times to come and Islamic law guides the life of millions of Muslims all over the world, then this argument alone is enough to justify that the doors of *Ijtihad* must remain open in the present times. The wide gap between the ideal and the practice of Islamic principles today can be bridged by digging deep into the concept of *Ijithad* and reviving different legal techniques of reinterpretation. Use of *Ijithad* and juristic techniques would also help in distinguishing between actual teachings of the Quran and customary practices which are adopted in the name of religion.

ISLAMIC NOTION OF DIGNITY OF LABOUR

Another important issue that needs to be discussed is the concept of dignity of labour and duties/responsibilities in Islam with reference to employer and employee. The principle of dignity of labour has been laid down in the Quran in unequivocal terms. Anyone who does not work should not hope to reap any fruit and that the worker should have his/her full reward: The Quran says:

> That man shall have nothing but what he strives for: and that his striving will soon be seen. Then he will be rewarded for it with the fullest reward.[169] So whoever does good works and he is a believer, there shall be no denying of his effort, and we surely write (it) down for him.[170]

The life of the Prophet Muhammad [PBUH] is a living example of the dignity of labour as he sets the example of personally performing all his household chores. He never despised any work, however humble, notwithstanding the dignity of his position as Prophet, and as a leader. He thus demonstrated through his personal example that all kinds of work are dignified.[171]

Equal importance is given to the regulation of relations between a labourer and his employer in terms of equality. Paying workers in domestic service their wages on time and to treat them with fairness comes under the category of *Faraiz* (obligation), i.e. a compulsory duty. Similarly, both are considered as two contracting parties, in which the employer is as much bound by the terms of the agreement as the worker. The Prophet laid down a general law relating to contracts:

> Muslims shall be bound by the conditions that they make.[172]

> Allah says: There are three persons whose adversary in dispute I shall be on the day of Resurrection: a person who makes a promise in My name then acts unfaithfully, and a person who sells a free person then devours his price, and a person who employs a servant and receives fully the labour due from him then he does not pay his remuneration.[173]

> No service carried with it any indignity, so much so that it was recommended that the servant may eat on the same table with his master.[174]

An example of paying remuneration to the employee is the case of Umar ibn-al-Kithab when he was appointed as a collector by the Prophet and offered remuneration. Umar refused to take it saying that he did not stand in need of it. The Prophet, however, told him to accept it and then give it away to charity if he liked.[175] The principle was thus laid down that every employee, every worker and every labourer was entitled to remuneration. Simultaneously it is expected that workers will be faithful and honest towards their employers. The Quran wants individuals to be trustworthy: 'Don't embezzle what has been entrusted to you.'[176] This applies not only to an item entrusted for safe-keeping but also to domestic workers who are given the charge of house keeping by their employers. Thus, Islam gives importance not just to rights or entitlements but it also stresses upon duties and obligations.

The examples cited above underpin the importance of a humane relationship between employer and employee and also pose a question for Islamic feminists to interrogate why these principles are ignored in those Muslim countries who derive their constitutional and legislative basis from religion. Islam, like the other monotheistic religions, emphasizes equity, justice, humanity, compassion, and dignity of labour which are also the foundational principles of human rights discourse. These principles can be translated in the laws and policies of the country. In the words of Moghadam 'these principles may *inspire* civil codes, political processes, social policies, and economic institutions'.[177] By including and providing protection to domestic workers in labour legislation a consonance with the Islamic and secular human rights discourse can be ascertained. However, what is yet to be seen is when these principles laid down in theory will be translated into actual lived realities.

LEGAL PLURALISM

Pakistan is a country where plural legal norms exist together and deeply influence women's lives. Women domestic workers thus live in a setting where a variety of norms have an impact on their lives. Legal pluralism is therefore a relevant tool for analysis of law in the context of women in domestic service. It challenges mainstream legal discourse, which represents law as positivist, uniform, formal and with certain universalistic rules, which are created within the framework of the modern nation state.[178] This view of the law excludes all other forms of normative ordering that exist in a society. Legal pluralism emerged as a reaction to European legal positivist philosophy, which reduced the law to state law.[179] The proponents of early classical legal pluralism argue that there is no one single legal ordering rather there are various legal orders that prevail and operate alongside the single legal system which is the state law in modern societies.[180]

The concept of legal pluralism, which originated in the late nineteenth and early twentieth century has been discussed and debated within legal anthropology and legal sociology. Hooker is of the view that legal pluralism is based on the idea of 'dual systems of law' in which the common law system was applied to Europeans and the customary law was seen in the context of colonized world.[181] Pospisil argues that society is made up of a collection of subgroups with their own legal systems which are different from those of other groups.[182] In this way there are 'different legal levels' in every society and every subgroup is associated with that legal system which regulates the conduct of its members. Smith's theory of legal pluralism is based on his concept of 'corporations'.[183] He argues that corporations exist in all parts of society, such as churches and schools. Members of such corporations derive their roles, rights, and responsibilities from these corporations which act as a form of political organization. Ehrlich refuses to accept the monopoly of the state on law. He provides a descriptive theory of legal pluralism in which he argues that peoples' behaviour is not necessarily ordered by the all comprising state law but by the inner orderings of associations which he termed as 'Living law'.[184]

Griffiths in his work makes a distinction between 'weak' and strong forms of legal pluralism.[185] He is of the view that early classical legal pluralism is weak because it relies upon a legal centralist model of law where state law remains dominant and hierarchal. Griffiths defines legal pluralism as 'that state of affairs, for any field, in which behaviour pursuant to more than one legal order occurs.'[186] These normative orders in Griffiths's view are as much law as those which are the part of the formal state system. Griffiths is more in line with Moore's description of legal pluralism. In Moore's view law should not be seen in isolation rather it should be seen in the context of society and culture where it exists in the form of customs and rules which have their own ways of inducing compliance.[187] Moore uses the term 'semi-autonomous social fields' to describe multiple systems of orderings in complex societies.[188] She uses this argument to refute the legal centralist claim that only state law has the force to ensure compliance.

Weak pluralism has also been criticized by Woodman who is of the view that this type of legal pluralism is static and does not explain the dynamic interaction between legal orders.[189] In Woodman's view 'legal pluralism in the strong sense consists of different legal orders such as the state law and the customary law of an ethnic group that coexist within the area over which the state claims jurisdiction.'[190] In Chiba's view classical legal pluralism focuses only on non-western societies. It should also be extended to western societies since 'unofficial laws' are present within the most sophisticated polity as well the less developed.'[191]

The last few decades has witnessed a shift in the legal pluralism paradigm from classical to new legal pluralism. Sally Merry states that debates concerning legal pluralism are no longer confined to indigenous law of the colonized but have moved into discussing the pluralist qualities of law in capitalist societies as well.[192] Proponents of this new form of pluralism study the pluralistic qualities of law in capitalist, urban, industrial and modern societies.[193] Amongst them Santos has linked law and globalization process in the present day world. Santos uses the term 'different legal orders and different forms of law' and considers legal pluralism as a cornerstone in the post-modern view of law.[194] He has produced a theory of legal pluralism in relation to the process of globalization in today's world. He argues that contemporary societies in today's world system are legal constellations in which law has become a complex and richer landscape operating in local, national, and global time spaces and has both a regulatory or repressive and emancipatory potential.[195] The law from each of the three time spaces overlaps with and interpenetrates law from the other time space, thus modern societies are being regulated by plurality of legal orders, which are interrelated.

Legal pluralism has also been used in studies undertaken in the area of gender relations. Griffiths's study of procreative relations between men and women in Botswana provides an insight into the study of law as gendered where both formal and informal legal systems work to the disadvantage of women.[196] Griffiths argues for reconfiguring law through integrating legal centralist and legal pluralist approaches while exploring the relationship between legal status and social context of women.[197] Griffiths attempts to link the difficulties women face in the legal arena to difficulties they face as social actors and considers that such linkages are crucial to understand women's experiences of the law.[198] Her analysis of individuals as social beings moves beyond the confines of law and looks into the economic and social disparities that govern the power relations between men and women in Botswana.

A number of Scandinavian scholars including Bentzon and Hellum have also used legal pluralism.[199] These scholars took up the task to understand pluralism in the context of colonization where customary law was changed for the sake of codification and law reform in Africa in particular. Bentzon et al. interests' in legal pluralism further led to the application of grounded theory methodology for empirical investigation that focuses on the lived experiences of women.[200] They argue that the use of grounded theory approach 'initiates a continuous dialogue and interaction as the research proceeds between the initial theory and the empirical data collected.'[201] A grounded theory approach would thus help in building new profiles of women which will provide a thorough understanding of the role that the law plays in their lives and how women cope with the plural, legal and social situations in which they live. The present study on domestic workers in Pakistan uses a similar approach and focuses on the lived experiences and voices of women domestic workers.[202]

In the African context another groundbreaking study of legal pluralism and women's human rights has been carried out by Hellum on the management of procreative problems in marriage and divorce faced by Zimbabwean women.[203] The study challenges the law and modernization theory which assumes that uniformly applied laws and development programmes would improve the position of women in law and society.[204] Based on the actual experiences of women and following a grounded theory methodology, this study assesses the efficacy of the International Convention on the Elimination of all Forms of Discrimination against Women with particular reference to its gender equality principle.[205] The study also identifies the existence of plural legal norms within the international human rights framework. It uncovers the tensions and conflicts between the international standards defining women's rights and grounded realities that exist in the form of customary norms and family-based arrangements in case of women's infertility.[206]

The presence of legal pluralism in Pakistan has been explored by Ali and Arif, Mehdi and Yilmaz.[207] These studies demonstrate the existence and impact of plural legal norms (in the form of customary practices, statutory law and religious norms) on women's lives in Pakistan.[208] Ali and Arif discuss the impact of parallel, dispute resolution systems/forums both at the formal state level under special laws as well as at the informal level under customary practices. They are of the view that the implications and consequences of this dual judicial system are more detrimental for women as the ambit of laws such as the Muslim Family Laws Ordinance and Family Law Courts has not been extended to Provincially Administered Tribal Areas.[209] Moreover, informal dispute resolution forums represent the interests of male elite therefore it is highly unlikely that women's complaints would be sympathetically heard.[210]

The law is also critiqued with reference to the Hudood Ordinances, which show how religion is politicized to serve the interests of men in Pakistan.[211] Mehdi examines the process of Islamization of law within the overall framework of Pakistani statehood, Islamic revivalism and pluralistic legal structures in the form of customary laws and practices.[212] She outlines the complexities of the legal processes and their social effect on women in Pakistan by examining reforms made in the area of constitutional, criminal, and family law in Pakistan. Mehdi argues that the gaps exist in legal norms because the Islamic provisions on the basis of which reforms were made to the formal law have been interpreted differently by the traditionalists and modernists.[213] As a result, complexities arise for those seeking justice under these so called Islamic laws of the state.

A more recent addition on legal pluralism has been Yilmaz's work in which he discusses the dynamics of Islamic legal pluralism in the post-modern age.[214] In the Pakistani context, by citing the changes made under Muslim personal laws, he argues that Pakistan provides an example of interaction of religious and local customary traditions with the role of the modern state. Yilmaz is of the view that in Pakistan traditional Muslim law has not been abandoned but there has been an attempt by the state to reform, limit, regulate and restrict it.[215] However, this has resulted in a debate between the traditionalists and modernists in the country where the former consider such reforms as repugnant to the basic teachings of Islam and the latter demand a complete secular legal system.[216] As a result, despite attempts by the state to codify Muslim personal law, there are still other non-legal norms that govern Muslim family law issues in Pakistan which clearly suggest the presence and strong influence of legal pluralism in Pakistan.

Bearing in mind the range of definitions and explanations of legal pluralism, following the definition of legal pluralism as given by Moore, the present study observes that, in the case of women domestic workers, the 'others' household' is the semi autonomous social field where plurality of norms exist in the shape of gender difference, class hierarchies and patriarchal systems due to which statutory regulations have had little impact on women's rights and in improving their work conditions. With legal pluralism as a framework for analysis it is argued that in the presence of these deeply entrenched practices legislation would fail to provide any protection to women in domestic service. It has been seen that so far the formal legal system in Pakistan has not provided the vast majority of disadvantaged women their rights. This further raises the question how yet another set of laws will help in improving the position of women domestic workers in Pakistan.

It is argued that the law alone as a simple set of rules cannot bring equality and remove all sorts of disparities in the presence of the deeper injustices that exist in the form of discriminatory customary practices, misinterpreted religious norms, patriarchy, gender, class and socio-economic differences. Advancing only legal solutions can complicate the situation for women domestic workers in Pakistan and it would bring more harm to them rather than providing any relief to their situations.

CONCLUSION

Feminist legal theories provide the basis for critiquing the law as a tool for empowerment for women and used in the present study to question the efficacy of proposing a law for women domestic workers in Pakistan. Aubert's and Sverdrup's studies compel one to think that formal law alone may not be a workable and effective solution for Pakistani women workers in domestic service.

A review of Third World feminist literature was helpful in identifying the point that a legal feminist perspective cannot co-exist with an exclusively essentialist approach towards women, which views women as a category and ignores their multiple identities. The law can only be effective if it recognizes the experiences of women and existence of other factors such as race, ethnicity, class, religion, and gender that constitute women's multiple identities. The discussion on the concept of women's agency negates claims about Third World women as mere passive victims. Women's apparent inability to take a stand or to make decisions is not because of some innate inferiority but due to the socio-economic structure of society. Third World women have the power to resist the dominant forces of society. What is required is to enhance women's agency and women's capacities by providing support structures so that the law can become accessible and be effectively implemented. The discussion on Islamic feminism leads us to the conclusion that there is no single, ethnocentric discourse on 'feminism' and it is more appropriate to speak of 'feminisms'. Feminisms must be more inclusive and accept the legitimacy of women's struggles on the local and trans-national levels. The feminist movement must take into account the diversity of criteria and legitimate interpretations within Islam. At the same time, non-Muslim feminists must remain on guard and not accept the most sexist and reactionary sectors of Islam as the only possible interpretation of Islam. This practice tends to hinder collaboration between Muslim women fighting for their rights and the global feminist movement. Moreover,

Islamic feminists need to explore and use various interpretative juristic techniques so that Islamic principles of human dignity and respect for labour can be highlighted and used in relation to women and work in Muslim societies.

The discussion on legal pluralism has helped in enriching understanding of the law in plural legal settings, with particular reference to the main research hypothesis, i.e. to question the efficacy of formal law in empowering women domestic workers in Pakistan. A plural legal framework also helps in analysing how customary practices and misinterpreted religious teachings, combined with poverty and illiteracy determine women domestic workers position in the Pakistani society. Such knowledge of both formal and informal laws/structures would then be useful in suggesting a way forward in Eberhard's words 'by rethinking law in a pluralistic and intercultural way' for bringing empowerment and change in the lives of women domestic workers in Pakistan.[217] It is in the light of the above themes that the theoretical framework of the present research is developed which will be linked to Part II of the study and the empirical findings from the field in Part III.

NOTES

1. Legal centralists such as Jeremy Bentham and John Austin believe that the state is the sole creator of laws. In their view, laws are commands from the government that create a duty in the governed and are backed by a threat of sanction from the government. In this way they define law primarily in terms of the power to control others. (For further detail see footnote 1178).
2. Feminism is not a monolithic term and over the years it has taken various shapes. Starting from liberal feminism to post-modern feminism, there has also been the emergence of new feminist perspectives in the form of Lesbian feminism, Black feminism, Third World feminism, Polyversal feminism and Islamic feminism. Throughout the movement, feminists have always engaged with the law, despite differences of opinion and diversity of perspectives. It is beyond the scope of this research to discuss all the various streams in feminism, therefore this section is restricted to some of the debates within the feminist legal thought which is more related to the present work in assessing the role of law.
3. For a detailed analysis of the different classificatory schemes of feminist legal thought, see: Chamallas, M. (1998), *Introduction to Feminist Legal Theory*, New York: Aspen Law and Business; Evans, J. (1995), *Feminist Theory Today: An Introduction to Second Wave Feminism*, London: Thousand Oaks, New Delhi: Sage Publications.
4. Roavh Andleu, L.S. (2000), reprinted (2001, 2002), *Law and Social Change*, London: Sage Publications, p. 74.
5. Ibid., p. 75.
6. Cain, P. (1989-1990), 'Feminism and the Limits of Equality,' *Georgia Law Review*, Vol. 24, p. 803. Also see Cain, P. (1991-1992), 'Feminist Legal Scholarship,' *Iowa Law Review*, Vol. 77, p. 19.

7. Ibid., p. 1154.
8. For instance see the works of feminist legal scholars such as Taylor, B., Rush, S. and Munro, R.J. (1999), *Feminist Jurisprudence, Women and the Law: Critical Essays, Research Agenda, and Bibliography*, Colo: F.B. Rothman; Bartlett, K.T. and Harris, A.P. (1998), *Gender and Law: Theory, Doctrine, Commentary*, New York: Aspen Law and Business, Fineman, M. and Thomsden, N. (1991), (ed.), *At the Boundaries of Law: Feminism and Legal Theory*, New York, London: Routledge; MacKinnon, C. (1987), *Feminism Unmodified: Discourses on Life and Law*, Cambridge: Harvard University Press; Barnett, H. (1998), *Introduction to Feminist Jurisprudence*, London: Cavendish; Smart, S. (1989), *Feminism and the Power of Law*, London: Routledge, pp. 29-44.
9. Stereotype images of women are always portrayed, and identified, with their roles as mothers, daughters, wives and sisters.
10. To support the argument this research study focuses on the works of feminist legal scholars such as MacKinnon, Smart, Naffine, Kapur, Chunn and Lancombe, Ali, Shaheed, Jilani, Jehangir, Prashar, Agnes Jhappan, Basu, Narsimhan and Mukhipadhyay etc.
11. MacKinnon, C. (1987), *Feminism Unmodified: Discourses on Life and Law*, Cambridge: Harvard University Press.
12. Ibid., pp. 81-92.
13. Ibid., p. 72.
14. Smart, C. (1992), 'The Woman of Legal Discourse,' *Social and Legal Studies*, Vol. 1, pp. 29-44.
15. Ibid., p. 32.
16. Ibid., p. 33.
17. Smart, C. (1989), *Feminism and the Power of Law*, London: Routledge, p. 88.
18. Ibid., p. 165.
19. Dahl, T.S. (1987), *Women's Law: An Introduction to Feminist Jurisprudence*, Oslo: Norwegian University Press.
20. Ibid., p. 14.
21. Ibid., p. 20.
22. Ibid., p. 32.
23. Chunn, D.E. and Lacombe, D. (2000), (ed.), *Law as a Gendering Practice*, Oxford: Oxford University Press. Also see Lessard, H. (2001), 'Review of Law as a Gendering Practice,' UBC *Law Review*, Vol. 35, p. 199.
24. Ibid., p. 202.
25. Ibid., p. 13.
26. Jhappan, R. (2002), 'The Equality Pit or the Rehabilitation of Justice,' in Naffine, N. (ed.), *Gender and Justice*, Dartmouth: Ashgate Publishing Company, pp. 169- 218. Also see Jhappan, R. (2002), *Women's Legal Strategies in Canada*, Toronto: University of Toronto Press.
27. Ibid., p. 190.
28. Stewart, A. (1996), 'Should Women Give up on the State? The African Experience,' in Rai, S. and Lievesley, G. (ed.), *Women and the State: International Perspectives*, London: Taylor and Francis, pp. 23-44.
29. Kapur, R. and Cossman, B. (1996), *Subversive Sites: Feminist Engagements with Law in India: Feminist Engagement with Law in India*, Sage (New Delhi, Thousand Oaks, London).
30. Ibid., pp. 19-21.
31. Ibid., p. 21.
32. Ibid., pp. 19-21.

33. Agnes, F. (1999), *Law and Gender Inequality: The Politics of Women's Rights in India*, Delhi: Oxford University Press, p. 24.
34. Basu, M. (2001), *Hindu Women and Marriage Law: From Sacrament to Contract*, New Delhi: New York: Oxford University Press.
35. Ibid., p. 149.
36. Ibid., pp. 146-7.
37. Mukhopadhyay, S. (1998), *In the Name of Justice: Women and Law in Society*, Delhi: Manohar, pp. 9-14.
38. Narasimhan, S. (1999), *Empowering Women: An Alternative Strategy From Rural India*, New Delhi: Sage Publications.
39. Ibid., p. 75.
40. Agnes, F. (1998), 'Violence against Women: A Review of Recent Enactments,' in Mukhopadhyay, S. (ed.), *In the Name of Justice: Women and Law in Society*, Delhi: Manohar, p. 82.
41. Ibid., p. 115.
42. Ali, S.S. (1997), 'A Critical Review of Family Laws in Pakistan: A Woman's Perspective,' in Shaheed, F. and. Mehdi, R (ed.), *Women's Law in Legal Education and Practice in Pakistan: North South Cooperation*, pp. 198-223; Jilani, H. (1998), 'Law as an Instrument of Social Control,' in Khan, N.S. et al. (ed.), *Locating the Self: Perspectives on Women and Multiple Identities*, Lahore: ASR Publications; Zia, S. (1995), 'Women and Law,' in Khan, N.S. et al. (ed.), *Unveiling the Issues*, Lahore: ASR Publications; Shaheed, F. (1997), 'The Interface of Culture, Customs and Law: Implications for Women and Activism,' in Shaheed, F. and Mehdi, R. (ed.), *Women's Law in Legal Education and Practice in Pakistan: North South Cooperation*, pp. 47-63; Shaheed, F. (1994), 'Controlled or Autonomous: Identity and the Experience of the Network, Women Living Under Muslim Laws,' *Signs*, Vol. 19, No. 4, pp. 997-1019; Jahangir, A. and Jilani, H. (1990), *The Hudood Ordinances: A Divine Sanction?* Lahore: Rohtas Books.
43. Ibid., p. 204.
44. Ibid., p. 209.
45. Ibid., p. 209.
46. Jilani, H., supra note 42, p. 102.
47. Ibid., p. 102.
48. Jilani, H., supra note 42, p. 104.
49. Zia, S., supra note 42, p. 76.
50. Ibid., p. 76.
51. Ibid., p. 76.
52. Shaheed, F., supra note 42, p. 999.
53. Ibid., p. 999.
54. Ibid., p. 1000.
55. Ibid.
56. Jehangir, A., supra note 42, p. 21.
57. For a detailed discussion on the successes and failures of women's movement in Pakistan, see Khan, N.S. et al. (1995), *A Celebration of Women: Essays and Abstracts from the Women Studies Conference March 1994*, Lahore: ASR Publications; Mumtaz, K. and Shaheed, F. (1987), *Women of Pakistan: One Step Forward Two Steps Back*, Pakistan: Vanguard Books (Pvt) Ltd., p. 43; Ali, S.S. (2000), 'Law, Islam and the Women's Movement in Pakistan,' in Rai, S.M. (ed.), *Gender and Democratisiation: International Perspectives*, London: Routledge, pp. 41-63; Zia, S. (1995), 'Some Experiences of the Women's Movement: Strategies for Success,' in Shaheed, F. et al.

(ed.), *Shaping Women's Lives: Laws, Practices and Strategies in Pakistan*, Lahore: Shirkat Gah, Women's Resource Centre.

58. Unfortunately, the laws are still in existence but the Women's Movement in Pakistan has been continuously pressuring successive governments in Pakistan to abolish these laws. The judiciary is also following a conscious approach when it comes to implementation of these laws in cases of rape and adultery.
59. Aubert, V. (1966), 'Some Social Functions of Legislation,' *Acta Sociologica*, Vol. 10, p. 104.
60. Ibid., p. 104.
61. Ibid., p. 101.
62. Sverdrup, T. (1990), 'Employees in Private Homes,' Working Papers in Women's Law (No. 33), Institute of Women's Law, University of Oslo, Norway, pp. 1-39.
63. Ibid., p. 27.
64. Ibid.
65. As cited by Kapur, R. and Cossman, B., supra note 29, p. 36.
66. For a detailed discussion on the history of feminist movement see Buechler, S.M. (1990), *Women's Movements in the United States: Woman Suffrage, Equal Rights, and Beyond*, New York: Rutgers University Press; Hoskyns, C. and Threlfall, M. (1996), *Mapping the Women's Movement: Feminist Politics and Social Transformation in the North*, New York: Verso; Marilley, S.M. (1996), *Woman Suffrage and the Origins of Liberal Feminism in the United States, 1820-1920*, Cambridge, Massachusetts: Harvard University Press.
67. Section 2 of the Act says 'Not withstanding any rule of custom or usage in all questions regarding succession (whether testate or intestate) special property of females, betrothal marriage: divorce: dower, adoption guardianship, minority, legitimacy or bastardy, family relations, wills, legacies, gifts usages or institutions including *waqfs*, trusts and property, the rule of decision shall be the Muslim personal law in cases where the parties are Muslim'.
68. Mehdi, R. (2002), *Gender and Property Law in Pakistan: Resources and Discourses*, Copenhagen: DJOF Publishing, p. 33.
69. Some other legislation included; The Government Servants (Marriages with Foreign Nationals) Rules 1962, The West Pakistan Family Courts Act, 1964, The West Pakistan Family Courts Rules, 1965, The Dowry and Bridal Gifts (Restriction) Act, 1976, and The Dowry and Bridal Gifts (Restriction) Rules, 1976.
70. Marriage Commission Report, *Gazette of Pakistan Extraordinary*, 20 June 1956.
71. Section 5, Section 4, Section 6, and Sections 7 and 8.
72. The Mines Act, 1923; The Maternity Benefit Act, 1961; The West Pakistan Maternity Benefit Act, 1958; The West Pakistan Maternity Benefit (Amendment) Act, 1985.
73. These laws were introduced by General Ziaul Haq, a military dictator who ruled the country for eleven years and promulgated a set of ordinances on 10 February 1979. The ordinances are a compilation of five separate laws: offences of theft and armed robbery; *zina* and rape; *qazf*; use and sale of alcohol; and, lastly, the procedure for whipping. It prescribes two sets of punishments: *hadd* (singular form of *hudood* referring to punishments in the Quran related to adultery and fornication, making false accusations, theft, and the consumption of alcohol) and *tazir*. The *hadd* punishment requires very specific evidence based either on the confession of the accused or the testimony of a specified number of eyewitnesses. In the case of *zina*, the number of eyewitnesses must be at least four. All witnesses for the *hadd* sentence must be adult male Muslims who are 'truthful persons and abstain from major sins.' If the accused is a non-Muslim, the witnesses may also be non-Muslim. The law either

presumes that non-Muslims will only rob or rape non-Muslims or the lawmakers wanted to leave less room for non-Muslim offenders to escape the *hadd* punishment. Punishments under *hadd* are severe: stoning to death in the case of rape and *zina* or amputation of one's hand for theft of a particular type.

74. For details, see chapter 3.
75. Cf. For details see section on 'Socio-religious constraints in chapter 3 and section on 'Women's Experiences of Formal and Informal Mechanisms of Justice' chapter 6.
76. The constitutional provisions are discussed in detail in chapter 4.
77. For instance imposing certain age limit conditions might result in the exclusion of women from jobs. Similarly, marital status should also be covered with sex, because married women with young children are often discriminated by the employers who feel that child rearing responsibility often leads to women's absence from her job.
78. Kapur, R. (2006), 'Revisioning the Role of Law in Women's Human Rights Struggles,' in Meckled-García, S. and Basak, C. (ed.), *The Legalization of Human Rights Multidisciplinary Human Rights and Human Rights Law*, London and New York: Routledge, p. 111.
79. Women's inhibition to access courts has been discussed in chapter 6. There are also other studies carried out in Pakistan that have thoroughly discussed the issue of access to justice for women in Pakistan. See for example Asia Foundations project on legal reforms, The Asia Foundation (2001), 'Improving Access to Justice under the Local Government Plan: Small Scale Technical Assistance', Islamabad.
80. 'Third World women' is a socio-political designation used for women of African, Asian and Latin American origin. It also includes Arab, Korean, Thai and Latvian women immigrants to the US, Europe and Australia. Often this term is used interchangeably for 'Women of Colour.' Mohanty defines Third World on geographical basis. According to her the nation states of Latin America, Sub-Saharan Africa, South Africa, South and South East Asia constitute the Third World including those immigrants living in the First World who have historic links with these geographic entities. Odim explains the term with reference to under developed/over exploited geopolitical identities, i.e. countries, regions, continents and even those oppressed nationalities from these areas who now live in the developed first world countries. Spivak is of the view that the term Third World was first of all used by those emerging from the old world order in order to establish a third way neither with the Eastern nor with the Western bloc in the world system. Spivak also challenges the inability of western intellectuals to mediate and understand the forms of culture and knowledge that exist in the Third World.
81. Mohanty, C. (1991), 'Under Western Eyes: Feminist Scholarship and Colonial Discourses,' in Mohanty, C. et al. (ed.), *Third World Women and the Politics of Feminism*, Indiana: Indiana University Press, pp. 51-71.
82. Ibid., p. 60.
83. Mohanty, C., Russo, T. and Torres, L. (1991), *Third World Women and the Politics of Feminism*, Indiana: Indiana University Press, p. 64.
84. Ladner, C., 'Westerner Feminists: Vanguards or Suppressors of Third World Women? www.wlu.ca/~wwwpolsc/facpages/abrown/CRP1Cladner.htm accessed on 19/03/03.
85. Ibid., p. 1.
86. Ibid.
87. Mohanty, C.T. (2003), *Feminism without Borders: Decolonizing Theory, Practicing Solidarity*, Durham, NC: Duke University Press.
88. Ibid., p. 143.
89. Ibid., p. 144.

90. Ibid., p. 226.
91. Conaghan, Joanne (2000), 'Reassessing the Feminist Theoretical Project in Law,' *Journal of Law and Society*, Vol. 27, No. 3, pp. 351-85.
92. Ibid., p. 373.
93. Ibid., p. 384.
94. The issue of multiple identities of women is also addressed by Tove Stang Dahl when she refers to different subgroups among women. While introducing 'Women's Law' as a discipline she distinguishes it from other disciplines on the ground that the group which Women's Law focuses on (that is the women) 'is a large and complex segment of the population which in turn has exceedingly many and extremely varied subgroups….women are elderly, immigrants, prisoners, patients…it is not one role, one interest, one function or one minority group that women's law serves in the way consumer law is concerned with consumers, patient law with patient etc.'
95. In 1990s, post-modern feminists including Elizabeth Schneider, Martha Mahoney, and Kathryn Abrams criticized the labelling of women as victims with reference to cases of battery, harassment, and abuse. They were of the view that without minimizing the harm/negative impact done by oppression, concept of 'woman's agency' can be helpful in presenting a realistic and dignified account of women's resistance to male domination.
96. Littleton, C.A. (1989), 'Book Review: Feminist Jurisprudence: The Difference Method Makes,' *Stanford Law Review*, Vol. 41, pp. 751- 66.
97. Cain, P., supra note 6, p. 19.
98. Elizabeth Schneider, Kathryn Abrams, and Martha Mahoney have discussed the concept of women's agency in relation to battered women and victims of sexual harassment and different coping strategies adopted by these women to deal with their exploitative situations.
99. Nafine, N. (March 2002), 'In Praise of Legal Feminism,' in *The Journal of the Law and Society of Legal Scholars*, Butterworths, Vol. 22, No. 1, p. 86.
100. Harris, A. (1991), 'Race and Essentialism in Feminist Legal Theory,' *Stanford Law Review*, Vol. 42, pp. 581-612.
101. Cf., see footnote 57.
102. Gardner, K. (1998), 'Women and Islamic Revivalism in Bangladeshi Community,' in Jeffery, P. and Basu, A. (ed.), *Appropriating Gender: Women's Activism and Politicized Religion in South Asia*, New York and London: Routledge; Raheja, G.G. and Gold, A. (1994), *Listen to the Herons' Words: Re-imagining Gender and Kinship in North India*, Berkeley: University of California Press. See also Haynes, D. and Prakash, G. (1991), (ed.), *Contesting Power: Resistance and Every Day Social Relations in South Asia*, Delhi: Oxford University Press; Karlekar, M. (1991), *Voices from Within: Early Personal Narratives of Bengali Women*, Delhi: Oxford University Press; Minault, G. (1986), *Voices of Silence, Delhi:* Chanakya; Weis, A. (1992), *Walls Within Walls: Life Histories of Working Women in the Old City of Lahore*, Oxford: Westview Press.
103. Chandra, S. (1999), *Enslaved Daughters: Colonialism, Law and Women's Rights*, New Delhi: Oxford University Press.
104. Kapur, R. (2005), 'The Tragedy of Victimization Rhetoric: Resurrecting the 'Native Subject in International/Post-Colonial Feminist Legal Politics,' *Harvard Human Rights Journal*, Vol. 15.
105. Ibid., p. 7.
106. Shaheed, F. (2001), 'Constructing Identities: Culture, Women's Agency and the Muslim World,' *Women Living under Muslim Laws*, Dossier 23-24, p. 2.
107. Ibid., p. 5.

108. WLUML Report (1995), 'Women's Law Initiatives in the Muslim World,' *Discussions from the International Meeting, Towards Beijing: Women, Law and Status in the Muslim World*, Lahore.
109. Hirch, S.F. (1998), *Pronouncing and Preserving: Gender and the Discourses of Disputing in an African Islamic Court*, Chicago: Chicago University Press.
110. Griffiths, A. (2001), 'Remaking Law: Gender, Ethnography and Legal Discourse,' *Law and Society Review*, Vol. 35, p. 495.
111. Other studies that reflect Muslim women as active agents who negotiate and resist their positions within their own worlds include Abu-Lughad, L. (1993), *Writing Women's World: Bedouin Stories*, Berkeley: University of California Press; Starr, J. (1992), *From Islamic Courts to the Palace of Justice*, Albany: State University of New York Press; Ong, A. (1995), 'State Verses Islam: Malay Families, Women's Bodies and the Body Politic in Malaysia,' in Ong, A. and Peletz, M.G. (ed.), *Bewitching Women, Pious Men: Gender and Politics in South East Asia*, California: University of California Press. As cited in Griffiths, A., supra note 120, p. 495.
112. The empirical data in chapter 6 supports this line of argument.
113. See case studies in chapter 6.
114. The term Islamic feminism appeared in the 1990s in various global locations. It was first used by Iranian scholars Afsaneh Najmabadeh and Ziba Mir-Hosseini who explained the rise and use of the term Islamic feminism in Iran by women writing in the Teheran women's journal *Zanan*. Later on Saudi Arabian scholar Mai Yamani used the term in her 1996 book *Feminism and Islam*. Turkish scholars Yesim Arat and Feride Acar in their articles, and Nilofer Gole in her book *The Forbidden Modern* (published in Turkish in 1991 and in English in 1996) used the term Islamic feminism in their writings in the 1990s to describe a new feminist paradigm they detected emerging in Turkey. South African activist Shamima Shaikh also has used the term Islamic feminism in her speeches and articles in the 1990s.
115. Pakistan emerged on the world map in the name of Islam, which became the Grund Norm of the new state and its society and came to be known as the ideology of Pakistan. At the time of framing the first constitution, this ideology was translated into words in precise form by the first Constituent Assembly of Pakistan in a resolution passed by it in the year 1949 which declared that sovereignty belongs to Allah. This resolution known as the 'Objectives Resolution', provided as follows: 'Whereas sovereignty over the entire universe belongs to Allah Almighty alone and the authority which He has delegated to the state of Pakistan, through its people for being exercised within the limits prescribed by Him is a sacred trust; 'Wherein the Muslims shall be enable to order their lives in the individual and collective spheres in accordance with the teachings and requirements of Islam as set out in the Holy Quran and the Sunnah.
116. Article 2-A states: 'The principles and provisions set out in the 'Objectives Resolution' reproduced in the Annex are hereby made a substantive part of the constitution'.
117. Kandiyoti, D. (1991), (ed.), *Women, Islam and the State*, London: Macmillan; Ahmad, L. *Women and Gender in Islam: Historical Roots of a Modern Debate*, New Haven: Yale University Press; Shaheed, F., supra note 42, p. 1012.
118. The Quran is the primary source of Islamic law. It was revealed to Prophet Muhammad [PBUH] over a span of almost twenty-three years. What distinguishes the Quran from other holy books is that it is preserved in its original form and not a single change has been made to it over the centuries. It consists of thirty chapters, 114 suras and 6666 verses, of which 500 verses deal with legal matters. The literal meaning of the word Shari'a is path, a watering place or a flowing stream. *Shari'a* law is derived from

the Quran and Sunnah of the Prophet, but it is not dìvine because *Shari'a* is the product of human interpretation of those sources. *Shari'a* law classically does not draw any distinction between religious and secular law. *Shari'a* covers all aspect of human life including religious as well as day-to-day life.

119. Pooya and Karam in their respective books on women in Iran and women in Egypt have distinguished between the three types of feminisms that have emerged in the Muslim world i.e. Islamic, Secular, and Muslim feminists. For a detailed discussion of the three terms see Pooya, M. (1999), *Women, Work and Islamism: Ideology and Resistance in Islam*, New York: Oxford University Press; Karam A.M. (1998), *Women, Islamisms and the State: Contemporary Feminisms in Egypt*, Great Britain: Mac Millan Press Ltd.
120. Rahman, F. (1983), 'Status of Women in Quran,' in Nashat, G. (ed.), *Women and Revolution in Iran*, Boulder, Col: Westview Press; Esposito, J.L. (1982), *Women in Muslim Family Law*, Syracuse: Syracuse University Press; AlHibri, A., 'A Study of Islamic History: Or How do We get into This Mess?', *Women Studies International Forum*, Vol. 5; Ahmed, L. (1992), *Women and Gender in Islam: Historical Roots of a Modern Debate*, New Haven: Yale University Press; Naim, A.A. (1990), *Towards an Islamic Reformation*, Syracuse: Syracuse University Press; Ali, S.S. (1999), *Gender and Human Rights in Islam and International Law: Equal Before Allah Unequal before Man?*, London: Kluver Law International.
121. Badran, M., Islamic Feminism: 'What's in a Name?', Al-Ahram Weekly Online, 17-23 January 2002, Issue No. 569. http://weekly.ahram.org.eg/2002/569/cu1.htm. Accessed on 28 December 2005.
122. Ibid.,
123. Yamani, M. (1996), *Feminism in Islam: Legal and Literary Perspectives*, United Kingdom: Ithaca Press.
124. The Arabic word *fiqh* means knowledge, understanding, and comprehension. It refers to the legal rulings of the Muslim scholars, based on their knowledge of the *Shari'a*; and as such is the third source of rulings. The science of *fiqh* started in the second century after *Hijrah*, when the Islamic state expanded and faced several issues which were not explicitly covered in the Quran and *Sunnah* of the Prophet.
125. Tohidi, N. (1991), 'Gender and Islamic Fundamentalism: Feminist Politics in Iran,' in *Third World Women and the Politics of Feminism*, (eds.), Chandra Talpady Mohanty, Ann Russo, and Lourdes Torres, Bloomington: Indiana University Press, pp. 251-67.
126. Feminism is a term which is often associated with the West and denotes the struggle for women's rights by the middle-class white women. However, by this association it is actually denying the fact that feminism exists in multiple forms not only in the West but also outside. When the feminist movement began in the West, women in other parts of the world were also struggling for their rights but their struggles were subsumed under the language of anti-colonialism and anti-imperialism. Feminism today has moved beyond the struggle for equality and liberal individualism of the white western woman. Now it has pluralized meanings in the form of struggles of Black women, Muslim women, lesbians and Latina women. To understand the position of women in an Islamic state it is therefore necessary to look into Islamic feminist debates along with the legal feminist approaches.
127. Badran, M., supra note 121.
128. Hussain, F. (1984), *Muslim Women*, Worcester: Croom Helm, p. 37.
129. This approach dominates in the writings of Ustad Taha, Aziza Al-Hibri, J.L Esposito, A., An-Na'im, and Riffat Hasan for detailed reference see footnote 1 in Ali, S.S.

(1999), *Gender and Human Rights in Islam and International Law: Equal before Allah Unequal before Man?* The Hague: Kluwer Law International, p. 42.

130. The Quran, 49: 13.
131. The Quran, 4: 1.
132. The Quran, 33: 35.
133. The Quran, 6: 97.
134. As cited by Ali, S.S., p. 49.
135. Ibid., p. 49.
136. Ali, S.S. (1997-1998), 'Women's Human Rights in Islam: Towards a Theoretical Framework,' in Cotran, E. and Mallat, C. (eds.), *Year Book of Islamic and Middle Eastern Law*, Vol. 4, The Hague. London, Boston: Kluwer Law International.
137. Ibid., p. 152.
138. The Quran, 7: 4. Women's economic rights in Islam are also discussed in detail in chapter 3.
139. The Quran, 4: 32.
140. The Quran, 2: 233.
141. For a description of women's role in the early days of Islam see Mernissi, F. (1993), (Mary Jo Lakeland, trans.), *The Forgotten Queens of Islam*, Oxford: Polity Press; Hussain, A. (1987), *The Status of Women in Islam*, Lahore: Lahore Publishing Company; Afshar, H. (1996), 'Islam and Feminism: An Analysis of Political Strategies,' in Yamani, M. (ed.), *Islam and Feminism: Legal and Literary Perspectives.* London: Ithaca Press, p. 199.
142. Siddiqui, A.H. (1989), *The Life of Muhammad*, Lahore: Islamic Publications Limited, p. 53.
143. Afshar, H. supra note 141, p. 199.
144. Hussain, A., supra note 141, p. 228.
145. His ideas are shared by other notable and influential *ulama'* including Yusuf Al-Qaradawi, Abdel-Haleem Abu Shaqua, and Hasan Turabi.
146. Haddad, Y.Y. and Esposito, J.L. (eds.), (1998), *Islam, Gender and Social Change*, New York: Oxford University Press.
147. Ibid., p. 8.
148. Engineer, A.A. (2004), (2nd ed.), *The Rights of Women in Islam,* India: New Dawn Press, p. 17.
149. Hassan, R. (1990), 'An Islamic Perspective', in Becher, J. (ed.), *Women, Religion and Sexuality: Studies on the Impact of Religious Teachings on Women*, Geneva: World Council of Churches Publications, pp. 93-128.
150. Ibid., p. 100.
151. Badran, M., supra note 121.
152. See for example the writings of Yageneh, Afshar, and Nashat, while examining Islamic Ideology and the role of religious leaders and the state in Iran, argue that the interpretation of Quranic verses by the Ulema in Iran represent women as subordinate and dependent on men.
153. Ali, S.S., '(Re) Claiming Our Histories: A Reflection on Women, Islam and Human Rights in Contemporary Muslim Communities,' paper for Human Rights Day, 10 December 2003, Islamabad, organized by INGAD. Available at http://sachet.org.pk/home/gender_columns/webcolumn_26.asp. Accessed on 20 April 2005.
154. The Quran, 4: 34.
155. Hassan, R., supra note 149, p. 102.
156. Ibid., p. 102.
157. Engineer, A.A., supra note 148, p. 7.

158. Ali, S.S., supra note 121, p. 50.
159. Afshar, H., supra note 121, p. 200.
160. The literal meaning of the term *ijtihad* is to strive for, struggle or to make strenuous effort. Linguistically *ijtihad* is derived from the lexical root 'j-h-d', the same root as *jihad*, holy war. In general usage, the word *ijtihad* denotes the uttermost effort, physical or mental, expanded in a particular activity. *Ijtihad* is a methodology that facilitates the application of human knowledge to be a source of law in a legal system based on divine knowledge. It is a tool for the reformation of law. For an extensive study of *ijtihad* as a source of Islamic law see: Fyzee, A. (1955), (2nd ed.), *Outlines of Muhammadan Law*, London: Oxford University Press; Coulson, N.J. (1964), *A History of Islamic Law*, Edinburgh: Edinburgh University Press; Schacht, J. (1964), *An Introduction to Islamic Law*, Oxford: Clarendon Press; Hallaq, W.B. (1995), 'Ijtihad,' *The Oxford Encyclopaedia of the Modern Islamic World*, Vol. 2; Hallaq, W.B. (1997), *A History of Islamic Legal Theories: An Introduction to Sunni Usul al-Fiqh*, Cambridge: Cambridge University Press; Weiss, B. (1978), 'Interpretation in Islamic Law: The Theory of Ijtihad,' *American Journal of Comparative Law*, Vol. 26, No. 2, pp. 199-212; Weiss, B. (1998), *The Spirit of Islamic Law*, London: University of Georgia Press.
161. The Quran, 10: 24.
162. As cited by Arvidsson, M. (2002), 'Ijtihad Reformation of Islamic Law in the 21st Century: The Case of Sudan,' master's thesis, Faculty of Law, University of Lund.
163. Ibid., p. 25.
164. Ali, S.S., supra note153.
165. Ibid.
166. Anderson, N.J.D. (1976), *Law Reform in the Muslim World*, London: Athlone Press; Pearl, D. and Meniski, F. (1998), (3rd ed.), *Muslim Family Law*, London: Sweet and Maxwell. As cited in Yilmaz, I. (2005), *Muslim Laws, Politics and Society in Modern Nation States: Dynamic Legal Pluralisms in England, Turkey and Pakistan*, United Kingdom: Ashgate, p. 43.
167. The *first* example of the use of *Takhayyur* is *Majalla* a collection of codified Hanafi law. In *Majalla* rules were derived not from the consensus of opinion of Hanafi scholars but from the divergent opinions of the Hanafi traditions. Other examples of *Takhayyur* include the Dissolution of Muslim Marriages Act 1939, the Moroccan Code of Personal Status 1958, the Jordanian Law of Family Rights 1951, Syrian Law of Personal Rights 1953 and the Ottoman Law of Family Rights 1917 and in Pakistan the Muslim Family Law Ordinance 1961.
168. One such effort to re-read the Quran and to reinterpret it has been made by 'Women Living under Muslim Laws' group in the form of a compilation called '*For Our Selves Women Reading the Quran*.'
169. The Quran, 53: 39-41.
170. The Quran, 21: 94.
171. The Holy Prophet [PBUH] did all kinds of work. No work was too low for him. He would milk his own goats, he would dust his house; he would tie his camel and look after it personally. He would assist his wife in her household duties. He would do the shopping, not only for his own household but also for his neighbours and friends. He worked like a labourer in the construction of the mosque. Again, when a ditch was being dug around Madinah to fortify it against heavy attack, he was seen at work among the rank and file.
172. Bukhari, 37: 14.
173. Bukhari, 34: 106.

174. Ibid., 49: 18.
175. Ibid., 94: 17.
176. The Quran, 8: 27.
177. Moghadam, V. (2002), 'Islamic Feminism and its Discontents: Notes on a Debate,' *Signs Journal of Women in Culture and Society*, Vol. 27, No. 4 pp. 1135-71.
178. Legal positivism has a long history and a broad influence. Its roots lie in the conventionalist political philosophies of Hobbes and Hume, later on elaborated by Jeremy Bentham (1748-1832) and then adopted, modified, and popularized by John Austin. According to their view the law is the command of a sovereign backed by force. By the mid-twentieth century, however, this account had lost its influence among working legal philosophers. Its emphasis on legislative institutions was replaced by a focus on law-applying institutions such as courts, and its insistence of the role of coercive force gave way to theories emphasizing the systematic and normative character of law. The most important architects of this revised positivism are the Austrian jurist Hans Kelsen (1881-1973), HLA. Hart (1907-92) and Joseph Raz among whom there are clear lines of influence, but also important contrasts. The importance of Legal positivism, however, is not confined to the philosophy of law. It can be seen throughout social theory, particularly in the works of Marx, Weber, and Durkheim, and also among many lawyers, including the American 'legal realists' and most contemporary feminist scholars. Although they disagree on many other points, these writers all acknowledge that the law is essentially a matter of social fact. Austin, J. (1832), *The Province of Jurisprudence Determined*, Cambridge: Cambridge University Press; Campbell, T. (1996), *The Legal Theory of Ethical Positivism*, Dartmouth: Aldershot; Dworkin, R. (1986), *Law's Empire*, Cambridge MA: Harvard University Press; Hart, HLA. (1994), (2nd ed.), *The Concept of Law*, Oxford: Clarendon Press; Kelsen, H. (1945), *General Theory of Law and State,* trans. A. Wedberg, repr. 1961, New York: Russell and Russell; Raz, J. (1979), *The Authority of Law*, Oxford: Clarendon Press.
179. Scholars such as Galanter and Griffiths name this mainstream legal discourse as 'legal centralist' or 'formalist' model of law. Galanter, M. (1981), 'Justice in Many Rooms: Private Ordering and Indigenous Law,' *Journal of Legal Pluralism and Unofficial Law*, Vol. 19, pp. 1-47; Griffiths, J. (1986), 'What Is Legal Pluralism?', *Journal of Legal Pluralism and Unofficial Law*, Vol. 25, pp. 1-55. The term state law refers to legislation, the legal system, judicial pronouncements and the legal profession and the term non state law refers to the understanding of law as customary law, local law, tribal or indigenous law, people's law, folk law and religious law. Legal pluralists argue that the law exists not only in the form of formal rules or state law but also in the form of unwritten laws/rules of a society that could take the form of customs, traditions or even economic and social pressures.
180. Mauss (1906) identified at least two legal systems among the Eskimos. Llewellyn and Heobel, (1941) are of the view that there are multiplicity of legal systems within a geographically limited society, even in the most homogenous societies there may be several legal systems operating at the same time. Bohannan (1967; 1967) sees state law as secondary and derivative. He developed the idea of 'differing realms of law' to illuminate the relationship between customs and law. In addition to the above scholars Gurvitch (1947), Malinowskil (1959), Nader (1965) also followed the classical legal pluralist approach. As cited by Yilmaz, I. (2005), *Muslim Laws, Politics and Society in Modern Nation States: Dynamic legal Pluralisms in England, Turkey and Pakistan*, Great Britain: Ashgate.

181. Hooker, M.B. (1975), *Legal Pluralism: An Introduction to Colonial and Neo-Colonial Laws*, Oxford: Clarendon Press.
182. Pospisil, L. (1978), 'The Structure of Society and Its Multiple Legal Systems,' in Gulliver, P.H (ed.), *Cross Examinations: Essays in Memory of Max Gluckman*, Leiden: EJ Brill, pp. 96-109.
183. Smith, M.G. (1969), 'Some Developments in the Analytic Framework of Pluralism,' in Kuper, L. and Smith, M.G. (ed.), *Pluralism in Africa*, Berkeley: University of California, pp. 415-458.
184. Ehrlich, E. (1936), *Fundamental Principles of Sociology of Law*, Cambridge: Harvard University Press.
185. Griffiths, J. (1986), 'What is Legal Pluralism', *Journal of Legal Pluralism*, Vol. 24, No. 1, pp. 1-55.
186. Ibid., p. 2.
187. Moore, S.F. (1973), 'Law and Social Change: The Semi Autonomous Field as an Appropriate Subject of Study,' *Law and Society Review*, Vol. 7, pp. 719-746.
188. Ibid., p. 721.
189. Woodman, G.R. (1997), 'Progress Through Complexity: Options for the Subjects of Legal Pluralism,' in Mehdi, R. and Shaheed, F. (eds.), *Women's Law and Practice in Legal Education in Pakistan*, Copenhagen-Denmark: New Social Science Monograph, p. 188.
190. Ibid., p. 190.
191. Chiba, M. (1989), *Legal Pluralism: Towards a General Theory Through Japanese Legal Culture*, Tokyo: Tokyo University Press.
192. Merry, S. A. (1988), 'Legal Pluralism,' *Law and Society Review*, Vol. 5, No. 22, p. 869.
193. Some of the literature on this new form of legal pluralism includes; Green House, C. and Strijbosch, F. (1998), 'Legal Pluralism in Industrialized Societies,' *Journal of Legal Pluralism*, Vol. 33.
194. Santos, B. (2002), (2nd ed.), *Toward a New Legal Common Sense: Law, Globalisation and Emancipation*, London: Butterworths, pp. 384-94.
195. Ibid., p. 385.
196. Griffiths, A. (1997), *In the Shadow of Marriage: Gender and Justice in an African Community*, Chicago: The University of Chicago Press.
197. Ibid., p. 211.
198. Ibid., p. 214.
199. Bentzon, A. et al. (1998), *Pursuing Grounded Theory in Law: South-North Experiences in Developing Women's Law*, Oslo: TANO Aschehoug, Harare, Zimbabwe: Mond Books; Hellum, A. (1999), *Women's Human Rights and Legal Pluralism in Africa: Mixed Norms and Identities in Infertility Management in Zimbabwe*, Tano, Aschehoug: Mond Books.
200. Ibid., p. 25.
201. Ibid., p. 81.
202. Cf. For further details about the use of grounded theory methodology see chapter 5 of the present study.
203. Hellum, A., supra note 199, p. 21.
204. Ibid., p. 45.
205. Ibid., p. 21.
206. Ibid., p. 30.
207. Ali, S.S. and Arif, K. (1998), 'Parallel Judicial Systems in Pakistan and Consequences for Human Rights.' in S. Zia et al. (eds.), *Shaping Women's Lives, Law, Practices and*

Strategies in Pakistan, Pakistan: Shirkat Gah, Women Resource Centre; Mehdi, R. (2001), *Gender and Property Law in Pakistan—Resources and Discourses*, Denmark: DJOF Publishing; Yilmaz, I. (2005), *Muslim Laws, Politics and Society in Modern Nation States: Dynamic Legal Pluralisms in England, Turkey and Pakistan*, England and USA: Ashgate Publishing House.

208. For further discussion on legal pluralism in Pakistan in the light of these studies, see chapter 3.
209. Ali, S.S. and Arif, K., supra note 207, p. 51.
210. Ibid., p. 51.
211. The Ordinance deals with rape and adultery. The offences under this law attract different punishments according to the evidence on which the conviction is based. In cases where the most severe (*hadd*) punishments may be imposed, the evidence of women is not admissible. In a rape case the onus of proof falls on the victim. If a woman fails to prove that she did not give her consent to intercourse, the court may convict her of illicit sexual intercourse.
212. Mehdi, R. (1994), *The Islamisation of the Law in Pakistan*, London: Curzon Press.
213. Ibid., pp. 47-50.
214. Yilmaz, I., supra note 207, p. 167.
215. Ibid., p. 167.
216. Ibid., p. 168.
217. Eberhard, C. (2001), 'Towards an Intercultural Theory: The Dialogue Challenge,' *Social and Legal Studies: An International Journal*. Vol. 10, No. 2, pp. 171-201.

2

Domestic Service in the Globalised World: Perspectives from the North and South

INTRODUCTION

Domestic service still exists in the former colonial world of the South and has re-emerged in the affluent, capitalist countries of the North. Although women form a very high percentage of domestic workers in Pakistan, literature on the subject is minimal, therefore literature from North and other South jurisdictions is used as a template to draw analogies with the situation of women domestic workers in Pakistan and subsequently tested through empirical work undertaken for this study. The literature reviewed points to the fact that across the North-South divide, domestic service has remained an underpaid and undervalued activity performed by disadvantaged social groups of society. It demonstrates that Coser's claim in 1973 of the obsolescence of the occupation of 'servants' was too optimistic.[1] It also shows that there are more commonalities than differences in this type of employment carried out globally, whether it is in the developing or developed countries. It also illustrates the roles of gender, class, race, and ethnicity in placing domestic service at the bottom of the employment ladder. The literature also suggests that globalization has brought changes in the migration process, which is no longer male-dominated, as women in large numbers from developing countries are migrating to developed countries in search of work (mostly in domestic service).

This chapter presents a review of various books, research studies and articles on the subject of domestic service in the North, including the United States of America, Canada and United Kingdom. It also examines literature from the South looking at studies carried out in South Africa on domestic workers in the context of race, as well as from newly industrialized South East Asian countries like Malaysia, Singapore and the oil-rich Gulf countries such as Saudi Arabia and Kuwait.[2] The chapter further analyses the literature from a South Asian perspective by looking at various studies carried out in India, Sri Lanka. and Pakistan.

DOMESTIC SERVICE IN THE UNITED STATES OF AMERICA

Domestic service in the US has always remained largely occupied by women. The first scholarly work on American domestic service was undertaken by Lucy Maynard Salmon.[3] In her work, Salmon offered a historical background of domestic service in the US and suggested reforms for solving the 'servant problem' in the light of her survey findings.[4] Salmon argued that domestic service was a peculiar institution where mostly women were employed, and due to its personal and isolated nature, domestic service had never been considered as a form of labour like any other employment in industry or other profession. Discussing the social disadvantages of domestic service, Salmon considered that the low social position given to this occupation was the most serious social disadvantage in this form of employment. Despite receiving board, lodging, and other incidental privileges, the domestic never became a part of the family. This was reflected in three ways. First, domestics had to follow certain rules set by the employer about the number of visitors received by the employee. The employee was also not allowed to entertain any of the visitors and finally as compared to other occupations there were no opportunities for personal development of the employee.[5]

Salmon further argued that the knowledge about household activity was generally considered as something that was gained through instinct, experience or learnt through traditions. At the same time considering domestic service as only women's domain were some of the explanations given for not taking this service as other occupations that required proper professional training.[6] Salmon emphasized that improvements in this service could only be made if domestic workers were professionally trained. However, the success of such professional training depends on an in-depth study of the intricacies and complexities that surround this service.[7]

What Salmon highlighted in her study of the eighteenth century appears to be universally true of domestic service even today as it is still considered to be a 'woman's job' due to the nature of work. It has also not been recognized or regulated as a profession on the pretext that it is carried out in the privacy of homes and apparently, a domestic worker is considered to be a part of the family and not an employee.

Katzman in his work argued that there was a re-emergence of domestic service in the US. His analysis of domestic service in the nineteenth century USA suggested that it was a highly personalized relationship between employers and employees and considering it a low cadre job resulted in the exploitation of domestic workers as compared to other workers in the informal sector in terms of working hours, wages and due to the isolated nature of the job. The domestic workers worked in the privacy of a home in a highly personalized relationship and received part of their payment in kind, and worked irregular hours. According to Katzman: 'The highly personalised nature of the servant's relationship with her employer and the low level of specialisation in domestic roles are both anomalous in a modern industrial society moving towards specialised and impersonal work relationships'.[8] He also drew attention to the presence of racial and ethnic discrimination and pointed out how domestic work had become predominantly a black women's occupation in the US.

Palmer, in her work on domestic service in the USA between 1920 and 1945, attempts to make linkages between gender, race, and domesticity.[9] She focuses on the inter-war years in America, which witnessed a change between household economies of the early 1900s and the post-Second World War era. The former was a period in which middle class housewives in America depended heavily on domestic workers. However, in the later period middle class women had to learn to do without domestic help as white women moved into other jobs as more opportunities for women were created in the labour market. This led to the creation of jobs as domestic workers for women of colour. However, hiring women of colour resulted in a racial superiority of white women over their black workers. Domestic service was considered as a degrading occupation because those who performed it were perceived to be an inferior race and are of lower class status.

Katzman's and Palmer's studies raise an important issue of racial discrimination among Black minorities in the USA. This is an important fact in relation to the present study as Christian and Hindu women domestic workers in Pakistan like the black workers in USA are also discriminated against and receive degrading treatment from employers on the basis of their religious identity. Christian workers are given the title of *Jamadars* (sweepers performing 'dirty' work). Cleaning is described as 'dirty, because it is performed by those who belong to the lower social class and even if they move into other jobs e.g. many Christian women are in the nursing profession, they are always designated as belonging to the *jamadar* or sweepers community.

MIGRATION AND DOMESTIC WORK

In USA, more recent literature deals mainly with the issue of migrant women domestic workers and suggests that paid domestic work in the global world is now reserved for women of colour from the poor developing countries.[10] This literature also addresses the issues of gender, race, and ethnicity as cross-cutting themes with regard to the position of domestic workers in the global economy.

The relationship between white women employers and women of colour who work as their domestic workers has been analysed by Rollins in her groundbreaking work.[11] Focusing on white women employers and black domestics in the US, she draws attention to the class hierarchies that existed in these women-to-women relationships in domestic service. Rollins considers this relationship as in the form of a 'subcontracting relation' between the woman employer and the woman employee, which in turn allows women employers to overcome some aspects of gender inequality/oppression without challenging the position of men. Rollins further argues that this relationship also diverts challenges of patriarchy, as men are not called upon to assume their share of domestic responsibility, so employing women in domestic service further leads to gender inequalities. She argues that 'By delegating an important locale of their subordination, the area of housework, the employer attempts to escape from its limitations. However, by delegating it to another woman she serves to reinforce the sexual stereotyping of housework'.[12] Rollins's study also provides a first hand knowledge of the exploitative nature of domestic work as it is based on her own experiences as a waged domestic worker. Examining the employer/employee relationship, she argues that it reflects maternal notions and demands deference, obligation, respect and loyalty from the employees. During the empirical research on women domestic workers in Pakistan, it was noticed that employers in Pakistan had similar expectations of loyalty, deference and respect from their domestic workers.

While reviewing Rollins's book, Ostrander raises two valid points the author fails to bring up (1) Rollins has not discussed the possibilities of organization and action to change the working conditions, although she mentions the anger and resentment expressed by employees towards their employers for mistreating them; and (2) she has not paid due attention to the public/private dichotomy that pushes domestic service completely into the private sphere, thus resulting in further exploitation of the domestics.[13] The issue of class hierarchies, shifting of responsibilities by women employers to women employees, and demands for respect and loyalty from employees by the employers are some of the core issues raised by Rollins. These issues are also relevant to the present study and were addressed by women domestic workers in Pakistan during their interviews and discussed in chapter six.

Parrenas in her cross-national comparative study discusses the experiences of Filipino domestic workers in Rome and Los Angeles.[14] She examines the phenomenon of migration in the globalized world and considers this global translocation of domestic workers an 'international division of reproductive labour' that emerges at the local, trans-national and global level. What distinguishes her study from other literature on migrant domestic workers is that she looks into the experiences of these migrant workers from the 'Dislocations' perspective.[15] Parrenas examines the institutional processes in which these dislocations are formed and argues that due to their dislocation these women have to live away from their families and suffer the pain of family separation, social exclusion and isolation in strange lands.[16] The strict immigration rules and low salaries given to Filipino domestics make it nearly impossible to bring the families of Filipino domestics together. As a result not only Filipino domestic workers suffer but in this process their children go through the trauma of being separated from their mothers for years. Other consequences of dislocation include the uncertain immigrant status with partial citizenship rights and downward mobility in terms of their previous jobs in the country of origin.[17]

An important and noteworthy aspect of Parrenas's book is the analysis of the global labour market, in which different occupations in domestic service, such as cleaning and caring services, provide benefits to both the sending and receiving countries. For receiving countries, domestic workers fulfil a labour market shortage in care-giving services for the young, disabled, and elderly, while for the supplying countries, domestic workers provide important economic benefits to the families they leave behind. Along with the receiving and sending governments who play a vital role in promoting such migration flows, the recruitment agents, overseas employment promoters, manpower suppliers and a host of other legal and illegal intermediaries profit from this situation. In comparison, in Pakistan there are very few agencies involved in specifically providing jobs to women domestic workers within the country and overseas. Unlike the Philippine government, the Pakistan government does not encourage women domestic workers to work in other countries, nor are there any statistics available from the recruitment agencies that send informal workers abroad especially to the Gulf countries.

Parrenas in her book highlights another dilemma of this international migration: The downward mobility amongst immigrant women. Women who migrate are better off in their own countries: for instance, they belong to middle-income groups, who have received at least graduate level college education and work as secretaries, clerks and in some cases as school teachers in their own countries. In foreign countries they experience a downward mobility in their careers as compared to their previous jobs. The jobs they perform in Los Angeles and Rome are of a very low level and are at the bottom of the occupation hierarchy, generally shunned by local women because of low rewards, inferior working conditions and limited job prospects and security.[18]

A similar argument is made by Glenn and Romero in their respective studies of Japanese and Chicana domestic workers.[19] They state that domestic service is not a means for upward mobility for migrant women domestic workers: rather, they experience 'occupational ghettoization.' For Glenn, domestic service serves as an entry point to the USA for these women workers, after which they are trapped into this service for generations as was the case of Japanese-American women till the 1970s. Romero in her thesis points out that chances of upward mobility or rises in earnings are scarce, as women are denied access to sources of information and other form of support, being socially segregated. As such, their financial condition remains stagnant.

Colen, in her study of West Indian women, differs from the arguments made by Glenn and Romero; that once the migrant women receive their green card status these women become occupationally mobile.[20] Colen describes how West Indian women working as nannies in New York go to school at night or on weekends to improve their qualifications, which would help them in finding white-collar jobs. Many of the women who were part of her study have now moved into clerical, industrial and health service jobs.

Sotelo's study reveals aspects of the working lives of migrant Latina women domestic workers in America, whose migration is often a family survival strategy due to the negative effects of the structural adjustment programmes in their home countries.[21] In her study she discusses the indifferent attitude of employers towards their domestic workers. She es that inequality among nations is a major factor for the globalization of paid domestic work. It has forced large numbers of women to leave behind their families and homes for better prospects. Another interesting aspect of Sotelo's study which is also relevant in case of domestic service in Pakistan is that Sotelo does not favour abolition of domestic service.[22] She emphatically suggests the need to take steps to improve the working conditions of domestic employees by implementing laws related to minimum wages and social security benefits and emphasizes the need to inculcate awareness among workers and employers of their rights and legal obligations.[23] Sotello draws attention to the fact that, government regulations in California exist in this area of employment but these are blatantly violated by employers. She argues that the strengthening of formal employment standards itself by lawmaking alone would not be effective unless employers are made aware of their obligations to follow the law in the case of domestic workers. Along with formal laws a personal recognition of domestic service as a paid and regulated employment category in which every worker has rights is needed. In her words 'public education and social acknowledgment' of paid domestic service is necessary and that could be achieved through public education programmes specifically focusing employers.[24]

In the present study on women domestic workers in Pakistan, the findings from the field clearly suggest that abolition of domestic service would not do any good to women domestic workers in Pakistan, rather it would deprive them of a means of earning a living. For the majority of women, domestic service is the only solution because of their inability to enter into any other profession due to lack of education, skills, and training. This lack of education and training is also strongly linked to their poverty and cultural constraints where girls' education is still not considered to be important. In such a situation performing domestic service in other households is the only alternative available to women unless they are equipped to enter other jobs whether in the formal or informal sector.

Chang's book critically examines the impact of welfare and immigration laws on not only domestic workers but also other women in low paid jobs such as nurses, janitors etc in the state of California.[25] She says that the 'Nanny Visa Programme' is as exploitative as any other programme in the past because workers are not allowed to change employers even if they are being maltreated by them.[26] Chang also holds the global economic systems responsible for the dismantling of social services in the First and Third World countries. She contends that the dismantling of the social services in the First World has created a demand for care workers which is filled by the migration of women in the domestic service sector. In Third World countries the dismantling of social services is imposed through Structural Adjustment Programmes as a condition for further loans by international financial institutions such as World Bank and International Monetary Fund.[27]

Ehrenreich and Hochschild's edited collection is another persuasive book which includes articles by various authors examining care work performed by migrant women in different countries.[28] The work performed by these nannies, maids, and sex workers is a proof of feminization of migration in the new economy. Hochschild in her article argues that like the brain drain a 'care drain' from Third World countries has also emerged.[29] However, this time the extraction is not of material resources but of something that cannot be measured and quantified, i.e. the love, maternal affection and care which these women workers bring with them.[30] Both the authors succinctly point out this new transition as follows:

> Women who migrate from country to country to work as maids not only bring their muscle power but an attentiveness to detail and to the human relationships in the household that might otherwise have been invested in their own families. Sex workers offer the simulation of sexual and romantic love, or at least transient sexual companionship. It is as if the wealthier parts of the world are running short on precious emotional and sexual resources and have had to turn to poorer regions for fresh supplies.[31]

Zarempka in her article in the same book considers present day domestic service as modern form of slavery where migrant workers from Third World countries are physically and mentally abused by their First World employers.[32] Zarempka raises serious questions about the immunity status granted to foreign diplomats in the USA who easily escape legal liability and cannot be challenged under the law because of the immunity given to them.[33] She also pinpoints that due to the uncertain immigrant status of these women it is not clear from where the citizenship rights of these women arise and which legal systems (whether of the sending or of the receiving country) they should accede to. She also points out the need for organizations and proper support systems for domestic workers as, at the moment, there are very few organizations and a loose network of churches, lawyers, social service agencies and some good Samaritans who have taken the initiative on their own to provide help to domestic workers.[34] Zarempka's article on the situation of migrant domestic workers in USA highlights the drawbacks in the legal protection. It also draws attention to the need for organized support networks because, in the absence of networks, women domestic workers would remain vulnerable and subject to exploitative work conditions.

Some of the common issues raised in the above-mentioned literature on migrant domestic workers in USA, including Chicanas, Filipinas, West Indian, Latinas and Japanese-American women, are low pay, poor working conditions and unpleasant and restrained employer/employee relations. These studies document the unsafe exploitative working conditions under which women domestic workers live and perform their duties in the affluent countries: for instance, when a domestic worker embarks on an overseas journey with or without a 'domestic worker contract' she faces violation of the contract terms and conditions, or the contract is otherwise substituted on arrival with discriminatory and unfair labour conditions. Most receiving countries in Asia and the Middle East do not allow migrant women workers to come with their families, therefore women have to emigrate in their own right, to become income-earners for their families and important foreign exchange contributors for their countries.[35]

The above studies raise important issues which are related to the situation of women domestic workers in Pakistan such as feminization of labour force, race and ethnicity, impact of migration and absence of legal protection and safety networks. The literature also reveals the exploitative working conditions where domestic workers are often paid sub-standard salaries, often on an irregular basis, or sometimes pay is withheld by employers; there are no days-off, and so income-related exploitation goes on. Due to their individualized work situations and isolated nature of work, they have no access to social support networks. Their food is inadequate, accommodation unsafe and uncomfortable, medical benefits are denied. There have been innumerable cases of sexual harassment and abuse, and excessive workload.[36]

SOME PERSPECTIVES ON DOMESTIC WORK IN BRITAIN

The discussion on the topic will begin by looking at the works of some historians and sociologists in Britain who have explored the phenomenon of domestic service in Victorian and Edwardian Britain. It will then move on to literature covering domestic service in contemporary Britain, where it is now an occupation filled locally as well as by migrant workers.

Ebery and Preston, and Hecht observe that in the early eighteenth and nineteenth centuries, domestic service in other households was one of the major reasons for the geographical and upward social mobility of rural migrants in England.[37] Domestic service was also considered an opportunity by rural families to spend some time in the cultured urban surroundings where they could get an opportunity to learn basic literacy as well as some new job skills. By contrast Davidoff in her work looks at domestic service from a gender and class perspective in Victorian and Edwardian England.[38] Her writing shows how domestic service played a key role in the construction of both middle class and working class women's identities as women. In her writings she aptly points out the paternal nature of the master-servant relationship where servants were considered to be under the protection of the master.[39] The master was expected to provide the food, shelter and wages, whereas servants were expected in reciprocation to be at the disposal of the master and to show loyalty and deference in all respects.[40]

In Britain, domestic service in recent times has taken a new shape. Gregson and Lowe document the resurgence of domestic service in contemporary Britain, where two main forms of domestic workers, i.e. nannies and cleaners, are being employed by middle-class families.[41] According to their study 30 to 40 per cent of middle-class families and those with dual careers, employ nannies and cleaners.[42] The increase in better opportunities of getting well paid jobs for educated women has added to the demand for domestic service. Working women hire such services to be able to spend more quality time with their family and children. Like Rollins's study, Gregson and Lowe also observe that the hiring and management of domestic workers remains the responsibility of female partners. This brings to light the nature of gender relations, where men reduce their participation in household chores to a negligible level.[43] Thus, engaging nannies and cleaners represent the restructuring of the traditional nature of the gender division of labour as men easily absolve themselves from childcare and household responsibilities.[44] This situation is similar to Pakistan where it is considered culturally inappropriate for men to help women in household chores. For working women in such a situation it is difficult to cope with household responsibilities as well as job pressures. Domestic service, being cheap labour, is affordable for many families. From the fieldwork, it clearly emerges that not only the well to do and affluent families employ domestic workers in Pakistan but even the middle and low income families employ domestic workers, if not as full-time or live-in but at least on part-time basis.

Anderson examines the status of domestic workers brought into Britain by employers, who are foreign nationals as well as local British nationals.[45] Britain is now amongst those developed countries that host domestic workers who come with their overseas employers, including diplomats, visitors, doctors, businessmen or other professionals. These employers are from the Gulf and Middle Eastern countries, Greece, Hong Kong, India, Italy, Nigeria, Singapore, the US, as well as the British nationals. Domestic workers enter the UK through two routes: either directly from their own home countries with their employers or via a second country where they are already employed by the same employer. Anderson also discusses the plight of migrant domestic workers who suffer due to the lack of proper policies.[46] Due to their visa status domestic workers are not allowed to change their employers nor can they file criminal proceedings against abusive employers who are granted diplomatic immunity because of their status.[47] Britain also does not allow the women domestic workers to bring along families, and therefore women domestics also suffer from isolation as they have to live away from their families.[48] On the contrary, if an employee escapes, then under immigration laws she becomes an 'unauthorised worker', 'over stayer' or both, who is liable to be deported.[49] Due to these legal complexities, domestic workers continue working for undesirable employers.

Phizaklea and Anderson have carried out a study on the impact of regulations affecting migrant domestic workers who enter the UK under certain immigration conditions.[50] The study examines the trans-national household strategies of migrant domestic workers based in London as they move from their undocumented status to having a legal status. Another recent work by Anderson covers domestic workers in the UK and five other European countries.[51] Drawing upon a Marxist feminist approach, Anderson examines working conditions of both live-in and day-workers and argues that there is a blatant exploitation of cheap labour from developing countries by middle class households in Europe.[52] The employers do not buy the labour of the domestic worker or according to Marxist theory 'the person in property' but they actually buy the whole person through the power to command.[53] Like her previous work, this book too compares domestic service with slavery and draws parallels between historical and contemporary forms of slavery in which domestic workers are exploited, abused, and denied personhood.[54] This contemporary form of slavery also reflects the racist behaviour of employers towards their employees.

Cox's work is a more recent addition to literature on domestic service in Britain.[55] In her two-stage research of paid domestic service in London she argues that with more women entering into professional jobs the demand for recruiting nannies, maids and *au pairs* has increased manifold in the UK. The other reasons for this rapid increase in migration of women in domestic service from developing countries to the developed countries are global economic trends that cause inequalities in income and access to decent employment in their own countries. Likewise, government policies of the receiving countries push responsibility for care onto individual families rather than providing for state based support.[56] Cox also examines the recruitment processes used by employers and methods used by domestic workers to find jobs, and how these contribute to the ghettoization of particular groups.[57]

In summation literature from the UK highlights the weaknesses in immigration laws and policies that affect the lives of migrant domestic workers. It is also relevant to the present study that questions the efficacy of law as a tool of empowerment for women in domestic service. It also draws attention to the fact that employing domestic help has increased in the era of global economy with more women entering into fulltime professional jobs. At the same time it also shows the gendered nature of domestic service where housework and childcare is still considered to be a woman's responsibility.

DOMESTIC SERVICE IN CANADA

Domestic service in Canada is also carried out mostly by migrant women from developing countries. Studies carried out in Canada examine in detail the programmes and procedures for employing migrant women domestic workers.[58] These programmes are criticized for their discriminatory policies which deny citizenship rights and provide very little legal protection to migrant domestic workers. As a result these workers live and work under inhumane conditions. In 1955, when women domestic workers from the Caribbean countries came to Canada they were given landed status upon arrival and were supposed to work for one year as domestic workers.[59] After one year they had the option to find a job in any other field or they could continue as domestic workers. Due to the long working hours, low salaries and isolated nature of the job, with no chances of progress or financial improvement, many women after the completion of one year left their jobs as domestic workers. There was thus always a shortage of workers in domestic service. However, in the 1970s instead of improving working conditions, the Canadian government stopped issuing immigrant landed status to these workers, instead recruiting them under a temporary employment visa programme.[60]

In the 1980s, when cases of abuse of domestic workers were reported, the Canadian employment and immigration minister announced a new policy for domestic workers under which they could apply for immigrant resident status after completion of two years of service as domestics.[61]

In 1992, the Canadian government rolled back its 'Domestic Workers Programme' and announced a new scheme named the 'Live-in-Care-Giver' programme (hereinafter referred as LCP).[62] Under this programme foreigners are allowed to work in Canada as live-in caregivers for a specified period of time, in return for which these workers are offered permanent residence worker status. However, there are three drawbacks in the programme—temporary status, the twenty-four-month work period and obligation to live in the employer's home.[63]

Cohen's study of 'women of colour' working as domestics in Canada looks at the issue of domestic work from a different perspective, as compared to other studies carried out thus far that highlight the gender, class and racial discrimination of domestic workers.[64] Cohen refers to three types of coping strategies: 'External—mobilising community resources and ties with people outside the labour situation, Internal—utilising resources from within work situations and Cognitive—altering the definition of the situation.'[65] She explores these strategies used by women domestic workers to cope with their working conditions and to deal with their employers.[66] By identifying these coping strategies Cohen emphasizes the strengths of women domestic workers, and suggests that they are not just passive victims but have the courage and ability to handle their situations.

Literature on various domestic workers programmes, laws, and policies in Canada supports the argument that laws and policies alone are not sufficient to provide protection to a vulnerable group of workers such as women domestic workers. It also shows that the government does not appear to have the workers' welfare at heart. The loopholes in policies also indicate that these are susceptible to misuse by employers who abuse domestic workers by making them work for long hours, deprive them of their independence and in some cases even subject them to physical and sexual harassment. Cohen's findings are also relevant to the present study as it supports the concept of women's agency discussed in the previous chapter (theoretical framework of this research).It is useful in exploring strategies adopted by women domestic workers in Pakistan for dealing with their employers.

PERSPECTIVES ON DOMESTIC SERVICE FROM THE SOUTH

The literature produced on domestic workers in countries in the South, for instance Malaysia, South Africa and Saudi Arabia, suggests as in the case of Filipino and Indonesian workers in Malaysia that the global move since the 1970s to encourage open markets and free trade is not only confined to manufactured goods but also includes utilization of services of migrant workers from developing countries. In Malaysia the middle class depends on the capitalist market for the provision of services by trans-national migrant workers.

Chin's book illustrates the case of Filipino and Indonesian domestic workers in the newly industrialized Malaysia. Chin discusses how the state elite and middle classes in their pursuit of a modern lifestyle, which is also the objective of the country's modernity project, try to justify the demand and treatment meted out to these workers.[67] The purchase and display of material goods define the modern middle-class lifestyle, and hiring foreign domestic workers is associated with social status. In other words, employing foreign domestic workers has become a status symbol in Malaysia.

Chin argues that the process of acquiring modernity by export-oriented development policies, which include both consumption of goods and services, has to be reshaped in order to save foreign migrant domestic workers from inhumane and abusive treatment by the Malaysian employers.[68] She argues that the social construction of 'migrant domestic workers' images as 'prostitutes or commodities' legitimizes maltreatment of these workers. However, these workers are not the passive recipients of employers' abuse and they react in various ways to challenge employers' attitudes and the consequent treatment of these workers as lesser human beings.[69] In Chin's words:

> We cannot assume, however, that all domestic workers are powerless to redefine employer-employee relations, hence they succumb to the dominative and exploitative aspects of un-legislated domestic service. The denial of civil political rights does not necessarily preclude the fact that foreign female

domestic workers can be political actors who engage in different forms of resistance that challenge or renegotiate employer/employee relations.[70]

Chin states that political action may not necessarily require a formal mode of conduct or a forum like a trade union through which collective action is carried out against discriminatory treatment.[71]

The case of South African domestic workers is also very interesting, where the complex interrelation of race, gender and class has oppressed black domestic workers. Gaitskell (et al.) and Cock in their respective works discuss domestic service in the light of class, race and gender relations. Gaitskell (et al.) argues that those who perform waged domestic service should be considered as 'waged workers' because this would help in conceptualizing domestic service as a form of employment.[72] They further argue that the nature of work done in a household either by the housewife or by a waged domestic is almost the same, yet the position and status of the two are very different. The employer is in a dominant position and exploits the worker in terms of wages, working hours, and hires and fires at will.

Cock, in her sociological research of women domestic workers in Eastern Cape, South Africa, analyses those social structures and historical processes against the backdrop of apartheid, which has suppressed and silenced these workers for a long time.[73] She discusses in detail the poor working conditions, deprivation and relations with the employers of women domestics in South Africa, which are further aggravated due to the convergence of racial and sexual domination. Cock uses the term 'ultra exploitability' for South African domestic workers who suffer on two counts, the sexist patriarchal ideology which considers women as secondary, inferior, subordinate and dependent, and the racist ideology that considers blacks as irresponsible, stupid and passive.[74] By discussing and raising the issue of unequal power relations between women against women (the white women as employers and black domestic workers,) the book poses certain serious questions to feminists and challenges the over-simplified feminist notion of 'sisterhood'.

Wright's study of domestic workers in Singapore reveals the fact that Singapore does not have sufficient legal and social support for migrant women.[75] The residence permits of domestic workers are linked to their employment, and subject to restrictions.[76]

Another investigation into the case of domestic workers in Singapore appears in the detailed report by Human Rights Watch.[77] According to this report, women domestic workers in Singapore coming from countries like Indonesia, the Philippines, and Sri Lanka suffer at the hands of their employers as well as employment agents.[78] Domestic workers are not covered by the main labour laws of the country and there is no law that regulates their terms of contract, working hours, holidays, and wages. As a result they have to work longer hours and in many cases seven days a week. Besides, there are many employment agencies both registered and unregistered that charge heavy fees in lieu of providing employment to domestic workers.

Silvey, in her study of Indonesian domestic workers in Saudi Arabia, analyses the trans-nationalization of women's migration and activism.[79] She looks at the ways in which activist groups in Indonesia construct and mobilize particular 'scale and spaces' in order to pressurize states for regulatory change.[80] On the one hand this study highlights the violence and abuse faced by Indonesian migrant women workers working in Saudi Arabia, while on the other hand it explores how migrant worker organizations in Indonesia have trans-nationalized their scope by joining pressure groups, using internet communication networks and international women's meetings. She also makes the point that women's migration in a trans-national sphere can be emancipatory, as they are able to earn more as compared to what they were earning at home, as well as possibly helping them to escape from oppressive local domestic relations.[81]

Jureidini and Moukarbel, in their study based on interviews with seventy Sri Lankan women working in Lebanon, reveal the legal and employment conditions of these women.[82] They argue that Sri Lankan domestic workers in Lebanon fall under the category of 'contract slavery' as defined by Bales.[83] Jureidini and Moukarbel further argue, that 'contract slavery' is ascertained by the abuse or violence, or threats of abuse or violence, that these women face at the hands of their employers.[84]

Describing the legal and administrative conditions, the researchers point out that domestic workers in Lebanon are not covered by the labour law as these are not applicable to private households.[85] Domestic workers arrive in Lebanon through employment agencies (both in Sri Lanka and Lebanon). Some Lebanese agencies have contacts with Sri Lankan agencies and they hire domestic workers from them after paying a certain fee.[86] In terms of providing support to women domestic workers there are only a few NGOs in Lebanon that provide legal assistance and a safe house for 'runaway' domestic workers. The Lebanese government has now established a computerized database which records the entries of domestic workers and names of their employers.[87]

To conclude, literature from the South reflects some important themes that are also the subject of analysis of the present study. Silveys's work highlights the role of networks and pressure groups which are needed to provide support to women domestic workers. Weaknesses of the legal system discussed in studies from Singapore, Hong Kong, and Taiwan reinforce the main argument of the present study that legislation is not sufficient and other factors have to be taken into consideration, such as socio economic conditions and gendered nature of domestic service.

DOMESTIC WORK IN THE SOUTH ASIAN CONTEXT

Domestic work is performed by women in all the neighbouring countries of Pakistan in the South Asian region. Women, who enter into domestic service, in India, Sri Lanka, or Pakistan, are in majority of cases poor, illiterate and have no formal training for any skilled labour. Therefore, the only way left for them is to earn a living by performing domestic service in other households. Some of the studies carried out in India on women domestic workers, who face discrimination on the basis of their class, gender, and ethnic or caste background, are discussed.

Widge's study emphasizes the need to recognize domestic work as a form of productive labour and raises the point that the position of women domestic workers can only be made stronger if they are organized in the form of associations and organizations, and by providing legal cover through legislative provisions.[88]

Raghuram's study of Indian domestic workers who migrate from other parts in India to Delhi examines how informal networks in the form of social relations are used as coping strategies by domestic workers among their own community as well as in their relations with employers.[89] Raghuram also points to how migration of some individuals opens channels of mobility for other members of the same caste or region. Early migrants provide support and assistance to new migrants in entering domestic service, by introducing them to prospective employers. Such support is also seen in the case of domestic workers in the US, UK and other countries that receive migrant workers. This is also in the case of subjects of the present study in which many domestic workers have migrated from rural parts of Pakistan to the cities.

Chigateri in her study of Dalit groups in Bangalore also takes account of Dalit women who perform domestic service.[90] Using Fraser's framework she points to the injustice of mal-distribution as one of the major causes of the appalling conditions of this working group. She argues that 'It is an injustice rooted in an economic order that does not provide for the basic needs of its citizens.' The women interviewed for her study hold the state responsible for the mal-distribution of government jobs. Had there been jobs for their men, the interviewees think that they would have been leading more stable and secure lives and that there would not have been a need for them to be involved in domestic service. These women also contest the association of domestic service as intrinsic to their communities. The reasons for such contestation are firstly, domestic service is not the type of work which these women traditionally perform in their communities. They do work outside the home in fields as agricultural workers and that work has more value as compared to domestic service. Secondly, employers do not show any respect or recognition to domestic work as 'work' they treat women domestics as menial workers. Finally, due to the negative valuation of this work these women want to distance themselves from domestic service.[91] Like India, in Pakistan also, compared to cleaning jobs or domestic service, agricultural labour is considered more respectable. Women interviewees of the present study mentioned that those who work in the field are more respected than those who work as domestic workers. Similarly, many domestic workers in Pakistan like their counterparts in India enter this service due to unemployment of their men.

Although Chigatri's study focuses on Dalits, yet it presents certain common features to the situation of women domestic workers in Pakistan, especially women who migrate from rural areas of Punjab where the caste system is still prevalent.[92] It is also applicable to the Pakistani Christian domestic workers because cleaning jobs, considered 'low work', are always associated with Christians in Pakistan.

Qayum and Ray in their study of domestic workers in Kolkata discuss the continuation of domestic servitude in the modern Kolkatan society.[93] They argue that the institution of domestic servitude in the modern Indian home and life signifies a 're-articulation of ideas and practices derived from the feudal and colonial past.'[94] However, the shift from spatial homes to smaller apartments, extended family structures to nuclear family and the change in employers from feudal landlords into a younger generation of corporate elite has affected the previous notions attached with domestic service.[95] Now employers keep only one or two workers due to the limitation of space which affects their privacy, and are forced to keep part-time workers. There are also tensions between the employer and the employee regarding expectations of loyalty, love, and care. The young generation of employers on the one hand wants this relationship to be impersonal and contractual but when it comes to the employee's rights, employers feel threatened as they still want their servants to be under their thumb. In this way the culture of servitude persists even in the modern democratic Kolkatan society.[96]

Historically in India the issue of domestic workers has also been raised by novelists and short story writers. One such collection of stories is by Wajida Tabassum, an Urdu short story writer from Hyderabad Deccan.[97] In these stories she brings to light some negative aspects of the otherwise very rich and glamorous culture of Deccan associated with the days of Nizams of Hyderabad. In the foreword to this book, Tabassum asserts that her purpose in writing these stories is to hold a mirror to the plight of downtrodden, poverty-stricken male and female servants working in upper class households on very meagre remuneration. She says,

> A poverty-stricken, downtrodden, cruelly treated class of society has always caught my attention. Its importance like the first but the lowest rung of the ladder cannot be ignored, because it is the first step that takes you to the top. No doubt the services rendered by domestic servants (especially females) relieve the middle class ladies of the drudgery of the household duties enabling them to take jobs to improve their financial conditions and living standards. Whereas upper class women feed their vanities, languish away their time and enjoy life at the cost of domestic servants.[98]

The writer, in one of her stories *'Utran'*, portrays how charities extended by the employers in a condescending way adversely affect the self-esteem of both male and female domestic servants. This degrading treatment in the long run shatters the personalities of some sensitive persons, like Chamki, a girl servant in the story.[99] Constant suppression and a persistent feeling of humiliation provokes her to be revengeful. Consequently, on the wedding day of Shehzadi Pasha when Chamki is wearing a new dress for the first time in her life her charming reflection in the mirror gives her confidence that she has never experienced before. Obsessed with the feeling of revenge she misuses her confidence by alluring the bridegroom into sex. Later on, almost in an hysterical fit, she bursts out telling Shehzadi Pasha what she has done only to make Shehzadi realize how it hurts when one is given leftovers, and in this case it is the bridegroom who by indulging into this act has become like a used and second-hand commodity. This story is also a reflection on the hypocrisy of high-class society, where men despite great claims of morality fail to resist such temptations and can also be linked to present day world where women domestic workers often become victims of sexual harassment by the employers.

'*Bhuki*' is the story of another class of female servants employed as wet nurse to breastfeed the babies of their employers.[100] Zainab, a nanny character in this story, is given the best food, clothing, and all sorts of physical comforts as she has to feed the employer's baby, but the tragic part of the story is that she is not allowed to feed her own child and, being under constant watch of another maid, she cannot even feed him secretly. As a result her child, who is bottle-fed, which does not suit him, deteriorates physically and dies. In present times this situation can be compared to what Ehrenriech and Hochschild refer to as 'extraction of love and care' from the poor and developing countries to meet the demands of the developed world where parents are unable to provide love and care to their children due to their career commitments and extremely busy lifestyles.

LITERATURE ON DOMESTIC WORK IN PAKISTAN

The issue of women domestic workers in Pakistan has so far received little scholarly or media attention. While searching for the literature only one research paper and a survey on domestic workers was found. The dearth of literature in Pakistan perhaps shows that scholars, researchers and educators, including the author, have enjoyed the services of domestic workers but have turned a blind eye to their problems. It can thus be argued that as a result of a conflict of interest employers have failed to raise a voice for regulating domestic service in Pakistan.

As mentioned above the only article found while searching for literature on women domestic workers in Pakistan during the last two decades was a paper by Ali and Khattak on women domestic workers in the NWFP, presented at a seminar on women's employment legislation.[101] In this paper the authors discuss the nature of domestic service, working conditions and the various types of domestic servants, for instance full-time, part-time and workers in urban and rural settings, in the light of a few case studies. While advocating the need for proper legislation that could cover these variations in existing conditions and types of domestic work, they argue that the 'public private dichotomy' and the 'cultural construction of self' are the two major reasons why domestic workers in Pakistan are not covered by the labour legislation.[102]

Ali and Khattak also emphasize that both employers and domestic servants should be registered with employment exchanges and these exchanges can also disseminate information regarding rights.[103] At the same time these workers should have their own associations that would provide them with support in terms of resolving disputes or in finding another job.[104]

A small survey of domestic workers in Karachi was carried out in 2003 by a non-governmental organisation based in Karachi.[105] The detailed report of the survey has not yet been published. However, some of the findings of the survey were shared in a two-day consultation workshop on rights of domestic workers, and published in the proceedings of that consultation.[106] Fifty-eight women domestic workers were interviewed. The data collected from these interviews identifies the different migrant communities who have migrated to Karachi from other parts of the country in search of jobs. It also discusses their appalling working conditions, low wages, working hours, and reasons for leaving jobs.

Domestic workers have also been included in a recent study on bonded labour in Pakistan.[107] This study draws attention to the linkage between bonded labour and domestic service. It shows how families who have debts to pay to landlords in rural areas are engaged in bonded labour. They are forced to work for free without receiving any remuneration as domestic workers to pay off their family debts. In this form of service, workers not only surrender their labour but also all control over their lives. It is for the landlord to decide who is going to work for him and he may send the domestic worker to his relatives or to other members of the family. In such situations women domestic workers, especially young girls are in a dangerous situation as they often become victims of sexual abuse.

The issue of domestic workers in Pakistan has received attention of Urdu novelists and playwrights who use the character of domestic workers especially female domestic workers in their stories and plays.[108] Some of the stories are based on well-known facts of history and go back to the Mughal era, in which beautiful young maids were trained in singing and dancing to please and add colour to the life of the palace. A famous case is that of Anarkali, a maid in the palace of the Mughal emperor Jalaluddin Akbar. Imtiaz Ali Taj, a renowned Pakistani playwright, depicted the story of Anarkali in his stage play.[109] The story depicts the reality that despite tall claims made by Mughal rulers of their services and reforms rendered to the cause of humanity, the joys and sometimes even the lives of these maids were sacrificed on the alter of the royal ego.[110] Anarkali was punished for her sincerity and devotion whereas others who yielded to the pressures survived and flourished with their timid hypocrisies.

This contrast shows that character and personalities are distorted in an environment of pressure, intimidation and exploitation. This issue was also raised by another Urdu short story writer Ismat Chughtai who comments on the psyche of male and female domestic workers who served her family for generations.[111] Chughtai says that servitude, stretched over generations, perpetrates the slave mentality. Her comment about her domestic workers is that: 'Their mentalities were enslaved with their bodies. They were born with slave mentalities and they lived with it.' She goes on to observe: 'Servants have dual personalities; one in the presence of their masters is servile, kissing the hands of their masters, and the other behind their back gives full vent to frustrations by abusing their masters'. This apparently negative remark of the writer rings of truth and reveals her sympathy for the downtrodden human beings whose personalities have been marred by maltreatment of their employers.

The theme of callousness of employers has been elaborated upon by various modern writers in different regional languages of Pakistan. Zaitoon Bano a Pashto[112] short story writer in one of her short stories refers to the death of a young maid called Basri who, after being seduced and impregnated, was thrust upon a burning oil stove and burnt alive by her debauched landlord master.[113] The matter was hushed up by concocting a story that the tragedy was an accident. Her parents were too poor and intimidated to call for justice.

In the course of the literary search for the present study, I also came across a poetic monologue of Ahmad Faraz entitled '*Kaneez*' (maid).[114] In this poem he portrays the advances of a drunken master towards his maid and her reactionary remarks in response, with a tinge of deep sarcasm.[115] The poem reflects the vulnerable position of women domestic workers who are sexually abused at the hands of employers.

These pieces of literature highlight the fact that the situation of women domestic workers is a socio-legal issue and writers and poets have been sensitive to their plight and have addressed it in their literary works. Sympathetic realization of this issue inspires creativity and adds to the significance of the issue. No doubt these literary creations in the form of poems and stories cannot be a substitute for practical measures to improve the living conditions of the female servants but the fact remains that they inspire a deep feeling of sympathy for them as well as highlight their insecurity and miseries. Literature is also a powerful source of raising awareness. In the context of women in domestic service, it acquires further significance as it highlights the problems of the vulnerable.

CONCLUSION

Literature from the Northern and Southern countries reflect the diverse nature of domestic service and suggests that domestic service as well as its problems is a global phenomenon. It also highlights the point that despite differences in socio-economic and geographical settings, there exist a number of commonalties between women domestic workers working in different settings in developed and developing countries. It is also to be noted that all studies irrespective of country of origin point to the inadequacy of a simple legal response to address the situation of women domestic workers. This appears to be the case even in countries of the North where the formal legal system as well as the state and its institutions are well developed and responsive (these states have failed to provide protection to migrant domestic workers). But as this review suggests the problem is socio legal; hence solutions too must look beyond the black letter law.

In America, Canada and Great Britain domestic work is carried out mostly by the immigrant population from South America and by women from South East Asia. The vast scale of migration has given rise to 'trans-national communities.' The literature on immigrant communities highlights the fact that immigrant women in domestic service suffer in particular, due to the weaknesses in the immigration laws and negligible protection available under the employment laws of the host countries. This literature also discusses the re emergence of domestic workers in USA because of large numbers of immigrant population in the country. Race is another important theme which is discussed in relation to black domestic workers in America as well as in relation to domestic service in South Africa.[116]

Some of the literature on paid domestic work also links domestic service to the old institution of slavery. This now exists in the form of 'domestic servitude' and 'contract slavery' and has become an essential part of the family structure of countries in the South as well as affluent, capitalist countries of the North.[117] However, despite their sufferings women in domestic service are not always oppressed victims. They are consistently struggling and have devised their own ways and strategies for coping with oppressive work conditions, which Cohen in her study refers to as 'Internal, External and Cognitive Strategies'.[118]

A comparison of women domestic workers in Pakistan with migrant women domestic workers in affluent countries of the world shows that first of all domestic workers in Pakistan do not go through the same agony and pain of being lonely in strange lands, as in most cases they have their own families with them. Secondly, the cultural environment remains the same, where they share the same values, customs, and language with their employers, as for example compared to a Caribbean woman or a Filipino working in the USA or in any other European country.

A second difference is that in the case of global migrant workers most of them are literate, many hold college degrees and have previously worked in better positions in their home countries, as clerks, secretaries, teachers and factory workers. For a better income abroad, they understate their qualifications to get a job and as a result those with higher skills end up in lower jobs. This also shows the downgrading or waste of human capital involved. By contrast, domestic workers in the present study are illiterate, come from very poor backgrounds, and cannot afford to send their children to schools. However, in Pakistan, migration from rural areas to the cities has been a source of upward social mobility in many cases.

Finally, women domestics in the developed world, such as the USA or Canada, have better opportunities for enhancing their capabilities, whereas Pakistani women domestic workers in the majority of the cases are deprived of such opportunities. Sotelo's study has shown that migrant domestic workers in America have a chance to attend schools at night or at weekends to improve their qualifications, which would help them in getting white-collar jobs. Such opportunities do not exist for women domestics in Pakistan, mainly because they do not have the resources: the men in their households also do not consider female education as important, and over and above this, there are no organizations or support groups available to these women domestic workers. Similarly, in welfare states such as Britain and other European countries local domestic workers being citizens of a welfare state, receive free health care and education for children which is not available to women domestic workers in Pakistan. Besides, they can also not be paid below the minimum wage standards because they are covered under the definition of worker and provided protection under the employment laws of the country.

The literature review also highlights its scarcity and need for more research on the issue of women domestic workers in Pakistan. This present link between law and literature is therefore a step to fill the existing gap in literature on women domestic workers in Pakistan.

NOTES

1. Coser, L. (1973), 'Servants: The Obsolescence of an Occupational Role,' *Social Forces*, Vol. 52, No. 1, pp. 31-40.
2. Some examples of the thriving feminist literature on global domestic workers are: Ehrenreich, B. and Hochschild, A.R. (2003), (eds.), *Global Women: Nannies and Maids in Global Economy*, Great Britain: Granta Books; Silvera, M. (1989), *Silenced: Talks with Working Class Caribbean Women about their Lives and Struggles as Domestic Workers in Canada*, Sister Vision Black Women and Women of Colour Press; Anderson, B. (1993), *Britain's Secret Slaves: An Investigation into the Plight of Overseas Domestic Workers*, London: Anti Slavery International and Kalayaan; Parrenas, R.S. (2001), *Servants of Globalization: Women, Migration and Domestic Work*, Stanford, California: Stanford University Press; Sanjek, R. and Colen, S. (1990), (eds.), 'At Work in Homes: Household Workers in World Perspective,' *American Ethnological Society Monograph Series*, No. 3, Chang, G. (2000), *Disposable Domestics: Immigrant Women Workers in the Global Economy*, Cambridge, Massachusetts: South End Press; Sotelo, P.H. (2001), *Domestica: Immigrant Workers Cleaning and Caring in the Shadows of Affluence*, Berkeley, Los Angeles, and London: University of California Press; Ehrenreich, B. (2001), *Nickel and Dimed: On (not) Getting by in America*, New York: Henry Holt and Company, LLC; Widge, A. (1995), *Women in the Informal Sector: Multi Disadvantages of Domestic Workers*, New Delhi: Indian Social Institute; Chin, C.B.N. (1998), *In Service and Servitude: Female Foreign Domestic Workers and the Malaysian 'Modernity' Project.* New York: Columbia University Press; Cock, J. (1989), *Maids and Madams: Domestic Workers under Apartheid*, London: The Women's Press; Arat Koc, S. (1997), 'From Mothers of the Nation to Migrant Workers,' in Bakan, A.B. and Stasiulis, A. (eds.), *Not One of the Family Foreign Domestic Workers* in *Canada*, Toronto: University of Toronto Press; Langewin, L. and Belleau, M.C. (2000), *Trafficking in Women in Canada: A Critical Analysis of the Legal Framework Governing Live-In Care-Givers and Mail Order Bride*, Quebec: Status of Women Canada.
3. Salmon, L.M. (1972), *Domestic Service*, New York: Arno Press. Some other studies on domestic service in the US include the works of Dudden, F.E. (1983), *Serving Women: Household Service in Nineteenth Century America*, Middletown, Connecticut: Wesleyan University Press; Sutherland, D. (1981), *Americans and their Servants: Domestic Service in the United States from 1800 to 1920*, Baton Rouge La. and London: Louisiana State University Press.
4. According to Salmon's survey, domestic service in America has passed through three distinct phases. The first phase was from the early colonization to the time of the American Revolution. The second phase was from revolution to 1850s and the third phase began from 1850 to the present time.
5. Salmon, supra note 3, pp. 151-53.
6. Ibid., pp. 254-6.
7. Ibid., pp. 261-2.
8. Katzman, D.M. (1978), *Seven Days a Week: Women and Domestic Service in Industrializing America*, New York: Oxford University Press.
9. Palmer, P. (1989), *Housewives and Domestic Servants in the United States 1920-1945*, Philadelphia: Temple University Press.
10. Cf., see footnote 2.
11. Rollins, J. (1985), *Women Using Other Women*, Philadelphia: Temple University Press.

12. Ibid., p. 73.
13. Ostrander, S.A. (1987), 'Book Review: Women Using Other Women,' *Contemporary Sociology*, Vol. 16, No. 1, pp. 51-53.
14. Parrenas, R.S., supra note 2, p. 11.
15. Ibid., p. 12.
16. Ibid., p. 12.
17. Ibid., p. 12.
18. Ibid., p. 19.
19. Glenn, E.N. (1986), *Issei, Nisei, War Bride, Three Generations of Japanese American Women in Domestic Service*, Philadelphia: Temple University Press; Romero, M. (1988), 'Days Work in the Suburbs: The Work Experience of Chicana Private House Keepers,' in Stratham, A., Miller, E. and Mauksch, H. (eds.), *The Worth of Women's Work: A Qualitative Synthesis*, Albany: State University of New York Press.
20. Colen, S. (1986), 'With Respect and Feelings: Voices of West Indian Childcare and Domestic Workers in New York,' in Cole, J. (ed.), *All American Women: Lines that Divide, Ties that Bind.* New York: Free Press. Some other important works of the author include Colen, S. (1995) 'Like a Mother to Them: Stratified Reproduction and West Indian Childcare Workers and Employers in New York.' in Ginsberg, F. and Rayna, R. (eds.), *Conceiving the New World Order: The Global Politics of Reproduction*, Berkeley: UC Press, pp. 8-102.
21. Sotelo, H.P. (2001), *Doméstica: Immigrant Workers Cleaning and Caring in the Shadow of Affluence*, Los Angeles: California University Press; Sotelo, H.P. (1994), 'Regulating the Unregulated: Domestic Workers Social Networks,' *Social Problems*, Vol. 41, pp. 50-64; Glenn, E.V. (2003), 'Book Review: Doméstica: Immigrant Workers Cleaning and Caring in the Shadows of Affluence,' *American Journal of Sociology*, Vol. 109, No. 3, pp. 791–3.
22. Ibid., p. 210.
23. Ibid., p. 211.
24. Ibid., p. 243.
25. Chang, G. (2000), *Disposable Domestics: Immigrant Women Workers in the Global Economy*, Cambridge, Mass: South End Press, p. 93.
26. The 'Bracero Programme of 1942 to 1964' and 'Guest Worker Programmes' such as the 'H-2a agricultural workers contract programme' were easily bypassed by employers to employ undocumented workers.
27. Chang, G., supra note 26, p. 16.
28. The essays in this book also focus on paid domestic work and sex work in other countries such as Sri Lanka, Philippines, Thailand, Vietnam, Hong Kong, the Dominican Republic, and Taiwan.
29. Hochschild, A.R. (2003), 'Love and Gold', in Ehrenreich, B. and Hochschild, A.R. (ed.), *Global Women: Nannies and Maids in Global Economy*, Great Britain: Granta Books, p. 17.
30. Ehrenreich, B. and Hochschild, A.R., supra note 2, p. 4.
31. Ibid., p. 4.
32. Zarempka, J. (2003), 'America's Dirty Work: Migrant Maids and Modern-Day Slavery,' in Ehrenreich, B. and Hochschild, A.R. (ed.), *Global Women: Nannies and Maids in Global Economy*, Great Britain: Granta Books, p. 145.
33. Ibid., p. 147.
34. Ibid., pp. 152-3.
35. The residence permit of these workers is linked to their employment, and subject to restrictions. Foreign domestic maids in a number of countries cannot change jobs

within two years of an employment contract. In some countries, for example Singapore, migrant women are prohibited from marrying local citizens. They are not allowed to become pregnant, and are subject to six-monthly pregnancy tests.

36. Sarah Balbagan, a 15-year old Filipino, was raped by her employer in the UAE, and Teresta Tristan, who worked under inhumane conditions with a British family in the UK are examples, which tell us about the deplorable working conditions of domestic workers in foreign lands.
37. Ebery, M. and Preston, B. (1976), 'Domestic Service in Late Victorian and Edwardian England 1871-1914,' *Reading Geographical Papers*, Reading University, Department of Geography; Hecht, J. (1956), *The Domestic Servant Class in Eighteenth Century England*, London: Routledge and Kegan Paul.
38. Davidoff, L. (1995), *Worlds Between: Historical Perspectives on Gender and Class*, Cambridge: Polity Press.
39. Ibid., pp. 18-19.
40. Cf., study of domestic workers in US also reflects the same attitude of employers towards their domestic workers.
41. Gregson, N. and Lowe, M. (1994), *Servicing the Middle Classes: Class, Gender and Waged Domestic Labour in Contemporary Britain*, London and New York: Routledge.
42. Ibid., p. 50.
43. Ibid., pp. 240-1.
44. Ibid., p. 241.
45. Anderson, B. (1993), *Britain's Secret Slaves: An Investigation into the Plight of Overseas Domestic Workers*, United Kingdom: No. 5 in ASI's Human Rights Series.
46. Ibid., pp. 41-56.
47. Ibid., p. 41.
48. Ibid., p. 46.
49. Ibid., p. 52.
50. Anderson, B. and Phizaklea, A. (1997), 'Migrant Domestic Workers: A European Perspective.' study supported by Equal Opportunities Unit, DGV and Leicester University.
51. Anderson, B. (2000), *Doing the Dirty Work: The Global Politics of Domestic Labour*, London and New York: Zed Books.
52. Ibid., p. 112.
53. Ibid., pp. 113-4.
54. Ibid., p. 133.
55. Cox, R. (2006), *Servant Problem: Domestic Employment in Global Economy*', London: I.B. Tauris and Co. Ltd.
56. Cox, R. 'The Servant Problem: A Return to Victorian Values' available at http://www.socialistworker.co.uk/article.php?article_id=8423 accessed on 4 September 2006.
57. Ibid.
58. Macklin, A. (1992), 'Foreign Domestic Worker: Surrogate Housewife or Mail Order Servant?', *MC Gill L*, Vol. 37; Bakan, A.B. and Stasiulis, A. (1997), (ed.), *Not One of the Family: Foreign Domestic Workers in Canada*, Toronto: University of Toronto Press, p. 53, Silvera, M. (1989), *Silenced: Talks with Working Class Caribbean Women about Their Lives and Struggles as Domestic Workers in Canada*, Toronto: Sister Vision, Black Women and Women of Colour Press.
59. Prior to Live-in-Care Programme, Foreign Domestic Movement Programme was enforced from 1971 to 1992.

60. This programme was basically for filling up the labour shortage in the informal sector, in which workers performed their jobs under inhumane working conditions and for low wages. Another drawback for workers of this visa programme was that each visa was issued for a specific job, a specific employer and for a definite period of time, and in the case of a change of a situation the worker was required to inform the immigration service immediately. Unlike the 'Domestic Scheme' of 1955 this temporary visa programme was a temporary solution to overcome a domestic labour shortage and was least concerned about the working conditions under which these workers performed their jobs.
61. There were certain gaps in this policy also, because the women who applied for the resident status were left at the will of an individual immigration officer who would evaluate their application and determine whether they had an aptitude for learning, adaptability to the Canadian lifestyle, and personal suitability. Under the new policy employers were bound to provide free time every week to the workers to attend night schools, and to contribute $20 per month towards their employee's education/training programmes, but in practice the employers hardly followed this rule.
62. Langewin, L. and Belleau, M.C. (2000), *Trafficking in Women in Canada: A Critical Analysis of the Legal Framework Governing Live in Care Givers and Mail Order Brides,* Quebec: *Status of Women Canada*, pp. 30-31.
63. This temporary status lasts for three years or a 24-month period, during which this female worker has to work as a live-in care worker, and another twelve months in waiting after filing her application for permanent status. During this period, the domestic worker lives neither as an immigrant nor as a visitor, and as such she is bound to serve the employer whose name appears on her work permit. If she wants to change the employer, she has to pay a fee and obtain a new work permit with the name of the new employers on it, who should have their offer of employment validated by the Human Resources centre. It usually takes a month to obtain a new work permit, but any delay in finding a new employer or delay in providing necessary documents delays further the possibility of applying for permanent residence at the end of the 24-month period by a corresponding length of time. Any time spent in working without a work permit is not counted towards the 24-month period. Similarly, the condition that the employer must stay as a live-in worker can lead to such abuses as unpaid long working hours, violation of privacy, greater dependence on employers and sexual harassment and assault.
64. Cohen, R. (1991), 'Women of Colour in White Households: Coping Strategies of Live-in Domestic Workers,' *Qualitative Sociology*, Vol. 14, No. 2, p. 197.
65. Ibid., p. 197.
66. Women of colour who were interviewed by Cohen for her study included eighteen Philippino women, thirty from the West Indies, one from Hong Kong, and one from Mexico.
67. Chin, C.B.N. (1998), *In Service and Servitude: Female Foreign Domestic Workers and the Malaysian 'Modernity' Project*, New York: Columbia University Press.
68. The employers make the lives of women domestic workers miserable by putting unnecessary restrictions on them, merely due to the fear that any leniency in days off or rest periods and socialising with friends might result in illegal activities among the foreign domestics.
69. Chin in chapter 5 'Infra Politics of Domestic service: Strategies of and Resistance to Control' discusses in detail how foreign domestic workers cope with their employers when they fail to treat them as humans.
70. Chin, C.B.N., supra note 68, p. 128.

71. In everyday life, the household is a political arena where *'the personal becomes the political'* when the domestic servant challenges the power structure and the superior and dominant status of the employer by adopting a variety of strategies.
72. Gaitskell, D., Kimbie, J., Maconachie, M. and Unterhalter, E. (1984), 'Class, Race and Gender Domestic Workers in South Africa,' *Review of African Political Economy*, Vol. 27, No. 28, pp. 86-108 as cited in Gregson, N. and Lowe, M., supra note 42, p. 69.
73. Cock, J. (1989), *Maids and Madams: Domestic Workers under Apartheid*, London: The Women's Press.
74. Both ideologies propagate the inferiority of the particular group, emphasizing their inability to perform certain roles and exercise certain authority.
75. Wright, C. (1996), 'Wong: Foreign Domestic Workers in Singapore,' *Asian and Pacific Migration Journal*, Vol. 5, No. 1, pp. 117-138.
76. Women have to emigrate in their own right, to become income-earners for their families and important foreign exchange contributors for their countries. In Singapore, migrant women are prohibited from marrying local citizens. They are not allowed to become pregnant, and are subject to six-monthly pregnancy tests.
77. Human Rights Watch (2005), 'Maid to Order: Ending Abuse against Migrant Domestic Workers in Singapore,' New York: Human Rights Watch.
78. Ibid., p. 5.
79. Silvey, R. (2004), 'Trans-National Migration and the Gender Politics of Scale: Indonesian Domestic Workers in Saudi Arabia.' *Singapore Journal of Tropical Geography.* Vol: 25, No:2. pp. 141-55.
80. Ibid., p. 150.
81. Ibid., p. 151.
82. Jureidini, R. and Moukarbel, N. (July 2004), 'Female Sri Lankan Domestic Workers in Lebanon: A Case of 'Contract Slavery', *Journal of Ethnic and Migrant Studies*, Vol. 30, No. 4. pp. 581-607.
83. The concept 'Contract Slavery' is taken by the authors from Bales, K. (2000), *Disposable People: New Slavery in the Global Economy*, Berkeley and Los Angeles, California: University of California Press, who argues that slavery exists even today in various and complex forms, and it focuses on big profits and cheap lives. It is not about owning people but about controlling them completely. Bales says that contracts are a legal fiction rather than legally binding employment agreements and conceal what are in reality conditions of slavery.
84. Abuse and violence can be in the form of psychological and emotional abuse as well as in some cases physical violence in the form of beatings or sexual assaults by male employers or male family members. The second condition is the denial of freedom of movement, as their passports are withheld by their employers, they are not allowed to go out of the employer's house, and in some cases are even locked in the house and not given the permission to develop any friendships or social relations outside the employment relationship. The third slave-like situation is the exploitative working conditions which include long working hours and being at the beck and call of the employer and his family all the time. Most women interviewed did not have a separate room and they slept either in the kitchen or in the children's room. Some domestics also complained that the employers withheld their payments and forced them to work even after the expiry of the contract.
85. Jureidini, R. and Moukarbel, N., supra note 83, p. 596.
86. These fees cover the costs of airfare, visa fee and the agency's commission. However there are no fixed commission rates and they vary from US$240 to $500 as there are

no government price-ceiling regulations in Lebanon. The workers are issued with a three-month visa with the employer's name on it as a sponsor. The employer then arranges for their 12-month work permit and resident status.

87. Ibid., p. 604.
88. Widge, A. (1995), *Women in the Informal Sector: Multi Disadvantages of Domestic Workers*, New Delhi: Indian Social Institute, p. 46.
89. Raghuram, P. (1993), *Coping Strategies of Domestic Workers: A Study of Three Settlements in Delhi Metropolitan Region, India*, PhD Thesis, Newcastle Upon Tyne, p. 359.
90. Chigateri, S. (2004), 'Uncovering Injustice: Towards a Dalit Feminist Politics in Bangalore,' PhD Thesis, University of Warwick.
91. Ibid., p. 120.
92. These women belong to the low caste such as *musalis*, and due to the nature of work they perform they are called as *Kami kameen.*
93. Qayum, S. and Ray, R. (2003), 'Grappling with Modernity: India's Respectable Classes and the Culture of Domestic Servitude,' *Ethnography*, Vol. 4, pp. 520-55.
94. Ibid., p. 521.
95. Notions such as servants are essential to a well-run and well-kept household; second, servants are 'part of the family' and bound to it by ties of affection, loyalty, and dependence; and third, servants comprise a category with distinctive lifestyles, desires, and habits.
96. Ibid., p. 529.
97. Tabassum, W. (1976), *Utran*, Lahore: Mehmood Publishers.
98. Ibid., p. 7.
99. Chamki is in her teens; being the daughter of a senior maid she is born and brought up in the same household of her mother's employer. Being a playmate and companion of Shehzadi Pasha, the only daughter of the employers, Chamki enjoys some privileges, yet she feels insulted by being given hand me downs. Her spontaneous and innocent complaints are hushed by her mother for fear of the employer's annoyance.
100. Ibid., pp. 98-112.
101. Ali, S.S. and Khattak, S., Ali S.S., and Khattak, S. (1993), 'Domestic Servants and The Need For Legislation: The Case of the North-West Frontier Province' published in the Report on 'The Workshop on Women and Employment Legislation in Pakistan', 11-13 February 1993, pp. 154-162.
102. Ibid., p. 154.
103. Ibid., p. 158.
104. Ibid., p. 160.
105. Lawyers for Human Rights and Legal Aid (hereafter referred as LHRLA)
106. 'National Consultation on Domestic Workers Rights,' 2-3 September 2003, Karachi: Pakistan, organized by Lawyers for Human Rights and Legal Aid (LHRLA).
107. 'Rapid Assessment Studies of Bonded Labour in Pakistan,' 2004. A study conducted by the Bonded Labour Research Forum in collaboration with the Ministry of Labour, Manpower and Overseas Pakistanis Government of Pakistan and International Labour organization.
108. Urdu is spoken in many parts of Indian subcontinent. A vast literature (prose and poetry) has been written in this language. Urdu is also the national language of Pakistan as well as one of the twenty-three languages of India.
109. Taj, Imtiaz Ali, '*AnarKali.*'
110. Anarkali, once admired by the emperor, became the target of his wrath, when her love affair with the crown prince Salim was disclosed. Anarkali challenged the ego of the emperor by reciprocating the love of the crown prince. As a result she was buried alive

whereas the crown prince was allowed to live and forget Anarkali with the passage of time, his only punishment being a comfortable temporary confinement within the walls of the castle. Maids like Anarkali often had to pay the price for the comforts they were provided in the palace. For instance they were used as tools for spying, concerning the intrigues of the members of the royal family. The rewards and punishments in these matters depended on the moods and whims of the princes and emperors. In this atmosphere of exploitation and disgrace few could keep their character and conscience intact and that too at the cost of their lives.

111. Chughtai, A. (1998), 'Ghubar i Karawan,' in *Khawateen ka Alami Adab: A Selection of Literary Creations of the Women Writers of the World*, Islamabad: Academy of Letters, p. 112.
112. Pashto is one of the regional languages and is spoken in the North West Frontier Province of Pakistan.
113. Bano, Z. (1998), 'Faslain', in Zaitoon Bano *Zinda Dukh*, Lahore: Maqbool Academy.
114. Ahmad Faraz an internationally renowned modern Urdu poet who has written not only romantic poetry but has also addressed political and social issues in his poetry.
115. Faraz, A. (1957), *Tanha Tanha*, Lahore: Malik Sons Publishers, p. 137.
116. Jacklyn, C., supra note 74.
117. Chang, C.B.N., supra note 68; Anderson, B., supra note 52.
118. Cohen, R., supra note 65.

Part II

In Pakistan during the past two decades there has been a change in the organization of work in the employment sector. More women have entered into professions which were once considered men's domain. Women's work and economic independence are now considered as essential for improving their status. However, the majority of women still remain amongst the lowest earners of society. Most women are concentrated in the unregulated informal sector thus the overall increase in the number of women entering into employment does not match with an improvement in quality of their employment. With this background in mind, this part attempts to initiate a discussion on women and their work situation in Pakistan by placing them in a wider societal context. It is argued that a variety of socio, legal and cultural factors shape women's position in the employment sector. Thus a link between the theoretical discussion on legal feminism, legal pluralism and Islamic perspectives on women's work carried out in the earlier chapter and the situation on the ground with regard to women's employment is sought to be established.

This chapter discusses the constitutional and legislative provisions in Pakistan with particular reference to women's work. It also discusses Pakistan's commitment to international human rights and labour rights standards. The chapter also highlights how customary practices influence the black letter law and displace Islamic teachings. It is further argued that selective use of Islam by the state and society has negatively affected women's status. The socio-cultural constraints, patriarchal influences and class hierarchies which influence the position of women and hinder the process of access to justice also form part of the discussion.

To assess the issue of women domestic workers in a wider context, the next chapter provides a contextual analysis of women and work situation in both formal and informal employment sectors in Pakistan.

3

Women and Work in Plural Legal Settings: A Critique of Constitutional, Legislative, and Socio-Cultural Frameworks

INTRODUCTION

The purpose of this chapter is to analyse women and work situation in a plural legal setting like Pakistan. In light of constitutional and legislative frameworks, customary practices, religious laws and socio-cultural constraints, it seeks to understand the position and rights of women in the workplace as well as society at large. By using these plural legal frameworks as a tool for analysis, it also aims at drawing linkages between the theoretical basis of this study and women's lived realities in Pakistan. It will be argued that in the presence of multiplicity of informal regulatory norms, formal law alone cannot be an effective tool for empowerment of women. For securing equal rights for women in the workplace through legislation, it is important to assess their socio-economic position in the society. It is equally pertinent to understand the impact of customary practices, socio cultural constraints, gender and class hierarchies which create a hindrance in the process of accessing justice.

CONSTITUTIONAL FRAMEWORK AND APPLICATION OF THE PRINCIPLES OF NON-DISCRIMINATION AND EQUAL OPPORTUNITY IN PAKISTAN

The constitution of Pakistan is a written constitution that draws inspiration from the Universal Declaration of Human Rights (hereinafter referred as UDHR)[1] incorporating about two-thirds of the thirty rights enumerated in it. The equality provisions incorporated in the present constitution were also included in its predecessor constitutions of 1962 and 1972. The chapter on fundamental rights and the principles of policy clearly state that women shall be provided with complete equality and at the same time the norm of non-discrimination is echoed in several provisions of the constitution.[2]

The 1973 constitutional provisions maintain constitutional guarantees of women's legal equality with men. Article 25 of the constitution specifically lays down that all citizens are equal before law and are entitled to equal protection of law and that 'There shall be no discrimination on grounds of sex alone.' The two phrases aim at prohibiting arbitrary distinctions. It means that not all differences in treatment can be held as discriminatory and at the same time equal treatment does not mean that all persons should be treated in the same manner.[3] In *Progress of Pakistan Co Ltd. v Registrar Joint Stock Companies*, it was held that 'all law implies classification for when it applies to a set of circumstances, it creates thereby a class, and equal protection means that this classification should be reasonable'.[4] In another case it was argued that classification of persons and things is in no way contrary to the equality doctrine, provided the classification is not arbitrary or capricious, is natural and reasonable and bears a fair and substantial relation to the object of the legislation.[5]

Mullally, while referring to the competing and conflicting nature of equality provisions in the 1973 constitution, raises the issue that on the one hand Article 25(2) prohibits discrimination on the basis of sex alone, while on the other hand Clause 3 of the same article creates an exception to the rule in favour of women and children by laying down that 'nothing in this article shall prevent the state from making any special provision for the protection of women and children'.[6] She further argues that these clauses raise issues regarding what constitutes a special measure and whether such clauses are mandatory or are merely an enabling clause?[7]

In addition to Article 25 there are other constitutional provisions that permit the state to adopt affirmative action measures that could help women in gaining meaningful equality with men. Article 34 provides that the state must take steps to ensure full participation of women in all spheres of life. Article 35 lays down responsibility on the state to protect the family, the marriage, the mother, and the child. Article 37(e) provides that the state shall make provisions for secure and humane conditions of work, ensuring that women and children are not employed in professions unsuited for their age and sex, and for maternity benefits for women in employment. Article 27 lays down that 'no citizen otherwise qualified shall be discriminated in the services of Pakistan on the grounds of race, religion, caste, sex, residence or place of birth...and posts may be reserved to secure adequate representation in the services.'

The principles of policy laid down in the constitution are only guiding principles or enabling provisions that confer a discretionary power on the state to take action. According to Article 29(2) of the constitution the application of the principles is subject to the availability of resources. This suggests that the principles of policy do not impose any strict legal obligation on the state to take affirmative action measures for the protection of women or other disadvantaged groups in the society. Furthermore, the women-specific articles in the constitution are generally articulated as a need to protect them. Women are bracketed together with children and other disadvantaged groups of society in need of special protection by the state. Taking women as a special category has resulted in reinforcing the stereotypical image of women as helpless and oppressed. Therefore there is need to find out whether judicial perspectives or attitudes reinforce occupational segregation and discrimination against women or whether the attitude of the courts has been in favour of women.

In the case of Shirin Munir, the restriction on women's seats in Medical Colleges was challenged.[8] The Supreme Court of Pakistan held that under protective measures a minimum number of seats could be reserved but no restriction should be imposed as to the maximum number of seats available to eligible female applicants. *Naseem Firdous v Punjab Small Industries Corporation*,[9] tested the application of the equality norm laid out in article 25 of the constitution of Pakistan in conjunction with Article 27 that safeguards against discrimination in services. In this case, the petitioner, already employed by the Punjab Small Industries Corporation in 1977 and promoted to the position of Assistant Director (Design) in 1983 was prevented from applying for the position of designer in the same department as the advertisement was restricted to 'male only' applicants. The plea of the employers was that the position of designer was essentially a 'male' job; this statement was made regardless of the fact that the petitioner, a woman, was already performing that very job for close to a decade. The court declared the justification of Article 27 as conflicting with the equality article of the constitution and hence invalid/illegal.

In the Shirin Dokht case the Sindh High Court was approached by an air hostess who challenged Regulation 25 of the Pakistan International Airlines Corporation Employees (Service and Discipline) Regulations 1985. Under this provision an air hostess has to retire on attaining the age of thirty-five years extended from time to time to forty-five, whereas their male colleagues in pay groups I to IV would retire at the age of sixty. The Sindh High Court declared this provision *ultra vires* of the constitution of Pakistan and decided in her favour.[10] The Court held that the action of respondents was in clear violation of Articles 25 and 27 of the constitution as both the articles guarantee equal protection and equality before law irrespective of sex and provide a safeguard against discrimination in services. Despite this decision (confirmed on appeal by the Supreme Court of Pakistan), Regulation 25 continued to be in operation until it was struck down again by the Supreme Court in *Pakistan International Airlines Corporation through Chairman and others v Samina Masood and others.*[11] The Supreme Court upheld equality for women in the workplace by stating:

> What we are practically confronted with is proved, rather admitted situation, that cabin crew consisting of male stewards and female Air Hostesses are in one and the same group performing exactly the same duties. Though belonging to the same category, yet being differently treated, is not a distinction based on intelligible differential but clearly is a distinction based on sex. In the same functional group performing the same duties and belonging to the same pay group, the retirement age of Air Hostesses being fixed differently is nothing but discrimination resorted to for the only reason that they are females. What learned counsel for the petitioner called an intelligible differentia is nothing but a differentia based on sex, glaringly offending the provisions of Article 25(2) of the Constitution. We believe, nothing could be a discrimination based on sex, better than what we have found in the present case....[12]

The above discussion on case law suggests that in Pakistan so far, only a few women have invoked equality provisions of the Constitution in matters related to equal opportunity or discrimination in the workplace. Ali and Shahid argue that the constitutional cases in which discriminatory practices were challenged in no way represent a norm in Pakistan followed by most women workers, but it does suggest that at least formal law is being used.[13] It is also interesting to note that the higher judiciary in Pakistan has used formal black letter law for the protection of women in the public sphere. They have applied equality and non-discriminatory provisions of the Constitution in favour of women. However, the situation changes when it comes to private sphere, for instance in family matters, the cultural and customary norms influence the judgments of the courts.

THE LABOUR POLICY FRAMEWORK IN PAKISTAN[14]

Before entering into a discussion on various laws pertaining to women's employment, it is essential to briefly discuss the various labour policies of different governments in Pakistan. Soon after the creation of the state, Mohammad Ali Jinnah, the first Governor-General of Pakistan, in his speech to the Karachi Chamber of Commerce on 27 April 1948, said:

> Government will seek to create conditions in which industry and trade may develop and prosper. I would like to call to your particular attention to the keen desire of the government of Pakistan to associate individual and private enterprise at every stage of industrialization.... I can no more visualize a Pakistan without traders than I can without cultivators and civil servants. I have no doubt that in Pakistan, traders and merchants will always be welcome and that they in building their own fortunes, will not forget their social responsibility for a fair and square deal to one and all, big and small.

The statement of the founder of Pakistan laid down parameters within which, interests and the rights of labour were to be dealt with. They were not to be subordinated to the interests of the ruling elites of Pakistan, but unfortunately, those who came into power in subsequent years refused to undertake any reforms, including land reforms, to change the archaic socio-economic structure inherited from their colonial masters. Workers were left to depend on the social conscience and goodwill of the industrialists, traders and the government. As a result there was no well-defined labour policy of the government until 1955.

In 1955 the first labour policy of the country was announced. This policy encouraged the growth of trade unionism; protection of workers' rights; settlement of industrial disputes and redress of workers' grievances through constitutional means, such as conciliation and arbitration; and it also provided for compliance with international labour standards ratified by Pakistan. Despite commitments made by the government most parts of the policy remained unimplemented till 1959. In February 1959, the second labour policy was announced by the first military dictator of the country, General Ayub Khan. No new initiatives were suggested in the new policy and it was a mere reiteration of the former policy.[15]

The third and fourth labour policies were announced in 1969 and 1972 by the respective governments of the time.[16] These policies were heavily tilted in favour of labour. At that time the primary objective of the governments was to take control of the situation therefore the package included measures to improve industrial relations on a rational, liberal and healthy basis, revision of minimum wages and other welfare measures, strengthening of the collective bargaining process through strong unionism and the need to limit the role of government. However, when in 1969 the Industrial Relations Ordinance was amended it failed to reflect any of the measures announced in the labour policy.[17] The 1972 policy failed to achieve a balance between workers' and employers' rights. Employers were not happy with the nationalization policy and demanded the power to hire and fire employees. This policy also led to the increased role of outsiders in trade unionism, low productivity and endless litigation between employer and employees due to unfair labour practices.

In subsequent years, the need to reform industrial relations was strongly felt to restore investor confidence. To achieve this, various steps were taken, which included the holding of three tripartite labour conferences in 1977, 1980 and 1988. During this period two labour commissions were also set up. In 1993 when Benazir Bhutto came into power two task forces were formed. After extensive tripartite consultations the task force came up with a report which was tabled before cabinet but the policy was not adopted. During the Nawaz Sharif rule from 1997 to 1999 a draft labour policy was prepared. Although the government pledged to remove all barriers in implementation of international labour standards and extended the right to form unions and collective bargaining to workers in the agricultural sector, all this proved to be mere rhetoric. The government did not consult representative organizations of employers and employees while nominating their representatives to the Commission on minimum wages and consolidation and codification of Labour laws.

After a lapse of thirteen years in 2001, a significant development was the holding of the 24th Pakistan Tripartite Conference culminating in useful recommendations for legislative, institutional, and administrative reforms. Recommendations included, extension of the coverage of labour laws to the informal sector and home based workers, an unconditional minimum wage for starter unskilled workers was recommended to the government as Rs 2500, and to bring laws in conformity with international labour standards. Some of these recommendations were adopted in the Labour Policy 2002. In 2005, a new draft of 'Labour Protection Policy' was prepared. The new labour policy draft aimed at complying with the fundamental principles and rights of labourers contained in the constitution, international conventions, and labour standards.[18] The policy aimed at consolidating existing labour laws into six basic laws.[19]

In accordance with the recommendations of the tripartite conference, which also became part of the labour policy, the government has changed the structure of the labour Judiciary. Labour Appellate Tribunals have been abolished and the High Courts have been given the power to hear appeals. Apart from the consolidation of laws and changes in the judicial structure, the policy for the first time addressed informal sector home-based and seasonal workers aiming at a gradual extension of coverage of labour welfare laws to these workers. However, domestic workers have yet to capture the attention of policymakers, as there was no mention of domestic workers in the labour policy. This shows a casual and indifferent attitude of the government towards a substantial class of workers whose service is not recognized nor are they provided any legal cover against exploitative employers and poor working conditions.

LABOUR LEGISLATION PERTAINING TO WOMEN IN PAKISTAN

Under the constitution, labour is regarded as a 'concurrent subject', which means that it is the responsibility of both the Federal and Provincial Governments. However, for the sake of uniformity, laws are enacted by the federal government stipulating that provincial governments may make rules and regulations of their own according to conditions prevailing in, or for specific requirements, of the provinces.[20]

Labour legislation in Pakistan is primarily based on a legal framework inherited from the British. The four basic labour laws are (1) The Factories Act 1938, (2) The Shops and Establishment Ordinance 1961, (3) The West Pakistan Industrial and Commercial Employment (Standing Order) Amendment Act 1974 and (4) The Industrial Relations Ordinance 2002.[21] None of these laws covers contract workers, casual workers, piece-rated workers, the self-employed (home-based or otherwise), workers in domestic service, and agricultural workers. These categories are neither covered in the industrial or commercial sector nor counted in the services sector. The only legal framework applicable to the agrarian economy is in the form of tenancy laws.[22]

The Payment of Wages Act 1936 regulates the payment of wages to certain classes of industrial workers. It applies to those workers whose monthly wages do not exceed Rs 3000 (US$51.68) and are employed in factories, railways, plantations, workshops and establishments of contractors.[23] The Act uses the term 'worker' which has a neutral meaning being defined as any person (without any reference to any particular sex).

However, Mullally believes that male and female workers in Pakistan still do not receive equal treatment.[24] The remuneration is not based on evaluation of the content of work rather it is based on the sex that performs work. In other words the universal principle of equal remuneration for work of equal value is not followed in Pakistan.

Some laws have been framed in the area of maternity for pregnant and nursing mother workers.[25] There are two central enactments, one federal, and the other provincial, providing maternity benefits to women employed in certain occupations. The Maternity Benefit Ordinance, 1958, entitles women workers to maternity leave with full pay. It also stipulates that upon completion of four months employment or qualifying period, a worker may have up to six weeks prenatal and postnatal leave during which she is paid a salary drawn on the basis of her last pay.[26] The Ordinance is applicable to all industrial and commercial establishments employing women, excluding tribal areas. It also places restrictions on the dismissal of a woman employee during her maternity leave. Similarly, the Mines Maternity Benefit Act, 1941, is applicable to women employed in mines in Pakistan.[27]

These protective measures notwithstanding, legislative provisions are seldom enforced. A drawback of the Maternity Benefit Ordinance, 1958, is that its provisions only cover a specific category of female workers, i.e. mine workers and women factory workers, whereas seasonal workers and domestic workers are not included. Export Processing Zones are also excluded from its scope. There also exist flaws in maternity benefits, employer's liability to pay compensation and protection of employment in case of dismissals. The rates payable are very low in view of the high rate of inflation that has increased daily living costs.[28]

Labour Laws do not recognize workers who are not in employment for a continuous number of days per year.[29] The law further requires that if a minimum number of workers are employed, only then the law would be applicable. To keep themselves out of the ambit of law, employers do not hire workers on full time basis, or the factory is broken up into smaller units to show that the workers employed are less than the required number for application of the law. Due to these inherent weaknesses, actual implementation of labour laws becomes extremely difficult and limited to much fewer workplaces.

The contract system deprives workers of legally based protection that they are entitled to: it deprives them of an award, a union-negotiated settlement and even a statutory law.[30] However, the superior courts in Pakistan, interpreting Section 20 of the West Pakistan Industrial and

Commercial Employment Standing Orders has made the employer li[illegible] whether or not the workmen of such an establishment are employed through a contractor.[31] The dilemma faced by domestic workers is that 'home' or 'private household' is not included in the definition of an establishment or workplace. Although the Provincial Employees Social Security Ordinance 1965 has broadened the definition of the term 'establishment' by defining it as 'an organization, industrial, commercial, agricultural, or otherwise', it does not specifically mention home or private household and use of the term 'otherwise' is ambiguous. Thus, women domestic workers who are in a way contract workers are denied legal protection.

The protective nature of labour legislation in Pakistan becomes more visible in laws related to night work and hazardous work. Night work is covered by Section 45 (1)(b) of the Factories Act prohibiting women from working after 7 p.m. to 5.30 a.m. in accordance with the International Labour Organisation (hereinafter referred to as ILO) Convention on Night Work 1921.[32] Women are also excluded from certain employment deemed hazardous to their health such as to work on or near machinery in motion.[33] Similarly, Sections 3, 4 and 5 of the 1963 West Pakistan Hazardous Occupation Rules prohibit employment of women in processes involving use of lead, chromium and sand blasting. The 1973 Mines (Amendment) Act does not allow a woman to work below the ground in any part of the mine. However women who hold managerial posts or are employed in health and welfare services and do not perform any manual work are exempted. Other protective legislation includes the 1923 Workmen's Compensation Act places women in the category of persons under legal disability and further states that any payment of a lump sum as compensation should be first deposited with the commissioner.[34]

A REVIEW OF INTERNATIONAL LABOUR AND HUMAN RIGHTS STANDARDS AND PAKISTAN'S COMMITMENT

Law and the legal institutions are no longer confined to local boundaries and are being influenced and shaped by regional and international institutions of power and information.[35] One such instance is the presence of international and regional treaties and conventions drafted by international institutions like the ILO, the United Nations Organization (hereinafter referred as UN) Organization of Islamic Countries (hereinafter referred as OIC) and regional bodies including South Asian Association of Regional Countries (hereinafter referred as SAARC). These conventions and treaties have proved instrumental in mobilizing disadvantaged groups and have been frequently referred to for challenging the state laws that are discriminatory in nature.[36]

ILO standards are the legal component in its strategy for governing globalization, promoting sustainable development, eradicating poverty, and ensuring that people can work in dignity and safety.[37] One of the primary goals of the ILO is to achieve gender equality. It aims at promoting opportunities for women and men to obtain decent and productive work in conditions of freedom, equity, security, and human dignity.[38] In the case of domestic workers at the moment a world-wide movement for the rights of migrant domestic workers has already begun in different parts of the world.[39] In 1965, the International Labour Conference adopted a resolution concerning the Conditions of Employment of Domestic Workers. This resolution recognized the 'urgent need' to establish minimum living standards 'compatible with the self-respect and human dignity which are essential to social justice', for domestic workers in both developed and developing countries.[40] However, there is no specific international legal convention developed by the ILO addressing right of domestic workers within their home countries and abroad.

The UN has adopted a series of conventions in the area of slavery, forced labour, trafficking and international migrant workers which provide some protection to those who enter as migrant domestic workers in different countries around the globe.[41] These conventions call on countries to respect the rights of migrants who seek employment abroad and they should not be abused and discriminated by their employers. The UN General Assembly has taken into account some of these and other rights of migrant workers when it adopted the International Convention for the Protection of the Rights of Migrant Workers and Members of Their Families (hereinafter referred as CMW).[42] The major human rights provisions of the CMW apply equally to documented and non-documented workers, who are to be protected by both sending and receiving countries where possible. Article 7 of the CMW requires states to respect and ensure migrant workers' rights enumerated therein without distinction on the basis of, *inter alia*, sex, race, national origin, and nationality.[43] Rights protected in the Convention include, the right to leave any state, including one's state of origin; 'the right to life'; the right to be free from 'torture or [from] cruel, inhuman or degrading treatment or punishment'; and the right to be free from 'being held in slavery or servitude or from performing forced or compulsory labour.'[44] Under the CMW, receiving countries are responsible for fully informing migrants of the conditions of their admission and stay, and guaranteeing equal access to all educational, health, and other social assistance programmes.[45]

Other UN documents providing protection in the area of employment are: Article 23 of the UDHR which states that, 'every one has the right to free choice of employment and to just and favourable conditions of work, and to protection against unemployment'.[46] The International Covenant on Civil and Political Rights (hereinafter referred as ICCPR) provides for non-discrimination and equal protection provisions.[47] Similarly, the International Covenant on Economic, Social, and Cultural Rights (hereinafter referred as ICESCR) includes non-discrimination provisions in the field of social and cultural rights.[48] One specific exception to this rule is carved out, however, in Article 2(3) of the Convention. Under this provision, developing countries, with due regard to human rights and their national economy, may determine to what extent they would guarantee the economic rights recognized in the present Covenant to non-nationals. This exception is limited to developing countries, and to economic rights but it certainly does not absolve the countries from its obligation to provide basic minimum needs of its citizens such as food, shelter, education, employment, and health etc.

The UN Convention on the Elimination of All Forms of Discrimination against Women (hereinafter referred as CEDAW) calls on states to adopt prohibitions on sex discrimination.[49] It requires state parties to modify social and cultural patterns of conduct, to eliminate prejudice and practices that are based on the inferiority of women, to provide women with rights equal to those of men in the fields of employment and family benefits, and to recognize the difficulties facing rural women in particular.[50] Article 11 mandates the end of discrimination in the field of employment, including the right to work, to employment opportunities, to equal remuneration, to free choice of profession and employment, to social security, and to protection of health, including maternal health, and also in regard to discrimination on the grounds of marriage or maternity. Pakistan being a party to the CEDAW is obliged to provide protection to domestic workers in terms of their working conditions, remuneration etc. Convention on the Elimination of All Forms of Racial Discrimination guarantees the rights to non-discrimination based on race, colour, or national or ethnic origin in work, to free choice of employment, to equal pay for equal work and just and favourable remuneration.

Besides recognition of the right to work, the various international instruments also require from the state parties to provide protection to women employees from harassment at the workplace. The CEDAW provides clear and robust protection against sexual assault and harassment. In its General Recommendation on Violence against Women (No. 19, 1992), it makes clear that gender-based violence fits within the definition of discrimination against women under CEDAW, and specifies that gender-based violence is violence that is directed against a woman because she is a woman or that affects women disproportionately. It includes acts that inflict physical, mental, or sexual harm or suffering, threats of such acts, coercion, and other deprivations of liberty. General Recommendation 19 states that sexual harassment in the workplace is a form of violence against women. The Committee explains that such conduct can be humiliating and may constitute a health and safety problem. Sexual harassment is discriminatory when the woman has reasonable grounds to believe that her objection to the harassment would disadvantage her in connection with her employment, including recruitment or promotion, or when it creates a hostile working environment.

The Committee also expressed special concern for the situation of domestic workers, whose working conditions should be monitored by state parties, in part to prevent sexual abuse. Similarly, the ICCPR and the ICESCR have interpreted the two Covenants' protections against sex discrimination as including a prohibition on gender-based violence.[51] The International Convention on the Elimination of All Forms of Racial Discrimination guarantees the right to security of person and protection against bodily harm; this norm applies equally for men and women.[52] The International Convention on the Protection of the Rights of All Migrant Workers and their Families requires states to protect migrant workers and their families from attacks on their physical security and safety. All migrant workers have the right to be free from torture, or cruel, inhuman or degrading treatment as well as they have the right to effective protection by the state against violence, physical injury, threats and intimidation, whether by public officials or by private individuals, groups or institutions.[53]

Besides ILO and UN treaties, the Parliamentary Assembly of the Council of Europe in 2001, for the first time took notice of a new form of slavery that has emerged in the form of domestic slavery. It noticed that despite provisions of the European Convention on Human Rights,[54] women domestic workers coming to Europe in search of jobs from different countries receive inhuman and degrading treatment at the hands of their employers.[55] In light of this situation the Committee made several recommendations to the Council of Ministers including; any form of slavery, forced marriage, and trafficking in human beings as criminal offences and to draw up a Domestic Workers Charter of Rights.[56] After these recommendations no steps were taken by the member states to address the plight of domestic workers. As a result the Assembly came up with another recommendation in 2004, in which it proposed several measures to deal with domestic servitude, mail-order brides and placement of *au-pairs*.[57]

Alongside UN, EU and ILO treaties there are some other human rights documents framed by the Organisation of Islamic Countries (hereinafter referred as OIC) such as the Universal Islamic Declaration of Human Rights (UIDHR), the Cairo Declaration, the Tehran Declaration, and the Islamabad Declaration.[58] UIDHR in its article 3 entitled, 'Right to Equality and Prohibition against Impermissible Discrimination', subsections (b) and (c) states that:

> All persons shall be entitled to equal wage for equal work...and no person shall be denied the opportunity to work or be discriminated against in any manner or exposed to greater physical risk by reason of religious belief, colour, race, origin, sex or language.

Ali and Shahid contend that the phrase 'impermissible discrimination' gives the impression that, where permissible, discrimination will be permitted.[59] This suggests that women may be discriminated against on the basis of literal, traditional readings of the religious text in Islam. The Cairo Declaration was adopted by OIC on 5 August 1990. It consists of a preamble and 25 articles and is similar in tone and substance to the UIDHR.

The Tehran Declaration recognizes that women may be heads of households thus moving away from the traditional statement of men alone are, or can be, providers and maintainers of households. It also emphasizes the fact that women's roles are not confined to motherhood as stated in Para 1.8 of the recommendations of the seminar to the 23rd Islamic Conference of Foreign Ministers:

> ...to effectively meet the requirements of women and encourage their participation in public life thus enabling them to reconcile their family and

> professional responsibilities with their political rights and participation in decision making.

The Islamabad Declaration recognizes the rights of Muslim women to participate in public and political life, including to be head of state and government.[60] It seeks to establish the interdependence and indivisibility of all three generations of rights. Both declarations are also important because they accept the presence of discriminatory laws and customary practices in Muslim countries and call for their eradication and promulgation of laws which are more supportive of women's participation in public life.

Various studies carried out on domestic workers indicate that generally international and regional standards have failed to address the problems of female domestic workers.[61] These studies point out that there is no specific international instrument on domestic workers and the absence of such a document has led to a wide range of diversity in the approaches of countries towards the regulation of domestic work, even among those that have enacted specific legislation for it. This also implies a lack of international monitoring of different national approaches. Blackett in her study notes that such being the case, some might perceive a paradox between arguing for specific regulation in national laws when international labour standards for the most part do not directly mention domestic workers or contemplate the specificity of their employment relationship.[62] It means that international labour standards are not specially tailored to improve the situation of domestic workers by taking into account their particular conditions of work and employment relations. At the same time many ILO member states also exclude domestic workers in national legislation to escape challenges to its laws in regular ILO observations. Taking a different approach, Satterwaite argues that though the Migrant Workers Convention is a significant development in international human rights law yet the single application of the convention in women migrant workers case would lead to compartmentalization of human rights treaties. An intersectionality approach is needed where advocates and scholars must focus on the entire range of human rights and insist that rights of migrant workers are already included in the standards set out in human rights treaties.[63] Such an approach would help in identifying and articulating a set of robust standards that would shift the focus from the single migrant variable to taking into account of other variables such as ethnicity, gender, race etc, that are relevant to women migrant workers.

At the regional level, SAARC, during the 11th Summit in Kathmandu in January 2002, adopted a Regional Convention on Combating the Crime of Trafficking in Women and Children for Prostitution.[64] The Convention calls for cooperation amongst member states in dealing with various aspects of prevention, interdiction, and suppression of trafficking in women and children. It also calls for prevention of use of women and children in international prostitution networks, particularly where countries of the region are the countries of origin, transit, and destination.[65] It also obliges states to provide for repatriation and rehabilitation of victims of trafficking.[66] Pursuant to a decision of the summit, the SAARC Autonomous Women's Advocacy Group (hereinafter referred as SAWAG) was formed, to advocate mainstreaming gender and make recommendation on gender related issues and programmes in the region.[67] Besides, under the revised Regional Integrated Programme of Action (RIPA) in January 2004 a new Technical Committee on Women, Youth, and Children was also formed to highlight the plight of the girl in South Asia and to hold gender related seminars, workshops, and training programmes. However, none of these bodies have so far paid any attention to the issue of women in domestic service.

Pakistan became a member of the ILO in 1947. It has so far ratified thirty-four ILO Conventions, of which thirty-three are in force in the country.[68] Pakistan is also a member of the UN but has not ratified the CMW and has failed to carry out its international commitment to bring at par its domestic legislation and polices with international labour standards.

Pakistan ratified the Equal Remuneration Convention, 1951 (No. 100) on 10 October 2001. This Convention defines the term equal remuneration for men and women workers for work of equal value, with reference to rates of remuneration established without discrimination based on sex. Under Article 2 of the Convention each member state while determining wages or salary of workers whether male or female, has an obligation to promote and ensure the application of this principle in its national laws or regulations, legally established or recognized machinery for wage determination, collective agreements between employers and workers or a combination of these various means. Pakistan despite being a party to this Convention has failed to implement this principle in its laws relating to minimum wages.

Pakistan is also a party to Hours of Work (Industry) Convention, 1919 (No. 1) but research studies carried out on industrial workers have shown that there is a gross violation in terms of working hours.[69] Pakistan is at the same time party to the Convention on Freedom of Association and Protection of the Right to Organize, 1948 (No. 87).[70] Article 2 of this Convention provides the right to workers and employers to form their own organizations. The preamble of the Convention recognizes the principle of 'freedom of association' as a means for improving conditions of labour and establishing peace. However, unions are either banned in some professions or have not been very effective in playing their role.[71]

Pakistan's efforts to fulfil its commitments in international treaties and conventions to promote women's free, equal and full participation in all walks of life are summed up in the National Plan for Action (NPA) announced in September 1998, the National Policy for Development and Empowerment of Women (March 2002) and the Ten-Year Perspective Plan (2001-2011). Section 5.4 of the National Policy emphasizes the need to recognize, count and make visible women's real economic contribution and productivity in both the formal and informal sectors of the economy and to take appropriate measures to include women workers in the rural and informal sectors of employment under the definition of the 'worker' and ensure healthy and safe conditions of work for women.

Government has also taken steps for the 'Economic Empowerment of Women', covering alleviation of poverty, access to credit, remunerated work, rural women of informal sector, and sustainable development.[72] However, when it comes to the case of women in domestic service specifically, despite its commitment to improve the situation of women in the informal employment sector we do not see any effort being made by the state to include them under the definition of 'worker' in the labour law of the country. The present study of domestic workers demonstrates that principles of non-discrimination and equality are violated by employers and no protection is provided to domestic workers in the workplace under the legislation. Discrimination is visible as women performing the same kind of work are paid much lower wages than their male counterparts. For example, a male cook receives double the salary of a woman domestic worker who does cooking and other kitchen related work. The same pattern is followed in the case of drivers and *chowkidars* (guard or a caretaker) who are always men. Similarly, the absence of any formal contracts between the employer and the employee also leads to the exploitation of domestic workers.

In light of the above discussion it becomes quite evident that the nature of domestic work necessitates the need for specific legislation. Legislation would help in regulating the relationship between the employer and employee, fixing of wages and improving other aspects of domestic service and would significantly reduce the vulnerability of the domestic worker in privacy of others' households. However, this specific legislation has to be both at the international as well as national level. Expecting national governments to legislate for domestic workers may not be enough, particularly since their agendas may be driven by concerns other than the protection of domestic workers' rights. It is therefore suggested that it is the responsibility of international organizations to provide an international framework for the protection of not only migrant domestic workers but also those who work within their own countries. Once the state parties ratify the international regulatory framework, they would ultimately be under an obligation to incorporate its principles into national law. But at the same time this would only happen if there is a strong political will to stop the exploitation of women domestic workers and if there is a fair justice system in the country to protect domestic workers' rights; otherwise nothing will change. It is therefore suggested that a two-prong strategy needs to be adopted by enacting laws at the international and national level as well as organizing domestic workers through building networks and alliances so that protection could be provided to domestic workers in every country.

CUSTOMARY PRACTICES AND THEIR IMPACT ON WOMEN'S WORK

In Pakistan both formal and informal laws coexist.[73] The formal laws, as well as informal norms, control and determine various aspects of women's lives in Pakistan, including their employment. The plethora of laws that govern women's lives in Pakistan affect their multiple identities and status. Ali, explaining the identity of a Pakistani woman, aptly sums up the position:

> Women in Pakistan have a layered identity; each layer outlining certain rights and obligations. She is simultaneously subject to various set of rules; the gap between the de jure and de facto rights within each set widening as one moves from constitutional law to Islamic law and customary law.[74]

In this situation the real issues of gender difference, class hierarchies and patriarchal systems which relegate women to a subordinate status cannot be addressed by simply suggesting a legal framework to remove these disparities. In the presence of these deeply entrenched practices women find it very hard to have access to justice, and legislation alone fails to provide any protection to women.

Zia argues that custom in Pakistani society is not distinct from faith, religion and self-identification.[75] Customary laws contradictory to religious doctrines are practiced as part of religion and considered to have religious sanction behind them.[76] The influence of customary practices on religious law can be determined from the fact that women are deprived of their religious right to give consent in marriage. At the time of *nikah* the woman's consent is taken by the male relatives who act as the *nikah* father or *nikah* brother and then represent her at the *nikah* ceremony.[77] Provisions of statutory law are violated, when the proviso dealing with the right to *Talaqi-Tafwiz* (delegated *talaq*) to the wife, is struck off. Dower under Islamic law is the sole right of the wife but under customary practice it is not given to the wife but the family of the bride takes away the money from the bridegroom.[78] *Swara* is a customary practice prevalent in the rural districts of North West Frontier Province (NWFP) such as Swabi, Bannu, Swat and the tribal areas, where a girl is given to another tribe to settle a dispute without *nikah* or proper marriage. *Vani* is another such practice where a girl is given to another tribe as compensation for settlement of a dispute.[79] These examples suggest that customs also serve the purpose of patriarchal control over women. As a result, customary practices have become a powerful source of exercising control and providing guidelines for interaction among members of society. Any digression from these norms leads to sanctions which are neither legitimate according to state law nor religion.

The patriarchal structure of society controls social relationships and power distribution between men and women. Patriarchy, or male domination, controls all facets of women's lives in Pakistani society. This intersects with a woman's roles and responsibilities within the family as well as her role as a member of her community. Impact of patriarchal forces particularly on women's lives is not homogenous and depends on their caste, class, religion, and geographical location. Patriarchy also limits a woman's ownership and control over property and economic resources; it constrains her mobility and access to education.[80]

Ali argues that the patriarchal discourses are not evenly spread in the society, and the nature and degree of women's oppression/subordination varies according to their class, region, and the rural/urban divide.[81] Patriarchal structures are relatively stronger in rural and tribal settings where local customs establish male authority and power over women's lives and women in these areas of Pakistan are even today exchanged, sold, and bought in marriages.[82]

The social, cultural pressures in Pakistani society are also responsible for the 'public/private' dichotomy. The public sphere includes waged work, labour market and the institutions whereas private consists of the home linked with kin and family. The public/private divide results in considerable control on women's employment, thus limiting the economic choices open to them. Many women still prefer to work from within their homes for instance home-based workers because they can earn a living without being exposed to the outside world.

It is also interesting to note that domestic service stands at the boundary between the public and private sphere. Domestic workers provide waged work but within the context of a household. For them the private territory of the employer counts as public domain. However, one of the reasons why some women prefer to work as domestic workers than in any other public employment sector is that working within a household is considered to be a more secure place for women as compared to working in any other employment sector in the public sphere. This division between the personal and the public adds to the vulnerability of women domestic workers because their work is a hidden form of employment performed within the four walls of other households, which leads to their isolation and invisibility. This dichotomy further leads to the devaluation of work performed within the private sphere. From the employer's point of view, most of them prefer to have women as their domestic workers because Pakistani society is a segregated society where it is not considered appropriate to allow a stranger into the privacy of the home. This shows that concepts such as women's honour, segregation between men and women and sanctity of the home are at play even at the level of day-to-day household chores.

The sexual division of labour within the household has hardly changed because either other women in the house take responsibility of the household chores or even in those cases where men share some of the burden, yet the ultimate responsibility for household work still lies with women.[83] Conventional views about women's role in society are still prevalent. Such views play an important role in confining the average Pakistani woman into the so-called 'traditional role' away from mainstream 'normal life'.[84] Saigol, while discussing the impact of traditional knowledge systems, argues that a woman is generally considered as a social burden or liability for the family and is always compelled to think that marriage is considered to be her only goal in life.[85] Elder women of the family try to feed in her mind the traditional concepts of being a 'woman' and, off and on, she is the recipient of such proverbs as 'a woman's voice must not be heard outside the four walls of her house.'[86] This suggests that social attitudes are a source of controlling and discriminating against women and deny women access to economic, social, and political power.

Findings from various studies carried out on women and work in Pakistan suggests that self-perception varies from job to job.[87] Educated and professional women consider that their jobs have helped in their personal growth, their jobs give them a sense of achievement, and they feel that they are making a positive contribution towards their families and towards society. Women belonging to this category are more career-oriented, they make an effort to move forward in their careers and do not want to waste their qualifications by remaining at home and not making use of their abilities.

In the informal sector the increased participation of women in paid work suggests that there is more acceptability of women moving to the public sphere, although this move is more economically driven rather than men's desire to see their women move forward in life.[88] Participation in the work force has improved women's own perceptions as they feel that they have gained confidence and experience of the outside world.[89] They also feel that they are contributing towards family incomes. However, their paid work in the informal sector lowers their self-esteem mainly because the jobs they perform are considered as low status jobs by society.

Although there is a visible change in the role of women, with more women entering the public sphere, still women are considered as supplementary earners. Findings from various studies carried out on women and work in Pakistan suggests that the notion that women are only supplementary earners is commonly accepted.[90] The occupational role of a woman is not considered as the primary role that she has to play. Her roles as a mother and wife are considered as her main responsibility. Within the cultural norms of Pakistani society, particularly rural Pakistan, men are supposed to be the providers and maintainers of women. If a woman goes out of the house to earn money it reflects adversely on the men of the household who are perceived to be too incompetent and not 'man enough' to support their women folk.

In cases where women are sole earners and men are not earning either due to illness, joblessness, or in some cases, drug addiction and laziness, they are still considered to be the head of the household. As a result, incidence of female-headed household goes unrecognized and undercounted.[91] The concept of head of household is used more as a social construct rather than one involving any monetary connotations.

In Pakistan, men's work is still more valued as compared to women's work. Women are made to believe that whatever they do for the family is their responsibility or duty; they should not expect any recognition or remuneration for it whether in the form of monetary benefit or otherwise.[92] The general trend among working class women is of underestimation of the value of their work or input towards the family. Patel in her study of women's property rights in India finds the same minimization of individual self by women as they do not identify with the notion that they are entitled to a share in parental property.[93] Women still consider men as breadwinners and heads of household and therefore in their perception only what men do is valuable both socially and economically. In other words, while employment appears to help women meet their daily needs, it maintains the status quo and has made little change in women's subordinate position.[94]

Restrictions on women's mobility and lack of female staff in financial institutions to cater to women customers/client are among some of the obstacles in carrying out economic activities independently. In some informal sector jobs women still fail to perceive themselves as 'workers' and do not recognize and value their contribution as workers or earning members of the family. Ahmed et al. in their study noticed that most women working as home-based workers do not think about themselves as employed and as workers only because they are carrying out that work in their own households and not in the public sphere, unlike factory workers or other women who come out of their homes to earn a living.[95]

Another important issue is that the concept of division of labour between men and women at home has still to be accepted. Although mostly due to economic reasons women have come out of their homes to support men and to share their economic burden, in return women do not get the same support at home for domestic chores. There is hardly any attitudinal change amongst men and this trend of non-cooperation exists across social and class boundaries.

Finally, the gender gap in the education sector is also a major contributing factor responsible for women's poor working conditions. The adult literacy rate for females in the country is a mere 28 per cent, a little more than half the figure for male literacy which is 53 per cent.[96] These figures depict the gender gap in education and indicate a strong bias against the female population of the country. The gender gap exists due to two main reasons (1) the inaccessibility and remote locations of schools, especially in rural areas that make parents reluctant to send their daughters to a far-off school and (2) education of girls is generally not considered essential, and in many parts of the country it is generally considered that daughters are better employed looking after their younger siblings and contributing to the housework, or even working in other people's homes, rather than studying. This example reflects legal pluralism at play where the constitution, law, as well as religion provides the right to education for all, but customs and social norms inhibit this right to the girl child. The situation cannot be changed by merely providing constitutional and legislative provisions for education or by improving the infrastructure of schools, rather the emphasis should be on removing entrenched gender bias in society. This again is not an easy task as many obsolete, but firmly entrenched, traditions contribute to the regressive thinking on a number of social issues, education among them. Attempts to remove these would be one way of bridging the gender gap and improving education ratios for females which in turn would lead to better job opportunities for women and empowerment of women.

CLASS STRUCTURES AND URBAN RURAL DIVISIONS IN PAKISTAN

In Pakistan there are various social classes with a wide disparity among them. The class system is complex as it depends on a variety of factors such as the socio-economic position as well as the geographic location.[97] The middle class consists of small landowners, small businessmen, educated men and women involved in middle-grade public and private sector jobs, whereas the working class (the majority of whom illiterate), are involved in low paid jobs and live on the verge of poverty. The upper-class women, belonging to the feudal rural class are in majority of the cases dependent on their husbands or the male protection of their household. Alvi, in his article denotes these women as those 'who are virtually reduced to the status of well-fed, well-dressed and well-ornamented slaves absolutely dependent on the whims of their husbands.'[98]

Women in urban areas belonging to families of industrialists, businessmen and bureaucrats, like their rural counterparts hardly take up any employment. They spend a leisurely life because they do not have to provide for the family and have domestic workers to take care of their household chores. Those who are educated have used educational institutions only as finishing schools or as a means of killing time. These women are seen in public places when accompanied by the male relatives as for instance while dining out in hotels or restaurants or spending time and money on shopping and other recreational activities.[99] Jalal argues that these women are submissive to their men which is socially rewarding for them as it affords privileges to them not available to lower-class women but their subservience has resulted in preserving the authoritative structures of society.[100]

The majority of Pakistani women in gainful employment belong to middle and working class families. These women can be divided into three categories: highly educated professionals such as doctors, teachers, engineers, bankers, lawyers, architects, civil servants, etc coming from upper or middle class families who take jobs and follow a career path. Rouse suggests that educated women, more than ever before, are opting for jobs as a matter of choice and not because of any economic need but for self-fulfilment and their own desire to make use of their qualifications.[101] On the other hand, women belonging to lower middle class or working class with less education or with no education at all are also seen contributing towards the family economy due to inflation in the cost of living. Women belonging to this class who are not highly educated are entering into low cadre office jobs such as secretarial and clerical jobs, and those who are illiterate work as home-based earners, cheap factory labour or domestic workers.

The issue of women domestic workers in Pakistan is also the outcome of class discrimination. Women domestic workers in Pakistan irrespective of their religious and ethnic diversity form a category of workers who belong to the lower socio-economic classes of society.[102] Women belonging to this lower working class are looked down upon due to their lower economic status and nature of work performed, in particular Christian workers who are called *jamadars*, *mehtar* or sweepers doing the 'dirty' cleaning job. They are expected to perform jobs that are considered as menial in society.[103]

Domestic workers are treated in a certain way and expected to work in a certain manner. Individually there may be many examples of charitable treatment, such as providing them with ample food or clothing, helping them to send their children to schools, and extra monetary help in case of sickness, emergency, or mishap. However, when it comes to their well-being in an organized manner a lack of interest is clearly visible on the part of the state/government, civil society groups as well as individual employers. The state's indifference is visible from domestic workers' absence in labour legislation as well as official national surveys. Similarly, no serious effort has been made on the part of NGOs, activists and women's movement in Pakistan to raise a voice for improving the situation of women domestic workers. Employers' indifference is because there is no check on monitoring how domestic workers are treated by their employers. It shows that people who can bring a change have a conflict of interest. One obvious reason for it is that employers do not want workers to be aware of their rights or to be protected by law. They fear that any such awareness and legal cover might encourage an uprising against the rich and the powerful. Secondly, if this sector is regularized and legal protection is given to these workers, the upper classes will not be able to use their services by paying meagre salaries, nor would domestic workers be at the disposal of employers who could throw them out of jobs whenever they so desire.

PARALLEL JUDICIAL FORUMS

The impact of parallel dispute resolution forums both at the formal state level under special laws as well as at the informal level under customary practices is to be discussed under this heading.[104] In 1947 when Pakistan came into being it also inherited some of the princely states of India as well as some of the tribal or frontier districts that were not part of the mainstream British Empire and had their own administrative and judicial systems.[105] As these parts were considered a potential threat to the British Empire, special laws were promulgated that are to-date enforced in these tribal territories.[106] After independence, special courts were established under special laws and were incorporated in the Constitution of Pakistan.[107]

Parallel forums exist not only at the formal level but also at an informal level in the form of *jirgas* and *panchayats*.[108] The impact of these judicial forums on women in Pakistan has been very negative because women hesitate to approach courts, even if aware of the existence of formal mechanisms of adjudication. Due to their restricted mobility, illiteracy, and inability to understand the official language of the court system, women end up depending on traditional forums for adjudication. These traditional mechanisms are all-male forums in which women do not have representation. Disputes regarding family and property are most often referred to these forums where decisions are made in favour of men. Cases of honour killings and rape are some of the examples reflecting male chauvinistic and patriarchal mindset of those sitting on these decision-making bodies.[109] The cases of Mukhtaran Mai and Solangi are two instances that challenge the existence and legitimacy of parallel judicial systems in the country and raise serious questions regarding the dispensation of justice to women in Pakistan.[110] These cases also show that women are always considered to be repositories of family honour which is always expected to be upheld by or affected by female members of the family.[111] The slightest misbehaviour (which by men's standards varies from talking to a male stranger or wanting to marry someone of her own choice) is interpreted by men as bringing disgrace and dishonour to the family and for which a woman can be punished in the form of losing her life.

The Sindh High Court (Sukkur Bench) has declared that all tribal *jirga*s are illicit, in fact the court has strictly banned any efforts to arrange any kind of *jirga.*[112] It has strictly bound the law enforcement agencies to take severe steps against *jirga*s. A recent development has been the move by the Supreme Court of Pakistan in which it has ordered the police chief to take action against members of a *panchayat* who ordered that a three-year-old girl be given in marriage to a 14-year-old boy and a woman be married to the younger brother of her alleged rapist under the customs of *vani* and *sawara.*[113] In the same case the chief justice also ordered the setting up of committees in all the district and *tehsils* comprising the presidents and secretaries-general of bar associations to receive complaints from victims of *vani* or *sawara* and to initiate action through sessions judges. All the session judges and district police officers were directed to co-operate with these committees. The federal government was also asked to amend Section 310 of the Pakistan Penal Code and Family Act, 1964, and to make provisions for the dissolution of marriages of women, who become victims of customary practices of *vani* or *swara.*

These decisions of the courts are of vital importance as they indicate flaws in administration of justice. Different governments (both civilian and military) have on several occasions failed to provide protection to the citizens and have remained indifferent to implementing the laws framed by parliament, so it is not surprising that the courts are trying to fill the gap. However, according to the report of the Human Rights Commission of Pakistan twenty-five *jirga*s were held after the judgment of the Sindh High Court. These were held under the supervision of MPAs, councillors, political party leaders and even ministers. Such blatant violations of the judgment raise serious concerns about the effectiveness of the legal system. It is also a clear example of the class hierarchy and dominant patriarchal structure, where the powerful can break the law without any fear of reprimand. Another major reason why these alternate mechanisms still flourish in Pakistan is due to slow judicial system and lacunae in law. However, the shortcomings of the formal legal and judicial system in the country do not in any case justify the existence of parallel judicial systems. What is needed is to take a more holistic view of the law to provide a fair and just legal and judicial process.

THE RHETORIC AND REALITY: ISLAMIC TEACHINGS AND THE SITUATION OF WOMEN'S WORK IN PAKISTAN

In plural legal societies like Pakistan, women's roles and positions are determined as much by customary norms and socio-economic factors as by religious teachings. However, religious teachings are often misinterpreted and the Quranic intent is subverted when it comes to women. Actual rules in practice that govern women's status and position are the result of customary practices and not the Quranic principles.

In the context of Pakistani Muslim women, Ali argues that 'the selective use of Islamic teachings' by religious leaders has not only strengthened and justified patriarchy but it has proved detrimental to women's wellbeing.[114] Despite clear instructions in the Quran, Hadith and examples from Islamic history, the reality is that, in many cases due to the patriarchal nature of Pakistani society and its family structure, women are considered as subordinate and it is males who have authority over females.[115] The customary practices must be clearly distinguished by looking at the religious text and *fiqh* in a more critical and objective manner.

Esposito, in his analysis of Islamic law and women's lives in the Islamic societies shows how Muslim family law reflected the social mores of the time, the traditional roles of men and women, and functions of the extended family in a patriarchal society.[116] Karmi in her work adopts a more critical approach by raising questions regarding the role of religion in maintaining patriarchy.[117]She does not seem to agree fully with the traditional view that Islam improved the status of women as compared to their position in the *jahilya* period. Karmi is also uncertain as to whether Islam facilitated or legitimized patriarchy, but accepts that Islam has been used by patriarchal society to legitimize its discrimination against women.

In the context of women and work, the Qur'an and Hadith literature (as discussed in Chapter 1) clearly suggest that there is no bar on women working outside the home and to earn a living. Muslim women have the privilege to earn money, the right to own property, to enter into legal contracts and to manage all their assets in any way they please. They can run their own businesses and no one has any claim on their earnings, including the husband. Examples from early Islamic history also reveal women's active socio-political and economic role and the fact that they were neither subjugated, nor denied their rights.[118] However, all these rights appear to be confined to theory but realities on the ground are different. In many cases women are prevented from entering the labour market by their male relatives. Women do not work because their husbands or fathers do not want them to work outside the house.[119]

Women are not given a share in agricultural land on the pretext, that dowry given at the time of marriage is their share of the property.[120] In cases where women own some property, it is usually controlled by men and women are expected to give power of attorney, or make a gift or relinquishment deeds in favour of the son, husband, father, brother or other male relatives. To stop such practice the Dissolution of Marriages Act 1939 (hereinafter referred as DMMA) provides protection to women where she can file a case for divorce on the ground of husband's interference in her property.

This discussion can be linked further to the case of women domestic workers where findings from the fieldwork suggest how the Islamic concept of dignity of labour is exploited by the employers. The way women domestic workers are degraded due to the type of work they perform especially those performing cleaning jobs (for example the Christian workers) shows how Islamic teachings are ignored when it comes to women and work related issues. Firstly, women domestic workers are denied social recognition and dignity. Conditions under which these workers live and work are a clear violation of the basic Islamic tenets of humanity, respect, and dignity of labour, as well as a reflection of the double standards of a society that claims to be Islamic.[21] Secondly, in many cases women do not have control over their earnings which are often taken away by men or spent according to the wishes of male members of male family members.[122] It is also noted that women cannot work without the permission from male members (findings from the fieldwork of this present study also provide evidence of it).

In Pakistani society it is a fallacy to say that women do not need to be gainfully employed because men have the primary responsibility to provide for their families. Such statements contradict reality. The basic family structure and economic system in today's society has changed. In the context of Pakistan, these statements are not true because nowadays both parents have to work in order to provide a living for the family as seen in the case of women in domestic service as well.

During the course of fieldwork the author also came across women workers who were single, separated, divorced with small children, or neglected wives of polygamous husbands. It is rare for women in these circumstances to afford the luxury of staying at home, secure in the comfort that some men in their lives, be it their fathers, brothers, ex-husbands or polygamous husbands will accept complete responsibility for maintaining them. They have to work and earn a living for the sake of the survival of their families. What needs to be emphasized instead is the sharing of responsibility between women and men and society as a whole in the upbringing of children and maintaining a harmonious household. There is nothing in a man's biological make-up that prevents him from being a nurturer and caregiver. The reason why men do not participate in housework and share childcare responsibilities is because they do not want to and are able to enforce their will on women who are conditioned to believe that it is their sole responsibility to preserve the marital relationship and family peace.

CONCLUSION

This chapter set out to explore women's work in plural legal settings. It highlights the fact that the law cannot exist in a vacuum, abstracted from the lived realities of women. Formal law cannot be a tool for empowerment for women in the presence of customary practices, patriarchy, and socio-cultural norms which are more powerful than legislation. Formal legislation therefore remains ineffective in the presence of legal pluralistic norms. Theoretically speaking the constitution does not make an unreasonable distinction between men and women. However, the discussion on constitutional and legislative frameworks in Pakistan highlights the fact that, in practice, despite many equality provisions, vast disparities exist that render women to a subordinate status. Labour laws are insufficient in many respects and are marked with problems such as unequal treatment of the two genders, with women workers at a disadvantage as compared to their male counterparts. The Domestic legislation does not expressly lay down the principle of equal remuneration for work of equal value.

The exclusion of domestic workers from labour laws highlights the vulnerability of these workers who have no recourse to legal protection under present labour laws. It also shows the lack of commitment on the part of the state towards social legislation. In the absence of any social legislation applicable to informal/casual workers, in particular domestic and agricultural workers, employers are not bound to provide any security of employment or to pay any benefits, bonuses or insurance to their employees.

The section on customary practices has helped in identifying the role these norms play in subordinating women's position in Pakistani society. It has further helped in understanding the role of patriarchy in controlling women's lives and their work situations. It also shows social attitudes regarding women further deepens gender differences and how class hierarchies determine whether women do or do not enter into employment sector. Improving women's own perception and the perception of society about their work is also important from the point of view of seeking legal redress under the constitutional and labour law provisions. Formal laws will remain an under-utilized and partially effective strategy for women seeking equal rights in the workplace, until perceptions towards women and work undergo a transformative process and women's work is valued and accepted as an important contribution to society.

The discussion on women, work, and Islam shows how religious teachings are ignored when it comes to women and especially those who belong to the lower social status.

In light of these discussions the next chapter provides a contextual analysis of women domestic worker's situation in Pakistan by looking at wider issues faced by women in both formal and informal employment sectors.

NOTES

1. Adopted and proclaimed by General Assembly resolution 217 A (III) of 10 December 1948.
2. The 1962 constitution deals with equality in Article 15. The same subject of equality became Article 22 in the interim 1972 constitution with the addition of Clause 3: that 'Nothing in this article shall prevent the state from enacting any special provision for the protection of women.' Later, in the 1973 constitution, the equality provision appears in Article 25 and the word 'children' is added to Clause 3.
3. Mullally, S. (1995), 'Separate Spheres: Protective Legislation for Women in Pakistan,' *Asian Year Book of International Law*, Vol. 4, Kluwer Law International, pp. 47-67.
4. PLD 1954 SC 5.
5. *Jibendra Kishore v Province of East Pakistan*, PLD 1957 SC 9.

6. Mullally, S., supra note 3, p. 55.
7. Ibid., p. 56.
8. PLD 1990 SC 295.
9. PLD 1995 Lah 584.
10. *Shirin Dokht v Government of Pakistan*, 1995 PLC (CS) 251.
11. PLD 2005 SC 831.
12. PLD 2005 SC 841.
13. Ali, S.S. and Shahid A. (2006), 'Women, Law and Empowerment: Securing Equal Rights for Women in the Workplace (A Case-Study of Women and Employment in Pakistan),' in Crick, P. (ed.), *Our Freedoms: A Decades Reflection on the Advancement of Human Rights*, International bar Association, p. 180.
14. Amjad, A. (2001), *Labour Legislation and Trade Unions in Pakistan*, Karachi: Oxford University Press and Ali, K. (2003), 'Labour Policy and Law in Pakistan: A Case of Distorted Perspectives and Priorities,' in SDPI, *Sustainable Development and Southern Realities: Past and Future in South Asia*, Islamabad: City Press.
15. General Ayub Khan was the first military dictator in Pakistan who came into power in 1958 after carrying out a military coup against the then civilian government.
16. The period between the 1960s and the 1970s was the most turbulent period in the history of industrial relations in Pakistan. Disputes and conflicts over pay and working conditions continued between the trade unions and management. Strikes, go-slows, lockouts, and litigation were the most distinctive features of employer-employee relations. The concept of employers and employees working together in close co-operation to ensure productivity, profitability, and growth of businesses and security of employment was largely non-existent.
17. The ordinance increased the number of workplaces where unions could not be formed. The procedures for registration and certification of unions were further tightened up, and in the name of strengthening collective bargaining, more than one union in a single plant was allowed.
18. Government of Pakistan, 'Labour Protection Policy 2005 (First Draft)' Ministry of Labour, Manpower, and Overseas Pakistanis, available at http://www.pakistan.gov.pk/divisions/labour-division/media/LP PolicyDraft020205.pdf accessed on 20 March 2006.
19. The six main categories are Industrial Relations, Employment Conditions, Wages, Human Resource Development, Occupational Safety, Health, Labour Welfare, and Social Protection.
20. The Federal Laws of Pakistan are published by the government in a document called the *Gazette of Pakistan*. The Ministry of Justice, Law and Parliamentary Affairs in addition publishes individual Acts through the Official Gazette.
21. Factories (Amendment) Act 1973 (No. 16) *Gazette of Pakistan, 1973-02-07, XX*, West Pakistan Shops and Establishments Ordinance 1969 (No. 8) *Gazette of West Pakistan, 1969-07-03, Extraordinary*, West Pakistan Industrial and Commercial Employment (Standing Orders) (Amendment) Act 1974 (No. 48), Pakistan Industrial Relations Ordinance 2002.
22. These laws are framed at the provincial level since agriculture is a provincial subject under the constitution and these laws basically deal with sharecropper's occupancy rights.
23. The main object is to regulate the payment of wages to certain classes of persons employed in industry. The provisions of the Act can be extended to other classes of workers by the Provincial Governments after giving three months notice to the employers of their intention to do so. The Act stipulates that wages to workers

employed in factories and on railways are to be paid within seven days of completion of the wages period, if the number of workers employed therein is less than 1,000. In other cases, the time limit for payment of wages to the workers is ten days.

24. Mullally, S., supra note 3, p. 59.
25. The laws include the Mines Maternity Benefit Act, 1941, the West Pakistan Maternity Benefit Ordinance, 1958, the West Pakistan Maternity Benefit Rules, 1961.
26. This provision is in consonance with Articles 3 and 4 of the ILO 1919 Maternity Benefit Convention (No. 3).
27. An 'Ordinance' is passed under Presidential Order without going through different stages of legislative process whereas an 'Act' is enacted after debate and discussion in the Parliament and passes through all stages of legislative process.
28. Khan, N.S. (1989), *Setting the Record Straight*, Lahore: ASR Publications, p. 2.
29. Factories Act 1938 is applicable only where 10 or more workers are employed. West Pakistan Industrial and Commercial Employment Ordinance 1968 is applicable only partially in industrial and commercial units where twenty or more workers are employed. It is fully applicable only where fifty or more workers are employed. Employees Old Age Benefits Act 1976 is applicable only on the establishment where ten or more workers are employed. The workers in the informal sector, e.g. small shops and/or workshops are also not covered under the labour laws.
30. Amjad, A. (2001), *Labour Legislation and Trade Unions in Pakistan*, Karachi: Oxford University Press, p. 175.
31. Ibid., p. 121.
32. ILO 1919 Night Work Convention, (No 4). This Convention concerning Employment of Women during the Night (Note: Date of coming into force: 13:06:1921. The Convention was revised in 1934 by Convention No. 41 and in 1948 by Convention (No. 89) Convention: C 004).
33. Factories (Amendment) Act 1973 (No. 16) *Gazette of Pakistan, 1973-02-07, XX.*
34. Commissioners are appointed under Section 20 of the Workmen's Compensation Act by the provincial government and possess all the powers of a civil court.
35. Santos, B., supra note 194, ch. 1, p. 163.
36. There are also other regional bodies like the European Commission on Human Rights, Inter American Commission and the African System but, as this research study is on Pakistan only SAARC at the regional level is discussed.
37. In 1919, the signatory nations to the Treaty of Versailles created the International Labour Organization (ILO). ILO has developed a comprehensive 'Decent Work Agenda' which aims to achieve decent work for all by promoting social dialogue, social protection and employment creation, as well as respect for international labour standards. The standards have grown into a comprehensive system of instruments on work and social policy, backed by a supervisory system designed to address all sorts of problems in their application at the national level. The ILO Governing Body has identified eight conventions as 'fundamental', covering subjects that are considered as fundamental principles and rights at work: freedom of association and the effective recognition of the right to collective bargaining; the elimination of all forms of forced or compulsory labour; the effective abolition of child labour; and the elimination of discrimination in respect of employment and occupation. These principles are also covered in the ILO's Declaration on Fundamental Principles and Rights at Work (1998). In 1995, the ILO launched a campaign to achieve universal ratification of these eight conventions. There are currently over 1,200 ratifications of these conventions, representing 86 per cent of the possible number of ratifications. Four other conventions have also been designated as priority Conventions and member

states are encouraged to ratify them as these are also considered important for the functioning of the international labour standards system. The overarching objective of the ILO has been re-phrased as the promotion of opportunities for women and men to obtain decent and productive work in conditions of freedom, equity, security, and human dignity. Decent work is the converging focus of the four strategic objectives, namely rights at work, employment, social protection, and social dialogue. Decent work is an organizing concept for the ILO in order to provide an overall framework for action in economic and social development.

38. The commitment to gender equality policy is shown in the form of four key instruments adopted by the ILO Discrimination (Employment and Occupation) Convention, 1958 (No. 111), Equal Remuneration Convention, 1951 (No. 100), Workers with Family Responsibilities Convention, 1981 (No. 156) and the Maternity Protection Convention, 2000 (No. 183).
39. Literature review of domestic service in chapter two of the present study shows that there are various organizations working for the rights of women in domestic service, such as Kalayaan in the UK or National Domestic Workers Movement in India to name a few.
40. ILO: Resolution concerning the Conditions of Employment of Domestic Workers, International Labour Conference, Geneva, 49th session, 1965.
41. Slavery, Servitude, Forced Labour and Similar Institutions and Practices Convention of 1926 (Slavery Convention of 1926), 60 LNTS 253, entered into force: 9 March 1927. Supplementary Convention on the Abolition of Slavery, the Slave Trade, and Institutions and Practices similar to Slavery. Economic and Social Council Resolution 608 (XXI) of 30 April 1956 and done at Geneva on 7 September 1956 (entered into force: 30 April 1957) in accordance with article 13. The United Nations Convention against Trans-national Organized Crime, supplemented by the Protocol to Prevent, Suppress and Punish Trafficking in Persons, especially Women and Children. G.A. res. 55/25, annex II, 55 UN GAOR Supp. (No. 49) at 60, UN Doc. A/45/49 (Vol. I) (2001) United Nations International Convention on the Protection of the Rights of All Migrant Workers and Members of Their Families, 1990. G.A. Res. 45/158, UN GAOR, 45th Sess., Supp. No. 49A, at 261, UN Doc. A/45/49 (1990) (entered into force 1 July 2003) [hereinafter CMW].
42. International Convention on the Protection of the Rights of All Migrant Workers and Members of Their Families, G.A. Res. 45/158, UN GAOR, 45th Sess., Supp. No. 49A, at 261, UN Doc. A/45/49 (1990) (entered into force 1 July 2003) [hereinafter CMW].
43. Article 7 of CMW also states that: 'The present Convention is applicable, except as otherwise provided hereafter, to all migrant workers and members of their families without distinction of any kind such as sex, race, colour, language, religion or conviction, political or other opinion, national, ethnic or social origin, nationality, age, economic position, property, marital status, birth or other status.'
44. See Articles 8, 9, 10, 11 of the CMW.
45. See Articles 37, 38, 43 of the CMW.
46. The United Nations Universal Declaration of Human Rights. Adopted and proclaimed by General Assembly Resolution 217 A (III) of 10 December 1948.
47. Under Article 2, each State Party 'undertakes to respect and to ensure to all individuals within its territory and subject to its jurisdiction the rights recognized within the present Convention, without distinction of any kind such as race, colour, sex, language, religion, political or other opinion, national or social origin, property, birth or other status.'

48. Article 2 of the ICESCR obliges States' Parties to 'undertake to guarantee that the rights enunciated in the present Convention will be exercised without discrimination of any kind as to race, colour, sex, language, religion, political or other opinion, national or social origin, property, birth or other status.'
49. Convention for the Elimination of All Forms of Discrimination against Women, adopted Dec. 18, 1979, 1249 UNTS 13 (entered into force 3 Sept. 1981). See Articles 2, 5, 11, 13.
50. See Articles 2, 5, 11, 13 of the CEDAW.
51. The Human Rights Committee has made clear that sexual harassment is a form of sexual discrimination prohibited under the Convention.
52. Article 5(b).
53. Article 10 and Article 16(2).
54. Article 4, paragraph 1 of the Convention for the Protection of Human Rights and Fundamental Freedoms (ECHR), prohibits slavery and servitude, Article 3 of the ECHR, provides that no one shall be subjected to torture or to inhuman or degrading treatment or punishment, and Article 6, proclaims the right of access to a court in civil and criminal matters, including cases where the employer enjoys immunity from jurisdiction.
55. Their passports are systematically confiscated, leaving them in a situation of total vulnerability with regard to their employers. Most of the victims of this new form of slavery are in an illegal situation, having been recruited by agencies and having borrowed money to pay for their journey. The Assembly also deplored the fact that a considerable number of victims work in embassies or in the homes of international civil servants who, under the Vienna Convention on Diplomatic Relations of 1961, enjoy immunity from jurisdiction and enforcement and are covered by the principle of inviolability of persons and property.
56. Recommendation 1523 (2001) adopted by the Parliamentary Assembly Committee, on 26 April 2001.
57. Recommendation No. 1663 (2004), adopted by the Parliamentary Assembly Committee, on 22 June 2004..
58. UIDHR adopted on 19 September 1981 by the Islamic Council consists of a preamble and 23 articles.
59. Ali, S.S. and Shahid, A., supra note 13, p. 183.
60. Adopted at the first Muslim Women Parliamentarians' Conference in Islamabad on 1-3 August 1995.
61. Lim, L.L. and Oishi, N. (1996), 'International Labour Migration of Asian Women: Distinctive Characteristics and Policy Concerns,' *Asian Women in Migration, Special Issue of Asian and Pacific Migration Journal*, Vol. 5, No. 1, pp. 85-116; Chew, L. (2003), 'Discussion Paper for Programme Consultation Meeting on the Protection of Domestic Workers Against the Threat of Forced Labour and Trafficking,' prepared for Anti-Slavery International in cooperation with the ILO's Special Action Programme to Combat Forced Labour; Ramirez-Machado, J.M. (2000), 'Domestic Work, Conditions of Work and Employment: a Legal Perspective,' unpublished draft manuscript, Geneva: International Labour Organization, Conditions of Work Branch.
62. Blackett, A. (1996), 'Making Domestic Work Visible: The Case for Specific Regulation,' ILO's Focus Programme on Social Dialogue, Labour Law and Labour Administration, Geneva: International Labour Organisation Available at http://www.ilo.org/public/english/dialogue/ifpdial/publ/infocus/domestic/html.

63. Satterwaite, M.L. (2005), 'Crossing Borders Claiming Rights: Using Human Rights Law to Empower Women Migrant Workers,' *Yale Human Rights and Development Law Journal*, Vol. 8, No. 1, available at www.westlaw.uk for a thorough discussion on the inter-sectionality approach. Also see Piper, N. and Iredale, R. (2003), 'Identification of the Obstacles to the Signing and Ratification of the UN Convention on the Protection of the Rights of All Migrant Workers and Members of their Families,' available at http://www.unesco.org/most/apmrn_unconv.htm; Taran, P.A. (2000), 'Status and Prospects for the UN Convention on Migrants' Rights,' *European Journal of Migration and Law*, Vol. 2, No. 85, pp. 92-103. Caldwell, P.M. (1991), 'A Hair Piece: Perspectives on the Intersection of Race and Gender,' *Duke Law Journal*, p. 365; Harris, A. (1990, 'Race and Essentialism in Feminist Legal Theory,' Stanford Law Review, Vol. 4, p. 581, as cited in Satterwaite, M.L.
64. The South Asian Association for Regional Cooperation (SAARC) was established when its Charter was formally adopted on 8 December 1985 by the Heads of State or Government of Bangladesh, Bhutan, India, Maldives, Nepal, Pakistan and Sri Lanka. SAARC provides a platform for the peoples of South Asia to work together in a spirit of friendship, trust, and understanding. It aims to accelerate the process of economic and social development in Member States.
65. Article 8.
66. Article 9.
67. The Group convened its First Meeting in June 2004 in Islamabad, and decided to commission a study incorporating issues such as women's citizenship, women's political representation, trafficking and sexual exploitation, gender and HIV/AIDS, female education and literacy, legal rights and economic empowerment and impact of globalization on women.
68. For a detailed list of the Conventions signed and ratified by Pakistan visit ILO website http://www.ilo.org/public/english/index.htm
69. Khan, N. (1989), *Setting the Record Straight*, Lahore: ASR Publications; Shahid, A. and Arif, K. (2001-2002), 'Women's Labour Legislation in NWFP: A Case Study of Women Industrial Workers in Peshawar District,' Research Project, Faculty of Law, University of Peshawar, Ahmed, N. Qaisrani, S. and Tahir, M. (1998), 'Social Protection for Women Workers in the Informal Home-based Sector in the Leather and Textile Industries,' Islamabad: Aurat Publication and Information Service Foundation.
70. Another example is of Convention 111 which, is in furtherance to the Right to Organize and Collective Bargaining Convention, 1949 (No. 98). The objective of this convention is to provide protection against acts of anti-union discrimination in respect of their employment. It includes providing protection against imposition of any conditions attached to the employment such as making the employment of a worker subject to the condition that he shall not join a union or shall relinquish trade union membership or dismissal on grounds of joining a trade union on employee's organization. It also provides protection against any acts of interference by workers and employers or each other's agents or members in their establishment, functioning or administration.
71. For a detailed discussion on Unions in Pakistan see chapter 4.
72. A 'National Fund for Advancement of Rural Women' (Jafakash Aurat) with seed money of Rs 100m, created by the government, has a special focus on rural women and the informal sector. The fund is operated through a couple of commercial banks (Khushhali and First Women Bank) and NGOs, the Aga Khan Rural Support Programme, simultaneously providing skill, employment and income to nearly 23,000

rural women and benefiting over 74,000 households. In addition, the Provision of safety Nets', 'Food Support Scheme', 75 per cent of which are benefiting women covering 1.2m rural households, '*Guzara* Allowance' and '*Zakat*' 70 per cent of which is benefiting 0.4m women, the Dastkari schools (700), established by Pakistan Bait-ul-Maal, are providing skill based training and ready income, specially to over 3,000 widows and indigents. The 'Crop Maximization Project', 'Integration of Agricultural Research and Extension Activities' and 'Introduction of Herbs as Crops' and the 'Training Programme' in rearing livestock and dairy animals are helping women's income generation. The Micro-Credit Scheme, introduced recently under the aegis of the Ministry of Women Development through commercial banks (Khushhali and First Women Bank) is expected to create a new entrepreneurial class among poor women on a local basis.

73. For the purpose of this research, formal laws include the constitution of Pakistan (1973), all statutory laws, Sharia laws as introduced by General Ziaul Haq and international conventions signed and ratified by the Government of Pakistan. Informal laws include both codified and un-codified customary practices, traditions, and cultural norms.
74. Ali, S.S., supra note 121, ch. 1, p. 173.
75. Zia, S. (1995), 'Women and Law,' in Khan, N.S. et al. (eds.), *Unveiling the Issues: Pakistani Women's Perspectives on Social, Political and Ideological Issues*, Lahore: ASR Publications, p. 73.
76. Ibid., p. 74.
77. *Nikah* is the formal ceremony of marriage in which both parties give their consent to marriage in the presence of witnesses, and a certain amount of dower is fixed.
78. In March 2004, a case was brought in front of a judge in Dadu in the Sindh province, regarding the sale of Akthiar, a 7-year-old girl to a 35-year-old man for marriage. The girl's mother appeared with her in court to protest the sale of her daughter by her husband to Ali Hassan, a resident of Mazdoorabad Moholla in Dadu, for Rs 18,000 ($300). Akthiar managed to escape. Since then Ali Hassan has attempted to kidnap her back, and her mother is seeking protection for her daughter. An investigation into the incident was called for by the judge. Numerous other incidents have been reported in the Annual reports of Human Rights Commission of Pakistan.
79. The Law and Justice Commission in its report stated that all individuals who contract marriage by *vani* or *swara* through a *jirga* or *panchayat* (informal dispute resolution councils comprising of community elders) should be liable to rigorous imprisonment. The Chief Justices of the High Courts were given instructions to ensure that the trial courts and appellate courts do not allow for a woman to be given in compensation. The Commission also came out with a draft amendment to Article 366-C of the Pakistan Penal Code. The text of the proposed amendment states 'Whosoever takes part in reconciliation or *panchayat* and thereby requires any person to offer and accepts, and whosoever offers and accepts in marriage a woman (above the age of 16) against her free will, or a female child in lieu of any concession to an accused person, or as a compensation for an act when such an act is an offence under the law, or as a Badal-e-Sulh shall be punished with either description for a term which may be extended to ten years and shall also be liable to fine.' However this amendment has not as yet been passed. Government of Pakistan. 'Law and Justice Commission of Pakistan, Annual Report 2002.' Law and Justice Commission, Islamabad, p. 40. Accessed at www.lcpj.gov.uk/reports/annual/htm
80. A 1995 survey of over 1000 households in the rural areas of the Punjab indicated that in nearly two-thirds of households, daughters did not inherit land. It was customary

for only sons to inherit and daughters did not exercise their rights. In some cases women's names were simply not included on revenue records after they inherited, or in others, they were persuaded to sign relinquishment deeds in favour of male family members. Out of 1000 women, only thirty-six owned land in their own name and only nine had the power to sell or trade their land without permission from male members. Cited in Mahbub ul Haq Development Centre's Annual Report, *Human Development in South Asia 2000: The Gender Question*, Karachi: Oxford University Press, p. 89.

81. Ali, S.S., supra note 5, 121, ch. 1, p. 175.
82. Paying bride price to the family of the woman is a common practice in rural areas of NWFP. It is a customary practice which is in contradiction to the Islamic requirement of *Haq Mehr* (Dower), which is to be paid to the wife.
83. Khattak, S. (2003), 'Women, Work and Empowerment.' in SDPI (ed.), *Sustainable Development and Southern Realities: Past and Future in South Asia*, Islamabad: City Press, p. 334.
84. Discrimination against women begins from the moment of birth, an occasion which is still greeted with sorrow and despair as compared to the birth of a male child which is an occasion for rejoicing and celebration in many parts of Pakistan. Discrimination takes many forms, beginning with lessons from early childhood to be submissive, obedient, and always ready to surrender, and ending with society placing hurdles in her way to prevent her from approaching courts for whatever rights are available to her.
85. Saigol, R. (1995), 'Domestic Knowledge Systems and Patriarchy,' in Khan, N. et al. (eds.), *Unveiling the Issues: Pakistani Women's Perspectives on Social, Political and Ideological Issues*, Lahore: ASR Publications, p. 142.
86. In Pakistani society girls and boys receive different instructions on values, norms and behaviour. Girls are always taught to be submissive, obedient, respectful, and courteous, whereas boys are taught to be aggressive, bold, and assertive. This distinction between a man and a woman leads to inequality between the two sexes in the society. Common proverbs are used such as '*doli bap ki ghar say aur janaza shohar kai ghar*, i.e. 'she must appear in a bridal suit from her father's house and will only emerge in her coffin from her husband's house' or the concept of *Agla Ghar* or next home referring to husband's home as if she has no house of her own.
87. Hafeez, S. (1989), *Women in Industry*, Islamabad: Women Division, Government of Pakistan; Khattak, S. and Sayeed, A. (2001), *Women's Work and Empowerment Issues in an Era of Economic Liberation*, Karachi: PILER; Hafeez, S. (1981), *Metropolitan Women of Pakistan*, Karachi: Royal Book Company; Khan, N.S. (1986), 'Women's Involvement in the Industrial Sector in Punjab—Status and Prospectus,' Lahore: ASR Publications; Khan, S.R. and Aftab, S. (1995), 'Structural Adjustment, Labour and the Poor in Pakistan,' Islamabad: Sustainable Development Policy Institute; Khattak, S. and Sayeed, A. (2000), 'Subcontracted Women Workers in the World Economy: The Case of Pakistan,' Islamabad: Sustainable Development Policy Institute.
88. Cf., chapter 4 of the present book.
89. Cf., chapter 6 of the present book.
90. Cf., footnote 87.
91. Federal Bureau of Statistics, Government of Pakistan has taken a few initiatives, such as the 1997 Labour Force Survey which now includes fourteen types of household labour as part of economic activity. This has raised labour force participation rate to 25.5 per cent, yet this estimate still understates the actual position.
92. Khattak, S. and Sayeed, A., supra note 87, p. 46.

93. Patel, R. (2000), 'Perceptions, Norms and Women's Property Rights in India: A Discussion of Legal Pluralism', in A. Stewart (ed.), *Gender, Law and Social Justice*, London: Blackstone Press Limited, p. 172.
94. Ibid., p. 46.
95. Ahmed, N. (1990), 'Women Home Based Piece Rate Workers: A Study of the Informal Sector of Pakistan: Problems and Policies,' Informal Sector Study No. 3, Fredrich Eburt Stifung, Islamabad.
96. The national primary school enrolment rate stands at 38 per cent for girls and 46 for boys. About 50 per cent of the pupils leave primary school before completing their course. Most of the dropouts are girls—about 59 per cent.
97. The class system in Pakistan inherited from the pre-partition Indian sub-continent is composed of mainly three categories. The upper class consists of feudal landlords, bureaucrats, and industrialists. The middle class consists of small landowners, small businessmen, educated men and women involved in middle-grade public and private sector jobs whereas the working class (majority of whom illiterate), are involved in low paid jobs and live on the verge of poverty.
98. Alvi, H., *Pakistani Women in the Present Changing Society*, www.ourworld.compuserve.com/homepages/sangat/pakwomen.htm accessed on 20 February 2003.
99. Ibid.
100. Jalal, A. (1991), 'The Convenience of Subservience: Women and the State of Pakistan,' in Kandiyoti, D. et al. (eds.), *Women Islam and State*, London: MacMillan Press, pp. 77-114.
101. Rouse, S. (1994), 'Gender Struggles, the State, Religion and Society,' in Bhasin, K. et al. (ed.), *Against All Odds: Essays on Women, Religion and Development from India and Pakistan*, Delhi: ISIS and Kali for Women, pp. 22-23.
102. During the fieldwork many women domestic workers mentioned that as they could not see their children and families suffering, due to unemployment and extreme poverty therefore, they have to come out of their homes and take up jobs in other households. Women also mentioned that many times they are ridiculed by their extended family members and neighbours for leaving their homes especially in Peshawar which is a more conservative area as compared to Karachi.
103. The two terms 'cleaning job' and 'dirty work' contradict each other, as persons who undertake cleaning jobs are shunned as 'dirty' and 'unclean'. Although not within the remit of this study, it is pertinent to note that the people who clean and are looked down upon belong to the untouchable Hindu communities of South Asia. Many of these converted to Christianity during colonial rule but continued their occupation of cleaning. This may be one of the reasons for the low status accorded to cleaners.
104. For a detailed discussion of parallel legal institutions see Ali, S.S. and Arif, K. (1998), 'Parallel Judicial Systems in Pakistan and Consequences for Human Rights,' in Shaheed, F. et al. (eds.), *Shaping Women's Lives: Laws, Practices and Strategies in Pakistan*, Lahore: Shirkat Gah.
105. Bahawalpur, Swat, Dir, and Chitral are the princely states that had acceded to Pakistan. Malakand, Swat, Dir, Kohistan, and Chitral are in the NWFP and are called as Provincially Administered Tribal Areas (PATA).
106. Frontiers Crime Regulations (Regulations III of 1901).
107. Formal parallel systems include the Federal Shariat Court established under Article 2A of the Constitution has been given the powers to determine whether or not existing legislation is in consonance with Islamic injunctions. Military Courts and Special Courts for speedy trials have also been established from time to time during martial law regimes in the country. A recent addition to these courts has been the

formation of Accountability Courts which were given extensive powers to arrest, investigate and prosecute try corruption cases and Military Courts to try suspected terrorists expeditiously. These special courts lacked essential due process and fundamental rights guarantees, including the right of appeal. They allow for detention periods of up to 90 days without charge and do not allow the accused to access counsel prior to the institution of formal charges. In February 1999, the Supreme Court of Pakistan declared Military Courts as unconstitutional and ordered their dissolution. The Military Courts were then replaced with Anti-Terrorist Courts. Through amendments to the Anti-Terrorist Act (ATA), the jurisdiction of Anti-Terrorist Courts was extended to cover the same types of offences as had been tried by Military Courts, and the executive completed the transition through an April 1999 ordinance transferring such cases to the Anti-Terrorist Courts. As was the case with Military Courts, Anti-Terrorist Courts were established to dispense summary justice, conducting trials within seven working days and are not required to adhere to due process or provide fair trial guarantees.

108. *Jirgas* and *panchayats* are informal dispute resolution forms like a council of elders comprised of influential and powerful men in the community who adjudicate disputes among members of their community.

109. Honour killings form part of what has been termed 'traditional justice,' a contested form of private retribution that many find unwanted and illegitimate. The overall concern and stress on honour necessitates strict adherence to cultural and customary norms. The family honour is threatened/challenged when a woman refuses to accept the family dictates and marries according to her own choice. *Karo-Kari* is a customary practice in the province of Sindh where women are murdered when they are accused of having an illicit relationship. Even Pakistani woman abroad do not escape the threat of honour killings by their male relatives. The Nottingham Crown Court in the United Kingdom in May 1999 sentenced a Pakistani woman and her grown-up son to life imprisonment for murdering her daughter, Rukhsana Naz, a pregnant mother of two children. Rukhsana was perceived to have brought shame on the family by having a sexual relationship outside marriage. Her brother reportedly strangled Rukhsana while her mother held her down.

110. Amanat Solangi, a 44-year-old gynaecologist, married Ghulam Mustafa Solangi, 47, who was a skin specialist on 30 November 2003, in the presence of her mother and several of his relatives. The marriage was solemnized under Muslim family law. However, Mir Mohammad Solangi, Dr Aamnat's eldest brother of many titles, Sardar of the Solangis, chairman of the Public Safety Committee, president of the Multan Bar Council and *nazim* of the union council refused to accept the marriage. This elder brother called a *jirga* to decide the couple's fate. The verdict given by the *jirga* was that the marriage would be recognized only if the couple paid 2 million rupees and if two girls were handed over to the family as compensation for the damaged honour of the family. Failure to comply would result in the stigma of *Karo-Kari* and death. The second recent case in point is of Mukhtaran Mai who was first gang-raped on the orders of the *jirga*, later the Multan Bench of the Lahore High Court acquitted five out of six accused who had been awarded death punishments by the Anti-Terrorist Court. The Federal Shariat Court then took a *suo moto* notice of the decision of the Multan Bench on the ground that it had no jurisdiction to hear the case as it was a case of Hudood Law. Later the Supreme Court of Pakistan took another *suo moto* notice of the case.

111. According to the Human Rights Commission of Pakistan's Annual Report 2004, the number of women murdered in the name of honour by male members of the family

was 464. The actions were justified on the pretext that these women had transgressed cultural norms. For further statistical information and annual reports visit http://www.hrcp-web.org/ar_2004.cfm.

112. The Sindh High Court imposed a ban on the holding of *jirgas* in April 2004 because of the sometimes inhumane sentences awarded to people, especially the women. But the ban has been blatantly ignored and nothing has been done about it so far.
113. 'SC Seeks Action against *Swara* and *Vani*,' www.dawn.com/ accessed on 20 May 2006.
114. Ali, S.S., supra note 121, Ch. 1, p. 183.
115. The Quranic verses, Hadith and examples from Islamic history have been discussed in detail in chapter 1.
116. Esposito, J. (1982), *Women in Muslim Family Law*, Syracuse NY: Syracuse University Press, p. 48.
117. Karmi, G. (1996), 'Women, Islam and Patriarchalism,' in Yamani, M. (ed.), *Feminism and Islam: Legal and Literary Perspectives*, New York: New York University Press, p. 82.
118. Cf., see details given in chapter 1.
119. Government of Pakistan (1998-99), *Pakistan Integrated Household Survey*, Federal Bureau of Statistics, Statistics Division, Islamabad.
120. For a detailed discussion on the customs and property rights of women in Pakistan see Mehdi, R. (2001), *Gender and Property Law in Pakistan: Resources and Discourses*, Copenhagen: DJØF Publications.
121. Cf., findings from the field further substantiate the point that women in domestic service are exploited and treated in a degrading manner by employers.
122. Cf., chapter 5 of the book.

4

A Contextual Analysis of the Key Issues in Women's Work

INTRODUCTION

This chapter will explore the limits of law as a tool for empowerment of women domestic workers by placing them in a wider context of women and work in different employment sectors in Pakistan. In light of discussions on plural legal frameworks, it evaluates the extent to which laws in the formal and informal employment sectors have helped in providing protection and improving women's position in the workplace. It also seeks to evaluate if constitutional and legislative provisions (available to women in the formal public sector and in the informal sector) are being implemented; and, if not, what are the reasons for non-implementation of laws. It examines the question whether employment is a path towards empowerment and if increased participation has resulted in improving women's status. To what extent has economic empowerment improved women's decision making power and does economic empowerment enables women to participate in the decision making process in the workplace as well as in home or in family matters are some of the issues discussed. This chapter also looks into women's mobility and further discusses the factors that inhibit women's participation in trade union activities.

WOMEN'S INCREASED PARTICIPATION IN EMPLOYMENT

The increased participation of women in formal and informal sectors and questions whether it has helped in empowering women workers in Pakistan are to be discussed in this section.[1] Women in Pakistan have progressed and expanded their capabilities in all walks of life in the past two decades. Despite being in a largely male-dominated society, women

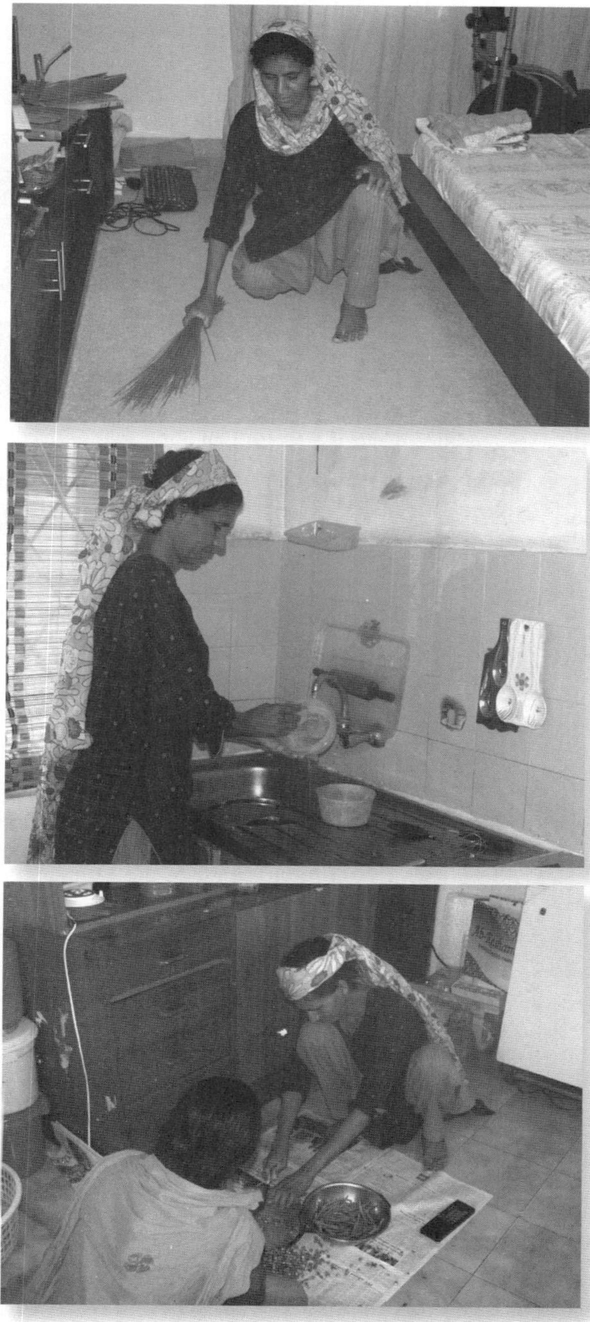

A woman domestic worker busy in household chores.

Women domestic workers from Bhit Islands

A woman domestic worker filling water cans

Broken wooden shed used as a toilet

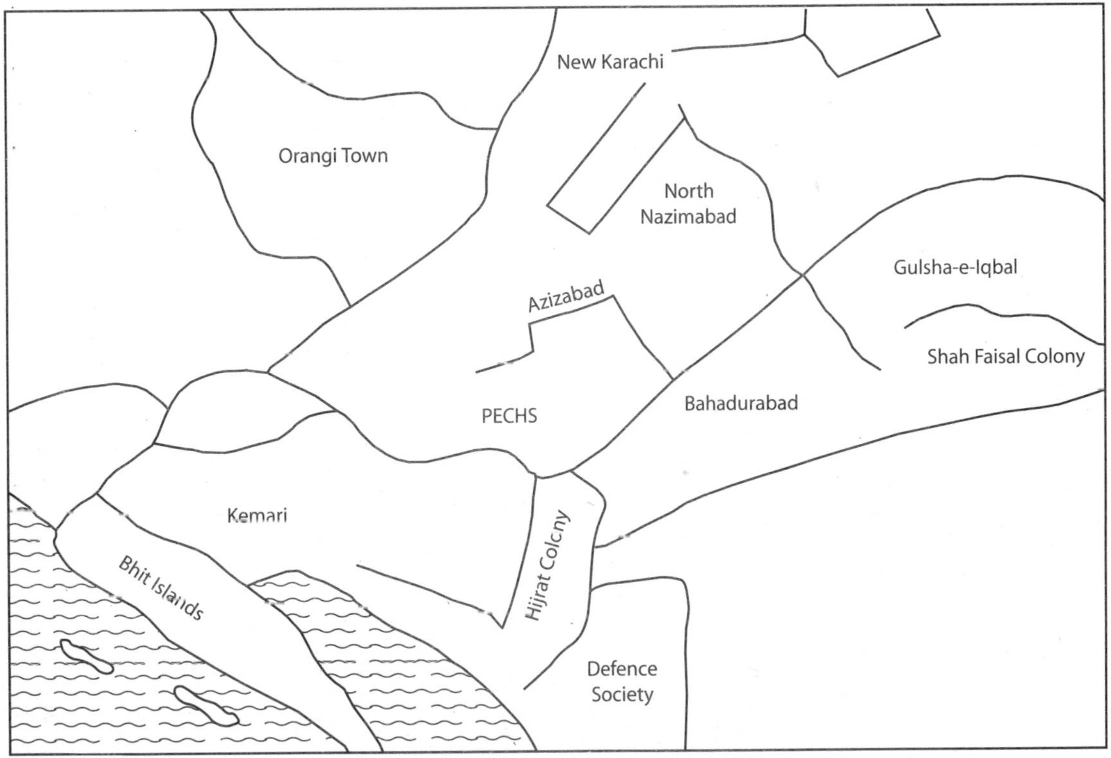

Map of Karachi with sampling location

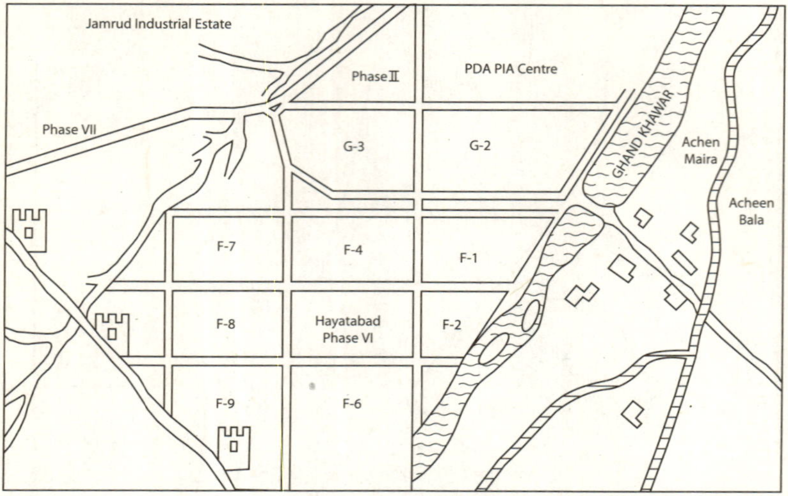

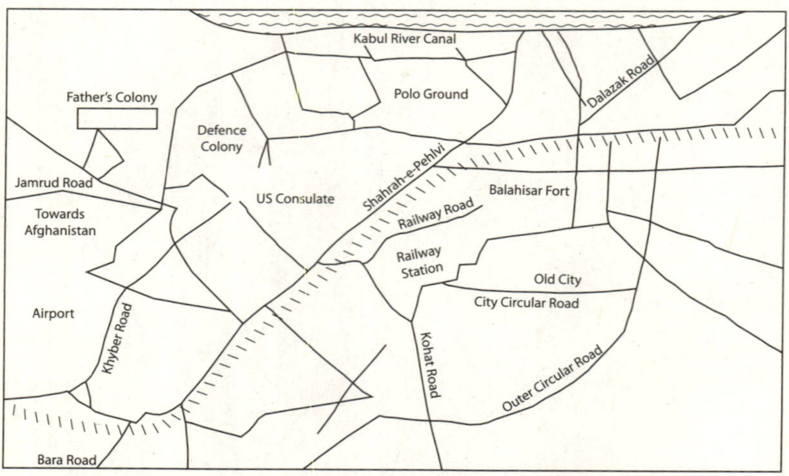

Maps of Peshawar with sampling location

in Pakistan are increasingly challenging the *status quo*, and struggling hard to create space for themselves in the public sphere. According to the report on the second quarter (Oct.-Dec. 2005) of the Labour Force Survey (LFS) 2005-6, the female participation rates have increased from 27.5 per cent in 2003-4 to 31 per cent in 2005.[2] The Gender-related Development Index rank (GDI) for Pakistan is 107 with a value of 0.508. The Gender Empowerment Measure rank (GEM) for Pakistan is 71 with a value of 0.379 and female economic activity rate is 36.7 per cent.[3] These figures also indicate an increase in the number of women participating in the employment sector. Table 4.1 shows the crude activity participation rates for male/female among rural and urban populations in Pakistan.

In urban areas more women are seen entering into professions which were once considered to be male only domains such as engineering, banking, internet computer technology, architecture, journalism, politics etc.

In public sector employment, educated and professional women are working in the federal and provincial civil service, judiciary, financial institutions, as consultants in national and international NGOs and donor agencies, and in public and private sector educational institutions.[4] In other formal public and private sectors, women are working as directors and managers right down to the level of clerks, administrative officers, receptionists, and peons. The First Women Bank, Women Police Stations and the Women's Post office in Karachi, are a few examples in the country that have all female employees.[5] Hafeez in her study says that women serving in these positions are an example of the fact that women have executive and managerial ability and this clearly negates the view that only men are capable of serving in these most valued administrative jobs.[6]

In the cities at least, women appear to be thriving in terms of their personal autonomy. From banking to telecommunications, and from civil service to service in the armed forces of Pakistan, female participation has increased at a greater pace than ever before. Literacy rates for urban women are now three times higher than their rural counterparts. These women have broken new ground and have entered fields which were once considered strictly the domain of men. They are a source of inspiration for other women because these women have taken themselves out of the general mould of the 'Pakistani Woman'. Also these women have helped in bringing attitudinal change within their own class and have made an indirect impact on other classes. In urban areas today the idea of a woman going out of the house for education or work is socially acceptable and that is why women from middle and lower middle classes are also seen

Table 4.1: Crude Activity Participation Rate

Area/Province	Annual (LFS) 2003-4			Quarterly July-Sep 2005-6			Quarterly Oct-Dec 2005-6			Half Yearly July-Dec 2005-6		
Pakistan	Total	Rural	Urban	Total	Rural	Urban	Total	Rural	Urban	Total	Rural	Urban
Total	30.4	31.0	29.2	32.8	33.9	30.7	32.7	34.1	29.9	32.8	34.0	30.3
Male	48.7	48.2	49.8	51.2	50.9	51.8	50.1	49.9	50.4	50.7	50.4	51.1
Female	11.2	13.2	7.0	13.8	16.7	7.9	14.5	1.6	8.1	14.1	17.2	8.0
Augmented Participation Rate												
Total	38.5	42.2	31.1	42.8	47.6	33.2	42.6	47.8	32.3	42.7	47.7	32.8
Female	27.5	35.8	10.8	30.7	39.6	12.5	31.3	40.7	12.4	31.0	40.1	12.5

Although persons ten years of age and over, reporting housekeeping and other related activities, are considered out of the labour force but from the perspective of time use, they are identified as employed if they have spent time on the specified fourteen agricultural and non-agricultural activities.

Source: *Labour Force Survey (LFS) 2005-6* (2nd Quarter Report Oct-Dec), Federal Bureau of Statistics, Government of Pakistan.

entering into employment which was once forbidden for them. This change shows that there is a realization of the importance and value of education. After receiving their education women want to make use of it and contribute towards the family income as well as develop their own careers.

Although there has been an increase in the number of women, yet compared to other countries in the South Asian region Pakistan has the lowest participation rate of women in employment sector. In the formal sector, for instance, only in Sri Lanka have women achieved near parity with 45 per cent of total formal sector employment whereas in Pakistan women occupy less than one-fifth of total public sector employment. Similarly, gender inequality persists in all employment sectors. The table below shows that except for the agriculture in all other areas of employment women are still behind men.

Table 4.2: Gender Inequality in Economic Activity

Female economic activity rate (% of male rate, ages 15 and above), 2002	44
Female employment in agriculture (as % of female labour force), 1995-2002	73
Male employment in agriculture (%), 1995-2002	44
Female employment in industry (as % of female labour force), 1995-2002	9
Male employment in industry (%), 1995-2002	20
Female employment in services (as % of female labour force), 1995-2002	18
Male employment in services (%), 1995-2002	36
Women contributing family workers (% of total), 1995-2002	33
Men contributing family workers (% of total), 1995-2002	67

Source: Human Development Report 2005.

The government of Pakistan has approved the proposal by the Ministry of Women Development, to reserve 10 per cent quota for women across the board in all its departments. This revised quota was approved on the existing 5 per cent. Apart from this, women can also compete in the remaining 90 per cent on open merit.[7] This quota system was introduced as an initial form of affirmative action to mitigate gender imbalance, facilitate entry of women into public sector employment, and remove existing barriers. With the passage of time such quotas could be progressively restricted once women are in a position to enter employment without any administrative crutches. It is a positive step taken by the government, however, it is yet to be seen how far this provision is implemented in practice.

Employment laws in the formal sector employment (in government and semi-government jobs) do not discriminate against men and women, and the same rules apply in terms of promotion, leave benefits and there is no difference in pay scales offered to men and women in the same grade. However, a recent detailed study on women's employment in the public sector reveals that despite equal legislation women are still discriminated when it comes to matters relating to promotions.[8] Similarly, posting/transferring women to far-flung areas away from their homes affect women's upward mobility. In some cases women have to forego chances of promotion by staying back in their home towns and sometimes even to resign as it becomes difficult for them to leave their families behind. Although some legal remedies are available and any kind of discrimination can be challenged, yet very few women have approached the courts to establish their rights. Ali and Shahid argue that courts being in the public sphere are not considered to be an appropriate place for women to appear.[9] Women in Pakistan are thus subject to competing ideas of rights, legality, and justice implemented through dominant patriarchal discourse facilitated by the state and its institutions.[10]

Other problems faced by women include non-availability of crèches, lack of transport facilities and separate toilets for women in the workplace.[11] Harassment at work and lack of conducive and safe environment for women within public sector offices is a major concern expressed by women employers. Cases of harassment are rarely reported because of societal pressures and as a result women face different forms of harassment from shouting, putting her down or insulting her in front of others, to demands of covert or overt sexual favours.

In the informal sector more job opportunities for women have been created in Pakistan.[12] Increased participation of women in the informal sector is due to trade liberalization and structural adjustment programmes (SAPs) which have a particular implication for women in the labour force in Pakistan.[13] Due to these policies and programmes there has been a feminization of the labour force in the informal sector which is not restricted to Pakistan. Acharya in her study of the Nepalese labour market and women's access to new and emerging economic opportunities argues that due to the liberalization process, on the one hand there has been an increase in the proportion of agricultural labourers while on the other hand there is decline in the number of production workers in cottage and household level manufacturing sector.[14] However, this increase of women's labour in the agricultural sector is disadvantageous for women because the remunerations received for agricultural labour are lower than in the non-agricultural sector.[15] Sadasivam in her article discusses how adjustment policies such as currency devaluation, price deregulation, privatization, export led growth strategies, etc., leave large sections of women poor in Third World countries.[16] She argues that a human rights agenda is missing in SAP's policies of international institutions, although due to the efforts of feminist economists the jargon of gender is being used in programmes and policies of these institutions albeit in a limited sense.[17]

Jhabwala and Sinha in their study look at the various effects of liberalization and globalization on women in the informal sector in India.[18] They are of the view that the impact of liberalization policies and globalisation has resulted in loss of existing employment without creation of new employment.[19] Secondly, due to mechanization and new technologies and skills the employment of manual workers is reduced and is displaced by workers who run the machines. The third effect is the informalization of work which displaces the better-paid, more protected workers and increases insecure and low-paid employment. Informalization benefits women in the informal sector in terms by creating more job opportunities. However, the types of jobs created in this way are irregular and low-paid for example in the manufacturing trades (except garments), the work is extremely irregular with an average deployment time is less than four months in a year. Finally, there has been creation of new employment opportunities in some new sectors without causing a loss to others or men in particular for example more jobs for women in handicrafts and personal services.[20] Yet this sector suffers from the problem of low wages, long working hours and lack of any legislative protection.

Chhachhi et al. in the Indian context also discuss SAPs and casualization of jobs in the industrial sector.[21] They deserve that as a result of SAPs, women are not employed on a permanent basis, have no contacts with unions and above all there is non-implementation of minimum wages legislation and other benefit provisions.[22] Pakistan implemented its stabilization and structural adjustment programme with support from multilateral institutions such as the International Monetary Fund (IMF) and the World Bank (WB) in the late eighties and nineties. Although there has been an increase in female employment in the informal sector, yet it has taken place outside the regular factory workforce and mainly in the form of temporary and contract workers. Since the 1980s more women have joined the industrial labour force mainly as unprotected contract and subcontract, un-skilled or semi-skilled workers, or as daily wagers.[23] Siddiqui et al. argue that this trend does not reflect welfare promotion for females because it indicates a deliberate policy by employers to exploit females as a cheap form of labour.[24]

Saigol says that a major aspect of SAPs is the deregulation of the labour market, and in that context the Export Promotions Zones (EPZs) or free-trade zones were established, where there are no medical facilities, no minimum wages, and no accident insurance.[25] As a result all the rights which are given to labour under the UN instruments and ILO conventions are taken away in this deregulation of the market.[26]

Another impact of SAPs is that women's entrance in the labour market is not exactly on the same terms and conditions as that of their male counterparts. Wide pay differences exist between men and women. If women perform the same type of work, they are paid less as than the men. Legislation also does not cover most of the women working in the informal sector such as home based workers, agricultural workers and domestic workers.[27] These factors also affect women in terms of activities they undertake, women's access, and control of resources and their decision-making power.

Studies carried out in different parts of Pakistan indicate that most women who work in industries are employed in low level, less skilled and low paid jobs. Khan's study of women industrial workers in Lahore provides an example of disparity between the wages of male and female employers performing the same type of jobs.[28] Women are kept in low skilled jobs mainly because of the culture of patriarchy that underestimates women's potentials.[29] A study of women industrial workers in Peshawar shows that women work for long hours but are paid low wages, in many industries they are employed for wages which do not meet the minimum wage standard set by the government.[30] Workplace safety and health/injury coverage is also not provided to most employees. Added to these problems are lack of flexible timings, poor transport arrangements, and non-existent child day care centres for industrial workers (the same problems are faced by formal workers as pointed out earlier). One of the main reasons for women workers' vulnerability and exploitation, as discussed in the previous chapter, is that there is little legislation concerning working conditions, workplace safety, and minimum wages and whatever legislation is available is hardly enforced.

Home-based workers and agricultural workers are not covered under labour laws of the country. Ahmed et al, in their study on home-based workers in leather and textile industries argue that in the absence of legislation and support structures home-based workers are not in a position to negotiate with employers, who are happy to engage women workers as they can keep the costs low and still maintain the quantity and quality of goods they produce.[31] Women who work in small units have their contractual arrangements on time-based wages while home-based workers contracts are on piece-rate basis. In the absence of any formal contracts, there is no fixation of working days or weeks because the factories for which they work are non-registered.

In the agriculture sector, where most women work, distinction between economic activities and non-economic activities is seldom clear. In rural areas of Pakistan, men own agricultural land and use family labour including women, for producing crops. The majority of rural women contribute towards agricultural economy without receiving any remuneration for the work done.[32] Nearly 69.9 per cent women work on family farms but their work is not paid because they perform different farm jobs as part of their family responsibilities; for instance most of the pre-harvest and post-harvest operations in which women indulge are carried out at home.[33] Participation of rural women in the agricultural sector in Pakistan has not made any significant improvement in their socio-economic positions. Women do not receive any cash income because it goes to the male head of the family or is received in kind by the entire family as a unit.[34] Gainful employment which helps in generating cash income and thus leading to self-reliance and confidence is not available to these women and they spend their entire lives as unpaid family workers.

Domestic service is another informal employment sector that employs mostly women as domestic workers. Review of official documents such as the Economic Survey, Labour Force Survey, Household Integrated Survey, Pakistan Social and Living Standards Survey to name a few, reveals the fact that domestic service in other households is not considered an area of employment, therefore no statistical information is available as to the total number of women domestic workers in Pakistan.[35] However, the fact that Pakistan is amongst those developing countries where most middle- and upper-class households employ women domestic workers itself speaks of the number of women engaged in this occupation.[36]

Increased participation of women in the employment sector has another interesting link with domestic service in Pakistan. Like other countries in the world, the increase in domestic workers in Pakistan is also associated with the growth of greater involvement in employment of middle-class women.[37] With growing employment opportunities more women are entering into the workforce. However, men at the same time have not yet accepted their role in carrying out household work and responsibilities. As a result there is more demand for domestic workers to take over the roles traditionally filled by women. This issue has also been discussed by Rollins in the context of American women, who argues that 'the personal nature of this relationship partly develops from the fact that the work done by domestic is a work which could otherwise be done by the employer herself.'[38] The responsibilities assigned to domestic workers are always seen as 'women's work' that is passed on from a wife to a waged worker.

The above discussion on women's increased participation in both formal and informal sectors shows that an increase in number of women does not lead to empowerment. It also raises questions regarding the efficacy of the law as a tool for empowerment for women because women continue to face discrimination despite being protected by the same laws that govern men's employment in the formal sector as well as in relation to industrial workers in the informal sector. If legislation has not worked in the case of formal sector and industrial sector then the question is how far would it be a useful tool for empowering women domestic workers? It further suggests that although domestic service is the largest employment category in Pakistan that employs women (as assessed in light of the number of households which employ them,) yet women domestic workers cannot be considered as empowered on the basis of their increased participation because the socio-economic and cultural constraints as well as lack of legal protection and non-availability of strong support structures render these women in a vulnerable situation.

WOMEN'S ROLE IN DECISION MAKING

This section analyses the role of women in decision making within the household and in the workplace. Women's increased participation is not only about increasing their numbers (whether it is in the formal sector or informal sector) but it is about their participation in decision-making leading towards their empowerment. The extent of female involvement in decision-making is an indicator of female autonomy and empowerment within the household, workplace and in the community at large.

The decision to enter into employment whether it is in the formal or informal employment sector in Pakistan, is not something that women can make on their own or according to their choice. They have to seek the permission of men in the household for instance husband, father, or brother. It is with their consent that women decide to enter into employment. This reflects the patriarchal nature of society (as discussed in the third chapter) which plays a negative role in constraining women's access and control over resources and decision-making power within and outside the household as well as in empowering women. Shah, Naqvi and Shehnaz in their respective studies on the different roles of women in Pakistan argue that husbands have a say in the wives' decision to enter the workforce especially when job responsibilities conflict with her roles as a mother or a wife.[39]

Sometimes women sacrifice or change their career due to family responsibilities. Many women lawyers for instance do not enter into the legal profession and opt for teaching as they find it less demanding compared to legal practice which involves long working hours and leaves them with less time for other household chores. This indicates that household responsibilities are always linked with women and men do not share or take responsibility for household chores.

Despite increased participation of upper, middle, and lower class women in formal and informal sectors of employment, women in general from all class backgrounds find it very difficult to have a say in the most important of all institutions, i.e. the family. Weiss in her article argues that for Pakistani women 'family' is the fulcrum for many activities, the location of honour, and the anchor of women's identity.[40] Women's mobility is still controlled by men in the family and they still need to seek the permission to come out of the house whether it is for an employment or any other purpose.[41]

In terms of decision-making at the formal public sector jobs, despite some positive trends of increased women's participation, very few women in Pakistan have reached higher positions in their careers or at decision-making levels. Women's limited participation in the decision making process is demonstrated overleaf by citing the example of women's employment in the District Management Group at the federal government level through statistics of the Establishment Division for June 2005. This table shows the number of women employed at the federal government cadres of the District Management and Secretariat Group.

Table 4.3: District Management Group

Basic Pay Scale (BPS) For Government Employees in Pakistan	Male	Female	Total
22	10	0	10
21	47	03	50
20	231	10	241
19	266	14	280
18	88	6	94
17	113	8	121

Source: Posting List 2005 Establishment Division, Government of Pakistan

These are the positions where most planning and development matters are decided but women are not fairly represented and given an opportunity to participate in decision-making level. As a result, women's needs are not addressed in policy and planning matters. Positive change leading towards empowerment can only be achieved if women are able to participate in open, transparent, and accountable decision-making processes of law and policymaking institutions. Their effective participation in decision-making processes would then influence institutional rules, norms, and practices and consequently shape the policy agenda and decisions. Without having a say in the decision-making process it would be extremely difficult to secure any rights for women and to redress gender disparities and change their lives.

Education and medicine are the two areas where women are employed in large numbers. In all girls' schools and colleges, women are appointed as heads of the institution, but in co-educational schools, colleges, departments and universities very few have been appointed as principals, chairpersons, or vice chancellors. There is information available on the number of school, college and university teachers in educational institutions in Pakistan, but none to the number of heads of institutions.[42] However, lack of information of the number of women in top-level positions or as heads of institutions indicates the scarcity of data on women's participation in different employment sectors. It also shows that women's contribution does not receive due recognition from society nor is it accounted for in national statistics.[43] Women remain invisible and receive no appreciation. Most of the data does not include women's work because it is counted as part of women's reproductive work like caring, nurturing, and household chores. Although there have been efforts to integrate gender specific questions and issues into data collection, the knowledge base remains limited as national statistics fail to present the different types of work women perform, or the amount of time they spend in both paid and unpaid labour.

In the informal sector women are employed in low cadre jobs in industrial units. Hardly any woman reaches the managerial level. One major reason for women's absence from such decision-making positions is that most women who are employed in the informal sector lack education and training. Most of them are also employed as casual workers or on part-time and contract basis which hinders their progress in careers compared to men who are employed as permanent or full-time workers. Employers admit that women perform their work more seriously, are more committed, honest and less threatening than male employees. However, due to lack of skills and their own family commitments women are employed not as permanent and full-time workers or considered for senior management posts. Another reason is that, due to patriarchal nature of society, men find it difficult to work under any woman.

As far as day-to-day family matters or household issues are concerned, such as providing for the daily needs of the family, education of children, and their marriages, women are consulted and they do have a say in these matters. Sattar and Kazi maintain that it is in the purchase of food that the highest percentage of women are consulted and 51 per cent of the women are the major decision makers in buying food and less than 20 per cent are consulted in the purchase of assets.[44] Thus the role of females decline when decisions regarding major financial matters such as buying or selling of property are taken. In the same study it was found that decision-making among rural women, whether it is related to family matters or farm issues, they hardly have a say. One of the reasons is that, gender hierarchy is so rigid within the household that women's earnings do not guarantee a shift in power relations between the genders. Kumari's study on women and work in Haryana district in India examines whether the development of agriculture has influenced work opportunities for women and subsequently their position in the power hierarchy.[45] The study reveals that most of the work that women perform remains secondary, unreported, unpaid, undervalued, and invisible. Women also remain excluded from participating in important decisions such as financial matters in the family.[46]

Naqvi and Shahnaz, and Kozel and Alderman in their respective studies have pointed out that women's say in family and financial matters also depends on factors such as age, marital status, and level of education.[47]

Women in old age groups have more say as compared to young women in the family; similarly, married women have more say as compared to a young unmarried female member of the family. Education also affects the decision making power of women. It increases the likelihood of women being in the labour force by three times more than the likelihood of a man being in the labour force.

HARASSMENT AT THE WORKPLACE

Harassment at workplace has been reported by women workers in various surveys and studies carried out in both public and private employment sectors. Harassment cuts across all boundaries—age, class, and position. Most of the working women in Pakistan at one time or other face harassment by their colleagues, bosses or employers. Mirza in her study of female office workers reveals that women in the workplace face harassment by employers and male colleagues which takes the form of passing comments or vulgar remarks to make women feel embarrassed, in some cases attempts to sexually abuse them, staring at women and passing dirty looks.[48] She also gives examples of women being turned down for the job because they were not fair (light-skinned) enough, or the bosses saying 'we want a pretty girl'. [49]

Alliance against Sexual Harassment at Workplaces (AASHA), a group of NGOs, which works to root out harassment of women, interviewed nurses, women employees of private and public organizations and salesgirls at plazas and malls.[50] The interviewees said they had faced sexual harassment by co-workers, patients, or relatives of patients and doctors. Only 11 per cent of the nurses denied harassment and 29 per cent refused to talk about it. According to the survey, the nurses are exposed to unwelcome physical advances and sexual innuendos on a routine basis. In some cases, the offenders show disgraceful and insulting behaviour towards them. However, the incidents are usually hushed up or blocked by the interference of other staff members who hold a grudge against the victim. According to this survey, a large number of women employed in other private and public sectors are routinely harassed by their bosses or senior colleagues. Pakistan as a party to the Women's Convention and UN Declaration on Violence against Women is under an obligation to take measures to protect women from sexual harassment and intimidation at the workplace. Absence of laws to tackle sexual harassment as a punishable crime has resulted in an increase of such occurrences, causing tremendous mental and psychological agony to women employees in all employment sectors.

WOMEN'S MOBILITY

The issue of women's mobility is multidimensional and it varies from the place where women live to places where they want to go. Class status also affects women's mobility. It is not possible to cover all dimensions of women's mobility in this section therefore it focuses on women's mobility from employment perspective only. Unsafe public transport affects women's mobility. Women have to bear sexually harassing acts while using public transport therefore public transport is not considered safe for women. The number of reserved seats for women are limited and it is considered inappropriate for women to sit next to men. To increase women's mobility, an all women transport facility could be provided. This would give some leeway to women so that they can come out of their homes and participate in public life.

Another reason for restricted mobility is the cultural pressure of the home being considered, as the most suitable place for women. The preconceived notion that the home is the best-suited place for women is still widely held where she is responsible for carrying out household chores and childcare. Due to lack of support from men in carrying out household chores, women cannot enter into paid employment. In many cases it is seen that women either have to wait till their children's schooling starts or they have to depend on outside help to carry out household responsibilities. In this way women remain confined to a private sphere and their mobility remains restricted. Khattak in her study found that many women therefore prefer to work in their own home-based establishments and are self-employed workers because it is more convenient to manage their household chores as well as earn a living for the family.[51] They also feel more secure in working from home instead of being exposed to the outside world. Most women also do not seek employment outside the home due to the objection of family members and people in the neighbourhood as well as the fear of creating a bad impression on the neighbourhood. Women impose this self-censorship as a defensive mechanism so that before anyone else raises an objection, they impose the same codes and restrictions upon themselves, which they are expected to follow.

A negative impact of restricting their movement to the home denies women the right to compete in the open market or look for better jobs.

In comparison women workers, such as domestic workers or factory workers, who step out of their houses in search of jobs, consider that this access to mobility has helped in seeking employment. It has also improved their self-confidence and understanding of the outside world. Women's mobility is also affected in areas where agricultural economy has prospered.

In rural areas it is only due to poverty denoted by low social status, that does not restrict women within their homes and they are allowed to earn some money to share living costs of the households. Jobs available to women are so low in the hierarchy of occupations that women engage in it due to dire economic necessity. Female agricultural workers are also considered as belonging to lower class/social status since it is a reflection of household poverty. Therefore, it is not surprising when women are drawn out of the agricultural sector as soon as the household's economic position improves. Men withdraw their women folk from the fields and traditional jobs like weeding, threshing of crops and cotton picking that were once performed by women are taken away from them. As a result, women's freedom of movement is restricted and they are confined to their homes.[52]

This situation suggests that in rural areas economic wellbeing is negatively associated with women's work participation. Women tend to lose their chances of work as the family achieves higher levels of income. Alvi, in his study mentions that, in the wake of the Green Revolution[53], many women have been withdrawn from participating in agricultural labour.[54] In rural areas, economic up-gradation has affected women in terms of losing their jobs, confining them to homes by restricting their mobility and asking them to observe *purdah* which is a status symbol for the rural population as it is strictly observed by the rural elite women.[55] As a result, women are excluded from social life and made completely dependent on their male family members. [56]

In the agricultural sector, women's mobility has been affected by the introduction of agricultural technology. Due to mechanization women have lost most of the labour intensive tasks that they used to perform in the agriculture sector.[57] It has also lead to the displacement of many peasant families who have now migrated from rural areas to urban areas in Pakistan. Many domestic workers in Karachi who migrated from interior Punjab have previously worked as agricultural labourers in their native villages.

ROLE OF UNIONS

Since the broader aim of this research study is to find out ways for empowering women domestic workers, this section looks at the experiences of women workers with regard to unions in other employment sectors in order to find out how solidarity among domestic workers could be achieved and how they can be empowered through organization. Could empowerment be achieved through the law alone or is there a need for organizing women domestic workers? Or are both interlinked and needed to achieve empowerment? What inhibitions do women workers have in participating in union activities? Do men co-workers encourage and support the idea of women's involvement in trade union activities? These are some of the questions addressed in this section.

In Pakistan there are 7,382 trade unions registered in the informal sector and they represent only 2.5 per cent of the total workforce with a total of 2134 female members as compared to 245,405 male members.[58] Since the 1990s, there has been a decline in the membership because of massive privatization and downsizing which are the outcome of the structural adjustment and liberalization policies of international financial institutions. Further, due to the establishment of export processing zones and Special Industrial Zones and contract labour, there has been a decrease in trade unions as can be seen in the table below.[59]

Table 4.4: Number of Union and Membership, 1993–1997

	1993	1994	1995	1996	1997
Total Registered Trade Union	-	7273	7246	7349	7355
Total Number of registered trade Union reporting	1685	1718	1718	1594	1534
Membership of the reporting Union	-	-	-	-	-
Total	374,731	325,677	337,617	293,530	296,257
Male	367,331	317,617	331,155	288,327	291,402
Female	7400	8060	6462	5203	4855

Source: Pakistan Statistical Year Book 2005, Federal Bureau of Statistics, Government of Pakistan, available at http://www.statpak.gov.pk/depts/fbs/publications/Year%20Book%202005/labour/12.18.pdf.

Table 4.5: Number of Union and Membership, 1998–2002

	1998	1999	2000	2001	2002
Total Registered Trade Union	7356	7382	7382	7382	7382
Total Number of registered trade Union reporting	1478	1493	1356	1260	1201
Membership of the reporting Union	305340	301104	301332	275646	247539
Total	305340	301104	301332	275646	247539
Male	298815	296617	296737	272007	245405
Female	6525	4487	4595	3639	2134

Source: Pakistan Statistical Year Book 2005, Federal Bureau of Statistics, Government of Pakistan, available at http://www.statpak.gov.pk/depts/fbs/publications/Year%20Book%202005/labour/12.18.pdf.

With this background, it is interesting to look at the position of women workers and their representation in trade unions. The representation of women both in terms of membership, as well as leadership, is minimal in the trade unions, which are heavily male dominated. The statistics above show that in 2002 the total number of female members was only 2134 as compared to 245,405 male union members. Hafeez argues that women are not encouraged to actively participate in union activities and male union leaders perceive a limited role for women workers in trade unions.[60] Findings of Hafeez's study point to the fact that male union leaders are of the view that women lack the experience to run organizational affairs, they do not understand the importance of contributions made by themselves as well as by male workers towards production, while some leaders consider unions to be a rowdy place not suitable for women and think that women will not be able to deal with such situations.[61] Other factors mentioned in the study that constrain women's participation in trade unions are restrictions from the family to participate in other job related activities, a double burden of work as women have to take care of all household chores, lack of extra time, pressure of employers in private factories and the fear of being expelled from their jobs. The case of first ever women trade union, formed at a garment factory in Karachi with the support of Women Workers Centre at PILER in 1990s and later on dissolved, is an example of the negative attitude of employers towards women workers and the constraints encountered by women workers in forming a union for themselves.[62] In the case of domestic workers in Pakistan, organizational support structures or unions are almost non-existent and as a result, their bargaining abilities are inadequate. They have very limited choice and have to work according to terms and conditions laid down by the employers. In the case of global/migrant domestic workers we find a number of NGOs and in some countries, like United Kingdom, the trade union movement provides support to them.

Women working in different employment sectors in Pakistan have always shown interest in trade union activities. Women workers in their interviews for different surveys and research studies have expressed the desire for more information on the activities and working of trade unions. The responsibilities or at least sharing of responsibilities at home and a decent, respectful attitude of male members at meetings would help in increasing women's participation at trade union level.[63]

Khattak in her study argues that women's ability to organize is reflected in the way women workers support each other at the workplace and within their own communities by helping each other to find jobs.[64] Organizational and strategizing skills are also shown through the 'committee system' where women pool together some amount of their wages as savings.[65]

In recent years more women have started participating in campaigns and protest meetings against the government which shows awareness, capability to organize and a solidarity for a common cause among women. Some of the examples are demonstrations organised by 'Fisher Folk Forum', 'All Karachi Hosiery and Garments Labour Association' and human rights organizations in Pakistan.[66] In organizing these demonstrations women are supported by different trade unions as well as different NGOs which shows the need for support structures for organizing women in Pakistan. There are also examples from other South Asian countries, for instances India, where the Self Employed Women's Association (SEWA) has organized home-based workers over the last twenty-five years. The struggle of *bidi* workers in India is also a case in point in which the workers were able to pressurize the government to pass a law for the protection of these workers.[67]

All these suggest that women have the potential to organize themselves. However, they need knowledge of the structures that can provide the means to challenge their conditions of work and help them in building up their capacity to empower themselves. They should know the laws and have an understanding of how the legal system works. This would help in understanding the role, working, and effectiveness of trade unions and collective action.

Finally in the wake of massive increase in women workers in the informal sector it is also essential to include and organize women because no trade union can establish itself and perform it's role without giving due representation to women workers.

CONCLUSION

This chapter has attempted to contextualize the issue of women domestic workers in a broader perspective by looking at the impact of increased participation, decision-making, self-perception, mobility, and role of unions on women in the formal and informal employment sectors in Pakistan.

The chapter also exposes the limits of the black letter law as an effective process and mechanism of empowerment for women in the workplace. It highlights the fact that despite the presence of constitutional and legislative provisions in the formal and some informal sectors in Pakistan, realities on ground reflect that securing equal rights for women in the workplace through employment laws alone is not an effective strategy. It is therefore pertinent to look at the possibility of using the law in conjunction with other socio-economic and political interventions.

Waged work and empowerment are often linked together and it is thought that women's employment would automatically lead to their empowerment. However, the analysis of women's increased participation in the employment sector in Pakistan demonstrates that there is no direct transition towards empowerment. Despite increased participation of women in both the formal and informal sectors of employment, the underlying structure remains the same. Women are exploited; gender stereotypes and hierarchies are systematically enforced by the state and society and these together hinder the process of real empowerment of women.

The decision-making role is also subject to societal pressures. In the formal sector some women have achieved high positions yet their participation in decision making is limited and the attitude of male colleagues is not very encouraging. Women in the informal sector, being part-time, contract, or casual workers, do not reach decision-making levels. At the household level, age and status in the family affect decision-making powers. From the point of view of effectiveness of laws, it is important that women are part of the legislative and policymaking processes; their voices must be heard and they must have a say in decision-making.

Women's mobility has helped them in gaining confidence and improving their knowledge of the world outside the confines of their homes. However, they do confront problems such as harassment, because of which some women prefer to work from home as has been seen in the case of home-based workers.

The chapter raises the importance of organizing women. It also emphasizes the need to have female representation on trade unions according to the percentage of women in the work force to ensure that they have a meaningful voice on all issues. It also pinpoints the need for networking and the joint responsibility of the government, NGOs, male union leaders and employers to facilitate women workers' representation in trade unions so that they are better represented and empowered to fight for their rights.

One important conclusion drawn is that the concept of women's own agency is demonstrated through women's participation and struggle for making a space for themselves within the public sphere. Linkage between the theoretical debate of women's agency, as discussed in the first chapter, and the grounded reality of women and the work situation in Pakistan, where women in all employment sectors are struggling hard to create a space for themselves, can thus be formed.

NOTES

1. Women's empowerment can be looked at from various dimensions. Better education, increased participation in employment, increased role in decision-making both at public and private level, women's access to mobility, resources, and control over resources are considered as necessary conditions for women's empowerment.
2. Women's labour force participation has risen at a greater rate than that of men since 1980. Pakistan's average annual female participation growth rate was 4 per cent in 1980-90, 4.9 per cent in 1990-5 and 5.1 per cent in 1995-8. There has been a substantial increase in 2001-2 in female participation rates to 25 per cent and in 2003-4 to 27.5 per cent and in 2005 it has risen to 31 per cent. (Source: *Labour Force Survey*, 2003-2004, Federal Bureau of Statistics and *Labour Force Survey (LFS) 2005-06*, Federal Bureau of Statistics, Government of Pakistan.)
3. The gender empowerment measure (GEM) reveals whether women take an active part in economic and political life. It focuses on gender inequality in key areas of economic and political participation and decision-making. It tracks the share of seats in parliament held by women; of female legislators, senior officials and managers; and of female professional and technical workers—and the gender disparity in earned income, reflecting economic independence. Source: UNDP (2005) *Human Development Report 2005*, New York: Oxford University Press.
4. Women civil servants, judges, women academics, engineers, doctors, bankers, lawyers, women police officers, women in the telecommunications services, Television Corporation and Broadcasting Corporation, women entrepreneurs, women in travel

agencies, advertising firms, newspaper agencies and research organizations, women working in financial institutions as charted accountants, bankers are examples of women working in the public sector.

5. As far as the performance of women in the First Women Bank and Post Office is concerned despite being in a male dominated society, they have been able to survive and have proved themselves as successful as any other competing body. However, the case of women police stations is a bit different. Women police stations have failed to serve the purpose for which they were established. For a detail discussion on female police stations see Taj, F. (2004), *Policing in Purdah: Women and Women Police Station in Peshawar, NWFP*. M. Phil Thesis, Center for Women's and Gender Research, University of Bergen Norway.
6. Hafeez, S., supra note 87, ch. 3, p. 73.
7. Information on increased quota is available at http://www.pakistan.gov.pk/ministries/ContentListing.jsp?MinID=17&cPath=182_413. Accessed on 12 December 2006.
8. National Commission on the Status of Women (2003), 'Inquiry Report on Status of Women Employment in Public Sector Organisations,' Islamabad: Government of Pakistan.
9. Ali, S.S. and Shahid, A., supra note 13, ch. 3, p. 176.
10. Ibid., p. 176.
11. Also see Ali, S.S. (2007), 'Where is the Toilet? Getting Down to Basics of Women's Human Rights,' in Hellum, A., Ali, S.S., Stewart, J. and Tsanga, A. (eds.), *Human Rights, Plural Legalities and Gendered Realities: Paths are Made by Walking*, Weaver Books.
12. The informal sector in Pakistan is defined for statistical purposes in terms of household enterprise and size of employment. In the informal sector most of the women work in textiles, garments, pharmaceuticals, sports and the factories of surgical tools. Women also work as domestic workers, agricultural and homes based workers. This definition, however excludes domestic workers, home based workers and agricultural workers. It clearly states 'excluded are household enterprises engaged in agricultural activities or engaged in non market production'. (Source: *Labour Force Survey 1996 97*, Federal Bureau of Statistics, Statistics Division, Government of Pakistan.)
13. In the late eighties and nineties like other developing countries, Pakistan also implemented structural adjustment programmes (SAPs) with support from multilateral institutions such as the International Monetary Fund (IMF) and the World Bank (WB). These adjustment programmes are adopted to reduce the fiscal deficit, improve the balance of payments, make the economic structure more productive and promote internal and external competitiveness. However these structural adjustment programmes did not succeed in improving the economic indicators like output growth, employment generation, poverty and others. For a detailed study on the impact of SAPS on women labour force see Siddique, R.and Hamid, S., 'Gender and Adjustment Policies: Evidence from Pakistan,' available at http://www.idrc.ca/en/ev-58038-201-1-DO_TOPIC.html.
14. Acharya, M. (2000), *Labour Market Development and Poverty with Focus on Opportunities for Women in Nepal*, Kathmandu: Tauka Prasad Acharya Memorial Foundation and Friedrich-Ebert-Shiftung, pp. 1-144.
15. Ibid., p. 20.
16. Sadasivam, B. (1997), 'The Impact of Structural Adjustment on Women: A Governance and Human Rights Agenda,' *Human Rights Quarterly*, Vol. 19, No. 3, pp. 630-650.
17. Ibid., p. 634.

18. Jhabvala, R. and Sinha, S., 'Liberalization and the Woman Worker,' Self Employed Women Association, Ahmad Abad, India, available at http://www.sewa.org/globalisation/pdf/LiberalizationandWomenWorker.pdf.
19. Thousands of women silk spinners and twisters of Bihar have lost their employment due to the import of 'China-Korea' silk yarn. Similarly in Gujarat, women gum collectors, who picked from the *prosposis julifera* (baval) trees, lost their employment due to the import of cheaper gum from Sudan.
20. Personal services include domestic work, cleaning and cooking services and care of children and the elderly.
21. Chhachhi, A. et al. (1997), 'Mediating Macro and the Micro: Industrial Restructuring and Women Workers Lives,' paper presented at the seminar on 'Policies and Strategies for Working Women in the Context of Industrial Restructuring,' 22-25 September 1997, Jamia Hamdard University, New Delhi, pp. 21- 22.
22. Ibid., p. 22.
23. After agriculture, industry is the second largest sector with highest percentage of women workers. In the first boom of industrialization in the 1960s women were taken into multinational pharmaceuticals and electronics, textiles and garments, food, rubber and plastic mainly on relatively secured permanent jobs.
24. Siddiqui, R. et al., 'Gender and Adjustment Policies: Evidence from Pakistan,' available at http://www.idrc.ca/en/ev-58038-201-1-DO_TOPIC.html. Accessed on 25 November 2006.
25. Saigol, R., 'Structural Adjustment Programmes and their Effect on Women Workers—Collusion of Patriarchy and Capitalism,' paper presented at Regional Conference on 'Impact of Economic Globalization on Women's Work and Empowerment Issues,' 22 and 23 November 2006, Best Western Hotel, Islamabad. Available at http://wmt.actionaid.org/wmt/pakistan/images/regionalconfernercedoc.pdf. Accessed on 31 January 2007.
26. Ibid.
27. Labour Legislation in Pakistan has been discussed in detail in chapter 3.
28. Khan, N., supra note 69, ch. 3, p. 48.
29. Ibid., p. 49.
30. Shahid, A. and Arif, K., (2001-2002), 'Women's Labour Legislation in NWFP: A Case Study of Women Industrial Workers in Peshawar District,' Research Project, Faculty of Law, University of Peshawar.
31. Ibid., p. 41.
32. Rural women participate in farming crops, livestock husbandry, cottage industry and other off-farm activities. Women often devote more time to these tasks than men do. They participate in all operations related to crop production such as sowing, transplanting, weeding, and harvesting, as well as in post-harvest operations such as threshing, drying, grinding, husking, and storage (including making mud bins for storage). Rural women in Pakistan carry out these tasks in addition to their normal domestic chores of cooking, taking care of the children, the elderly and disabled, fetching water and fuel, cleaning and maintaining the house as well as some of its construction.
33. For statistical information as to number of women employed in agriculture and forestry, see Table 8: Distribution of Employed: Major Industry Divisions, Labour Force Survey 2005-6 (Quarterly Report, Oct.-Dec.).
34. Government of Pakistan, (1997), *Ninth Five Year Plan (1998 2003) Report on the Working Group on Women's Development*, Government of Pakistan, Planning Commission Islamabad, p. 26.

35. Government of Pakistan, *Economic Survey 2005-06*, Ministry of Finance; Government of Pakistan. *Integrated Household Survey (PIHS) 2001-2002*, Federal Bureau of Statistics, Government of Pakistan. *Household Integrated Economic Survey (HIES) 2001-2002*, Federal Bureau of Statistics, Government of Pakistan. *Labour Force Survey of Pakistan (2005-2006) Quarterly Report (Oct-Dec 2005)*, Federal Bureau of Statistics, Government of Pakistan. *Pakistan Social and Living Standards Measurement Survey 2004-05*, Federal Bureau of Statistics.
36. The estimated population of the country is 152.3 million, whereas the total labour force consists of 45.23 million persons out of which, male participation activity rate is 40.74 per cent and female participation rate is 11.16 per cent. (Source: Government of Pakistan. *Economic Survey 2004-2005*, Ministry of Finance, Islamabad.) The total number of households in Pakistan according to size and urban-rural residence is 20,374,970, out of which urban households are 7,370,202 and rural households are 13,004,768. (Source: Pakistan Demographic Survey 2003.) Available at http://www.statpak.gov.pk/depts/fbs/statistics/pds2003/table-03.pdf accessed on 5 July 2006.
37. Although there is no statistical information available, this argument is supported by the fieldwork for the present study carried out in two cities in Pakistan.
38. Rollins, J., supra note 11, ch. 2, p. 154.
39. Shah, N.M. (1986), 'Changes in Women Role in Pakistan: Are the Volume and Pace Adequate?' *Pakistan Development Review*, Vol. 25, No. 3; Naqvi, Z.F. and Shehnaz, L., 'How Do Women Decide to Work in Pakistan,' available at www.pide.org.pk/pdf/psde per cent2018AGM/HowDoWomenDecideToWorkInPakistan.pdf.
40. Weiss, A.M. (2001), 'Gendered Power Relations: Perpetuation and Renegotiation,' in Weiss, A. and Gilani, Z. (ed.), *Power and Civil Society in Pakistan*, Karachi: Oxford University Press, p. 66.
41. Ibid., p. 68.
42. See Table 10.3 Economic Survey of Pakistan 2004-5 available at http://www.finance.gov.pk/survey/sur_chap_05-06/11-education.PDF.
43. Surveys and data collections in Pakistan suffer from conceptual, methodological, and definitional flaws. The main reason being that the term 'work' has been defined in varied ways from source to source. Traditionally work has been defined as activities for 'pay or profit' and in official statistics the term economic activity is used rather than work. This income-oriented approach includes only those who are in a wage and salaries, self-employment outside home for profit and self-employment in cultivation and household industries for profit. Exclusion of activities from the definition of work, which are carried out for self consumption affect women more for instance activities such as firewood/fodder collection, procurement of water which, are for self consumption are not considered as work if they are for self consumption. Other factors responsible for poor data include, publication of data with a considerable time lag, unsuitable methods of data collection where usually both respondents and enumerators are male, some work is of seasonal nature and the workers are piece rate workers and at the time of study they may not be working and as a result are not counted in the data. Another problem is that men neither give exact information about women in their households to research teams, nor are the teams given permission to interview women particularly in rural areas. Such denial of access affects the quality and reliability of the data. The issue of poor data systems in Pakistan has been discussed by Mumtaz K. and Shaheed, F. (1998), 'Gauging the Economic Participation Rate of Women in Pakistan,' in Naheed, K. (ed.), *Women Myth and Realities*, Lahore: Hawwah Associates, pp. 133-141; Feeney, G. and Alam, I., 'Fertility, Population, Growth and Accuracy of

Census Enumeration in Pakistan: 1961-1998,' available at http://www.gfeeney.com/pubs/2003-pakistan-fertility-2/2003-pakistan-fertility-2.pdf. Accessed on 08/09/05.

44. Sattar, Z. and Kazi, S. (1997), *Women's Autonomy, Livelihood, and Fertility: A Case of Rural Punjab*, Islamabad: Pakistan Institute of Development Economics.
45. Kumari, R. (1998), *Gender, Work and Power Relations: A Case Study of Haryana*, New Delhi: Har-Anand Publications, p. 220.
46. Ibid., p. 225.
47. Naqvi, Z.F. and Shahnaz, L., supra note 39, p. 10. Kozel, V. and Alderman, H. (1990), 'Factors Determining Work Participation and Labour Supply Decisions in Pakistan's Urban Areas,' *The Pakistan Development Review*, Vol. 29, No. 1, pp. 1-18.
48. Mirza, J. (2002), *Between Chaddor and Market: Female Office Workers in Lahore*, Karachi: Oxford University Press.
49. Ibid., p. 152.
50. 'Situational Analysis—Sexual Harassment at the Workplace', (2007), published by Alliance Against Sexual Harassment at Workplaces (AASHA).
51. Khattak, S., supra note 83, ch. 3, p. 326.
52. Ibid., p. 388.
53. The term Green Revolution is used to describe the transformation of agriculture in many developing nations that led to significant increases in agricultural production between the 1940s and 1960s. However the increased level of mechanization on larger farms made possible by the Green Revolution resulted in unemployment for many agricultural workers. This situation also led to migration of smallholder farmers and landless farm workers from rural to urban areas.
54. Alvi, H., supra note 98, ch. 3.
55. Ibid., p. 1.
56. Ibid., p. 2.
57. The introduction of tractors, combine harvesters etc. has appropriated women of their traditional role in farming and no alternative jobs have been created for women in rural areas. Due to this mechanization, women are invariably displaced not only from direct agricultural work but also in supposedly household work like grinding grains.
58. Source: Pakistan Statistical Year Book 2005
59. For a detailed discussion on the impact of globalization in the informal sector in Pakistan see Hasan, A. (2003), 'The Changing Nature of the Informal Sector in Karachi Due to Global Restructuring and Liberalisation,' *The Journal*, available at http://www.nipa-khi.edu.pk/journal1.asp
60. Hafeez, S., supra note 87, ch. 3, p. 162.
61. Ibid., pp. 162-3.
62. For a detailed discussion on the background and difficulties faced by the women who formed this union see Parveen, F. and Ali, K. (1993), 'Research in Action: Organising Women Factory Workers in Pakistan,' *AlMushir*, Vol. 35, No. 1.
63. Various studies on industrial workers, subcontracted workers and kiln workers have been conducted by Pakistan Institute for Labour, Education and Research (PILER), Sustainable Development Policy Institute (SDPI), Applied Social Research Institute (ASR) and other research and policy oriented organizations. These studies discuss in detail the role of unions, women's interest in organizing themselves and reasons for the absence of women from participating in trade union activities.
64. Khattak, S., supra note 83, ch. 3, p. 345.
65. This system of monthly savings is also adopted by women domestic workers and has been discussed in chapter 6.

66. Pakistan Fisher Folk Forum [PFF] is a registered organization. Since its inception, PFF has been active in the awareness, mobilization and community organization for the protection as well as sustainable management of the fisheries and other community livelihoods through advocacy, participatory research, information dissemination and participatory community development processes. All Karachi Hosiery and Garments Labour Association (AKHGLA) formed in 1998 to support hosiery and garment industries in Karachi.
67. The *Bidi* and Cigar Workers (Conditions of Employment) Act 1975. *Bidi* workers are further protected under the Minimum Wages Act that ensures their rate of payment, *Bidi* and Cigar Welfare Fund Act provides a fund for welfare including medical help, housing, and scholarships for children.

Part III

This part of the study sets the stage for the case study on women domestic workers in Pakistan, where domestic service is an informal employment sector employing a large number of women as domestic workers. This employment is carried out in the privacy of homes and as these workers are not covered by the definition of a 'worker' under labour laws of the country, therefore they remain vulnerable to exploitation. Other contributing factors towards their vulnerability include poor socio-economic conditions and class hierarchies. Besides, the voices of women domestic workers have always remained unheard and hardly any research has been carried out that looks into the lived realities of women domestic workers. With this background in mind, empirical data was collected to support the main research question i.e. to what extent the law can bring empowerment to women domestic workers in Pakistan.

Chapter 5 analyses the data in the light of the main themes which emerged during the interviews. A few case studies to support the findings of the empirical research have also been included in this chapter.

Chapter 6 suggests a way forward by looking into non-legal and legal strategies to make the law an effective tool for empowerment of women domestic workers in Pakistan.

5

Challenging Silences: Listening to Untold Stories of Women Domestic Workers in Pakistan

INTRODUCTION

By using the grounded theory methodology, and in light of women domestic workers' lived realities, this chapter provides an analysis of some of the key themes and sub-themes that have emerged from the data collected in the form of interviews with women domestic workers, employers, activists, academics/researchers and government officials. This chapter discusses the nature of work, working hours, wage structure, and commuting difficulties faced by women. It also focuses on the nature of employer-employee relations, which are unique and complex as there is no formal contractual arrangement between the employers and domestic workers. The class dynamics in Pakistani society, and how it affects the employer-employee relation, also form part of the discussion. The chapter also examines the situation of domestic workers in terms of access to justice and looks into other issues such as the factors that force women into domestic service, harassment at the workplace, women's self-perception and their decision-making power, workers' relations with male family members, childcare responsibilities. The experiences of women domestic workers belonging to religious minorities, i.e. Christian and Hindu domestic workers are also looked at. Finally, the chapter discusses a few case studies of women in domestic service and represents issues such as the exploitative nature of domestic work, domestic work as a hereditary/intergenerational activity, hard work, and continuous struggle, lack of support systems vis-à-vis the vulnerability of their children and also their experience of the justice system.

EXPLOITATIVE CONDITIONS OF DOMESTIC SERVICE AND JOB INSECURITY

This section discusses the nature of domestic service and conditions of work such as working hours, wages, paid holiday, sick leave, extra work, and commuting difficulties. Domestic service is based on an informal verbal contract between the employer and the worker. There is no written contract even if the job is provided through an employment agency. In Pakistan there are very few employment agencies facilitating domestic workers. In a big city like Karachi, there is only one such agency.[1] This employment agency only keeps a record of the domestic worker, consisting of a copy of the identity card, fingerprints, address, and the employment form duly attested by the area councillor. However, the form does not include any details about the nature of the job, working hours and salaries. This record is given to the area police station and a copy of it is kept by the employment agency. There is no document that can be called a written contract. Very few prospective employees approach employment agencies because they cannot afford to pay the fee nor do many know about the existence of such agencies, as these are small in number. Usually domestic workers get jobs through friends, neighbours and relatives who are already working as domestic workers in different residential areas.

Working under inhumane conditions, subsisting on very low wages as well as burdened with their own household responsibilities, both men and women carry out paid (and in some cases even unpaid employment, when it is linked to debt bondage or working in return for accommodation) domestic work in other households in Pakistan. However, like other countries in the world, it is women who are engaged in greater numbers as compared to their male counterparts.[2] Their main duties include cleaning, cooking, looking after the elderly and the children, whereas men work as gardeners, drivers and gate keepers/guards and some times as cooks. Women domestic workers are also discriminated from their male counterparts in domestic service such as cooks who receive more wages as compared to a woman domestic worker. Employing a male cook also blurs the issue of privacy in the home. By employing a male cook, the outsider becomes the insider. (Thus, employing male servants becomes an exception to the rule of privacy).

There is no fixed wage structure for full-time, part-time or live-in domestic workers and it varies according to localities, economic status of employer, and the nature of jobs they perform. Wages vary from five hundred rupees to five thousand rupees per month depending on the type of work they perform and on the number of working hours.[3] Those who work as full-time workers starting at 7 o'clock in the morning to 5 o'clock in the evening earn between fifteen hundred rupees to three thousand rupees per month. Time schedules vary according to the needs of both employer and employee, as in some cases they start their work at eight or nine in the morning and finish by six, whereas live-in workers are engaged for the day and night. They either get a day off a week, or sometimes a month, or fortnightly depending upon the will of the employer. Those who are live-in-workers (who stay through the day and night) are paid between three thousand to five thousand rupees. Women who work as part-time workers for only two to three hours (doing just one job either cleaning, laundry or dishwashing) are paid between five hundred to thousand rupees per task. Such type of work is called '*chota kaam*' or part-time work.

Child-carers or nannies are better paid compared to those engaged in other household chores. The reason for this wage difference could be either that these women have previous experience of childcare or because they are employed as live-in workers. Those who hire young girls as child-carers do not pay them the same salary as they would pay to a nanny. Although young girls do the same amount of work and even sometimes more work, as for instance the *begum sahib/malakan/bibi* (women employer or lady of the house) would ask her to sweep the room or do some dusting when the baby is asleep. The chart below provides a comparison of the wage difference among domestic workers in two cities, Karachi and Peshawar, where the fieldwork for this study was carried out.

Table 5.1: Wage Chart

Types of Workers	Karachi	Peshawar
Full-Time Worker	Rs 2500 to 3500	Rs 2000 to 3000
Part-Time Worker	Rs 700 to 1000	Rs 500 to 800
Live-in Worker	Rs 4000 to 5000	Rs 3000 to 4000

Source: Based on the findings from the field work carried out in the two cities in 2004.

Wages also vary according to the work, position of the employer and residential areas where they work. ZB who works as a nanny in Karachi for an affluent family gets Rs 5000 per month compared to her previous job with a middle-class family where she performed the same duties but was only getting Rs 3000. Similarly N who works in Peshawar as a nanny for a Chinese couple gets Rs 3500. N's salary is higher than that of other nannies because her employers are foreigners and pay slightly higher wages than the local residents. There are wage differences among live-in workers and part-time workers. Live-in workers are asked to do work which otherwise is not part of their job. They are often denied proper rest time, given leftovers to eat and not provided a proper place to sleep and are on duty almost twenty-four hours and seven days a week. S whose family still lives in Punjab came to Karachi six months ago in search of a job with the help of a relative. She is now working as a live-in migrant worker. Her day starts at 6 o'clock in the morning and she works till 10 to 11 o' clock at night without any rest time in the afternoon or evening. The only time she gets to relax is while having her lunch or tea. On a good day (which comes very occasionally), i.e. when her employer is in a good mood, she is allowed to watch television for half an hour in the evening, but that too is subject to the condition that *Sahib Ji* (her employer's husband) is not at home. She is often sent to the nearby shops to purchase groceries. When she took the job, she was not informed that buying groceries was also included in her duties. She does not receive any bonus or extra salary for the additional work that she does. Her extra work also includes cleaning the car every Sunday when the driver is not around. Her employer exploits her because she knows that S is new in the city, without family and not familiar with the locality. Live-in workers like S also experience social isolation, as many employers do not allow them to visit their families and friends or other co-employees in the neighbourhood. The employers do this because they fear that by socializing with other co-workers they would compare the salaries paid to them and their co-workers and could then demand more. This interaction with other co-workers would also give them a chance to find other jobs for themselves. Besides, employers also feel threatened about their own privacy as domestic workers often gossip around and talk about employer's family matters with others.

UZ, another domestic worker, in her interview told me that she also works on Sundays. Her employers do not however give her any extra payment for working on a Sunday whereas women working in factories are paid overtime. When she started her part-time job, her employer said that she would pay her extra money if she works on Sundays. She started working on Sundays but after a month when she asked for the payment, the employer refused to pay her saying, '*yeh koi sarkari nokri nahi key tum over time maang rahi ho. Mein aik paisa faltoo nahi doon gi aur agar tum kaam nahi karna chati to mein aur nokarani dhhoond loon gi*' (This is not a government job that you are asking for over time. I am not going to pay you a single penny and if you don't want to continue I will find another maid).

UZ's experience suggests that in the absence of any formal contractual arrangements women domestic workers can be easily exploited in terms of wages and working hours. Jobs also remain insecure as a worker can be fired for petty reasons at any time and is at the mercy of the employer who knows very well that a workforce is always available and he/she can get another worker (more or less for the same salary and sometimes even lower.) The concept of a reserved labour force is a basis for exploitation because the employer and worker both know that none of the workers are indispensable: if one is fired or if a worker refuses to continue there is another person to take her place.

K has been working for different households for the past five years. She was thrown out of a job by one of her employers when she was unable to work for a month. She informed her employer about her illness and, as a replacement, she started sending her twelve-year-old daughter to do the work but her employer was not happy with this temporary arrangement and found another maid. Consequently, it took her two months to find another job.

Both UZ and K mentioned that after this experience, they too have become careful and before taking a job, they do try to find an employer who does not live in a joint family system. They also prefer working in houses where the woman employer herself is in employment because then in her absence during the daytime, they can do their work more freely and without constant surveillance.

An issue that arose during discussion with the respondents was about providing for medical or healthcare. As there is no written contract between the employer and employee, women domestic workers are at the mercy of employers when they get sick. When BB was sick, her employer only gave her five hundred rupees for the medical tests, which was not only insufficient but the amount was later deducted from her salary. M, whose husband is a scavenger and has five children, complained that if she takes a day or two off in case of illness, her employer deducts from her salary. For her a day's salary of a few rupees means a lot because with it she can at least buy milk for her youngest son.

Transport or commuting is another problem. As these workers cannot afford to pay for bus fares they mostly walk to work. It usually takes forty-five minutes to an hour for women who come from Acheena village to get to Hayatabad. Similarly, women who live in Hijrat Colony prefer going on foot to their workplace, if they are working in more than one household. They prefer to work either in the same apartment buildings or in nearby houses. Women who come from Bhit Islands have it even worse as they have to travel daily by boats/launches to Kemari, from where they get buses for Clifton and Defence Housing Authority areas. It costs them twenty rupees daily. A few employers give them their bus fares everyday but most do not. The women are always on the lookout for households who are willing to pay the fare in addition to the salaries because otherwise a major chunk of their income goes towards transportation.

Women domestic workers also complain that most of the time they get leftovers to eat and only hand-me-down clothing. Zeenat said '*Mujhe bacha hua khana leiney per aitraz nahi laikin agar khana itna baasi ho aur kharab ho chukka ho to aisa khana kha kar bemar ho jani sey behtr hai ki usay phenk diya jai.*' (I have no objection in taking leftover food but if the left over is rotten then its better not to eat such food and get sick…its better to throw it away). Another domestic worker commented that '*itna baasi khana to hum apni janwar ko bhi dein to wo beemar ho jai.*' (We do not give such rotten food even to our animals). Another comment was '*kabhi basi khana leney sey inkar karo to begum sahib ko buht bura lagta hai aur hum ko batein sunatein hein key humarey nakhray ho gai hein*' (If we refuse to take rotten food the employer doesn't like it and tells us off by saying that we have become proud and arrogant).

Women domestic workers also raised the issue that whenever any extra help is provided in the form of a loan or otherwise as charity, the employer expects the worker to do extra work. Dasgupta in her study argues that 'unlike a construction worker or a factory worker, a housemaid does not become bonded due to any debt or loan she takes from the employer: no house wife can insist on the repayment of all the money that she has given in advance before the maid leaves the service'.[4] Her point of view is true to the extent that there are no bonds or written documentation involved but that does not suggest that extending such favours is always on sympathetic grounds or without any expectations from the employees. Most of the respondents' interviews mentioned that whenever they take some money in advance or as a loan they are expected to perform extra work and all the time they get constant reminders from the employer of this extra favour. K in her interview said '*Malikan jab bhi madad karti hai to phir hum sey chahti hai kay hum us ka faltoo ka kam bhi karein aur jab kabhi karaz lein to her maheinaiy tunkhua katthey hein aur kabhi kabhi to chuti walaiy din bhi kam par bula lethein hein*'. (Employers expect us to do work in return for what they have otherwise given to us as a charity and if we take a loan it is deducted from our salary every month and sometimes we are asked to work on our day off as well).

In some cases women domestic workers are only compensated in kind and not in cash. This practice is very common in villages where in return for their services, women are given grain for working in the landlord's household all year round. NJ who lives in Acheena mentioned in her interview that after her husband's death she started working in the house of a *Khan* (village landlord). She would grind wheat and help her *Bibi* (the landlord's wife) with household chores. In return for her services, she was given leftover food at the end of the day and two bags of wheat once a year. After working for the Khan for two years, she realized that such an arrangement was untenable. Despite her hard work she was not paid in cash and whatever she received in kind was not enough to fulfil her daily needs. She needed money to send her son to school and for other household expenses. Therefore, she decided to look for work outside her village, as she knew that some neighbours were working as domestic workers in nearby Hayatabad Township. She is now able to earn one thousand rupees a month, but she still grinds the wheat for the Khan's wife three days a week in exchange for a loan she took a few months ago. She is now given only one sack of grain instead of two as she has stopped doing the household chores.

Employers' had their own views on the issue of wages and working hours. A schoolteacher argued that employing a domestic worker even at a low wage should be seen as a measure to combat poverty and unemployment. If the minimum wage is set too high, some households will not be able to afford a domestic worker, which will lead to more unemployment and even greater poverty. Many unemployed workers are desperate to get jobs and are willing to work for less than the stipulated minimum wage to earn a little income. She also felt that domestic jobs are more beneficial than other informal sector jobs because domestic workers get food, shelter, and clothing, which is not the case in most jobs. In advancing this line of argument, the teacher ignored the fact that, if a minimum wage or working hours are not set then this sector will never become regulated and an environment conducive to exploitation will be maintained. Another employer claimed that a minimum wage rule will have a negative impact by reducing job opportunities for women domestic workers because there is always surplus labour available.

However, it is argued that the issue of wages should not be considered in isolation and needs to be examined from various angles. Firstly, when there is surplus labour available, there is also more demand for domestic workers. With more women entering into employment, they need help at home to carry out household chores. Secondly, if employers cannot afford a full-time worker they can hire a woman domestic worker on a part-time basis. Thirdly, a woman domestic worker can earn more or less the same amount of money by working part-time in two or three households. Another possibility is that if a woman in domestic service is working part-time she can make use of her extra time by learning some other skills such as sewing and that skill can be used for earning a living along with domestic service.

A housewife, when interviewed, said very sarcastically that women domestic workers are already paid well. She thought that there is no need to increase their salaries, as most of them do not have any formal training and whatever skills they have are actually improved only when they work in employers' households. Another employer who is a housewife complained that middle income groups or the salaried class in Pakistan is not highly paid therefore it was not possible for them to pay good wages to domestic workers.

Another form of exploitation of domestic work is seen in the form of child domestic labour. In many cases, domestic workers bring their young daughters with them to assist and help them with their work. The domestic work done by the 'girl child' is not seen as hazardous nor one of the 'worst forms' of child labour. Neither the employers nor the parents of the girl child take it as an exploitation of children and are not bothered about minimum age legislation and children's employment legislation.

When asked why they bring their daughters to the workplace and make them work, a common response received from the majority of the women, both in Peshawar and Karachi was '*Humarey pass school behjney ka khrcha to hai nahi...is sey acha hai key wo kuch kaam seekh lein is sey humary bhi madad ho jati hai aur hum aik ghar ki bajai do gharoon mein kam kar letien hein* (We don't have enough money to send them to school...by accompanying us at least they will learn the skill of doing domestic chores and it also is a help to us because we can then take in more than one job).'

Making the girl child work as a domestic worker has in many cases become an intergenerational activity. There are women whose mothers have spent their lives as domestic workers and now daughters and grand daughters too are involved in the same labour. The case of AZ and BJ is a clear example of involving the younger generation in domestic labour.[5]

Most domestic workers have little or no record of their employment; there are no official registration systems which could prove their work history. As a result, if an untoward incident such as robbery or theft occurs in which a domestic worker is suspected then without a record it becomes very difficult to trace them. Employers in their interviews raised the concern regarding increased cases of theft and robbery in which domestic workers are either directly involved or play a role in facilitating such crimes. An employer shared her own experience when her house was burgled and she was robbed of cash, jewellery, and other expensive household items due to connivance of her maid.

Employers stressed the need for putting in place a system of registration at local police stations of domestic workers with all their personal details and copies of ID cards. Such steps could help in reigning in the crime rate to some extent. Due to the informal verbal contractual nature of domestic service, in many cases employers do not know or take the trouble of keeping a record of where the domestic worker lives, where she comes from etc. As a result, when such incidents happen, it becomes difficult to trace their whereabouts. When this was discussed with domestic workers, they tried to defend themselves by saying that not everyone is involved in such activities and it is a rare event. One woman worker said '*Chori kar kar hum apney aulad ka pet sari umer key liyay nahi pal sakrey Agar hum aisey kam karney lag jaien to phir humey nokri koi nahi de ga*' (We can't feed our children for all their lives by theft alone. If we get involved in such activities then who will trust us and would give us jobs?). Such incidents have a negative impact on them because their employers also start suspecting them which affects their relationship. When asked about registering their details at the police station domestic workers showed their willingness for it. However, they wanted an assurance that they would not be harassed by the police. One domestic worker raised the issue that '*police hamesha zor waloan ka sath deti hai hum ghariboan ki kon soonta hai*' (police help those who are influential and no one listens to the poor). Domestic workers wanted that registration to also include clauses regarding their working hours, salaries and treatment at the workplace so that a check is kept both on employers as well as on domestic workers.

EMPLOYER/EMPLOYEE RELATIONS

The employer—employee relations in domestic work are unique and complex. Raghuram, in her study of domestic workers in the metropolitan area of Delhi, argues that 'the relationship between employer and employee is essentially contradictory and is marked by authority on the one hand and servility on the other. It is not regulated by any formal contractual arrangement'.[6] Findings of the present study also point to the same fact that the employer—employee relation in domestic service is imbalanced and leaves the employee in a very weak position.

One of the objectives of this research study was to provide a basis for workable relations between the worker and the employer. It was therefore essential to find out the views of both employers and domestic workers about their relations with each other: whether a formal contract was an acceptable solution to both the parties and would it secure the purpose of protecting domestic workers from being exploited by the employers and vice versa.

During the interviews, almost every employer started by asserting that in most cases their relation with their employee was based on goodwill: both parties being women they could share the joys and sorrows of womanhood together. Many employers claimed that due to the personalized nature of the relationship, they were 'kind and caring' not only to their domestic worker but also towards their families and children. They claimed that clothes and food were always given to the domestic workers. Besides, in case of illness the domestic worker and her family members were provided medical care.

To verify this 'personalized' relationship women domestic workers were asked whether they were getting any help from their employers. They accepted that there had been goodwill gestures on the part of employers on different occasions but in some cases employers expected more services from the domestic worker in return for the help extended. PR was conscious of the fact that whenever her *begum sahib* buys her clothes and slippers to wear, she starts asking her to do extra work in the house, for instance, cleaning and sorting out the storage area or box room. The employers wanted them to be wholly and solely at their disposal in delivering these services. In such cases, priority was given to the convenience of the employer, whereas the capacity and convenience of the employee was not given any consideration.

A women's rights activist, in her interview said that employers do exert a lot of pressure on their workers because they know that the worker, due to her low socio-economic status, has no negotiating power. The only recourse domestic workers have is to leave the job and look for another. However, that they will do only as a last resort when the situation really gets out of hand and it becomes impossible to work (in that situation). Women domestic workers also continue to work despite knowing that they are being exploited because they are well aware of the fact that they are not in a position to access justice through the courts, nor is there any legal protection available to them.

HONESTY, RELIABILITY, TRUST, AND EFFICIENCY

When employers were asked what criteria they had in mind in hiring a domestic worker, the response was that they try to make sure that he/she is honest, reliable, efficient, and hardworking. However all employers complained that in most cases loyalty, reliability, honesty and efficiency were missing. Some employers allege that the kind of loyal servants their ancestors used to have in their households are no longer available. This could be partly due to the fact that by migrating to cities both employers and employees may not come from the same village or town and could be complete strangers. As a result, a bond which existed among the employer and employee on the basis of knowing each other and belonging to the same community or area is lacking. Lack of reliability and trust could be due to the informal nature of the contract that the workers take advantage of, for example, being absent from work without prior notice, or leaving the job without giving any reason or notice in advance. In the absence of any formal contract, they give up their job for slightly better pay elsewhere without informing the employer beforehand and have no regard for the extra help extended to them in their difficulties. Once they learn the skills, they leave the job for the sake of some extra money, without realising that their previous employer had trained them in all the skills and that they would be left with no help.

Unreliability of domestic workers and the way they take advantage of the situation can be assessed from the comments of a housewife who sarcastically said that 'when guests are around or whenever we throw a dinner party for our friends or relatives or on special occasions such as *Eid*, the domestic workers would come because they know that the guests would tip them. On days other than festivals, they would disappear without informing the employer or previous notice or would demand a day off after the party. Similarly, when they go on leave they never turn up for duty on time. They will ask for a day off and not return for three days.

Another housewife pointed out that domestic workers do not miss the chance of stealing small things such as children's clothes or toys, or dry food stuff from the kitchen and smuggle them away in their bags every day when they leave for home. This comment was reminiscent of a domestic worker who quit a job because everyday when she left for home the guard or *chowkidar* of the bungalow was asked by the Begum Sahib to search her bag, which she found very insulting. The wife of a senior bureaucrat complained that women domestic workers are always inquisitive about their employer's family matters. Privacy of their family is affected by employing women domestics because while working for the employer and staying in the employers' house they come to know about the employer's internal family matters. It is difficult to keep privacy in their presence and they often disclose family matters while gossiping with other servants in the neighbourhood.

Also noticeable was a general feeling of distrust among employers about their employees. Most employers felt that workers were hypocrites and good at manipulation.

> If you treat them nicely they start taking you for granted. Most of them are never thankful for the extra help given to them in the form of cash or kind. Their problems never end and they are constantly in need of help. They keep on demanding monetary help on a regular basis. It also happens that they are often deceptive and ask for extra monetary help by concocting stories, as for example they would say that their child is ill and they need money for medicines or they have to pay the children's fee otherwise his/her name would be struck off. In reality, it is only a made-up story to gain the sympathy of the employer and extract money from him/her because the child is not even admitted in the school or he/she is not sick.

This feeling of distrust in some cases also gives rise to an indifferent attitude on the part of the employer towards the employee, which can be judged from this comment by a housewife. 'It is always better to keep a distance, the more you ask them about their family, or be sympathetic to them, the more demanding they become.'

The wife of a senior bureaucrat in her interview tried to explain and justify why she is not in favour of employing women domestic workers. Firstly, she prefers a male cook over a woman because she thinks that there are not many job opportunities for men, and as men are supposed to be the primary earners, they should be given a chance to earn a living. Secondly, she prefers male cooks because in Pakistani society there is segregation of the sexes. A male servant can easily attend male guests without inhibition whereas it often becomes a problem for female workers who are shy and reluctant to serve male guests. Thirdly, keeping a girl or woman also becomes a liability. One has to keep an eye on her interaction with male servants and male members of the family.

A general complaint of employers was that if domestic workers are left on their own to do work, they never complete it. They handle things carelessly such as crockery and waste food items or detergents for cleaning, laundry and dishwashing because they think that employers have sufficient resources and such a minor loss or damage would not make any difference to them. Some employers also complained that domestic workers who come from rural areas simply do not know anything about modern household living. They do not know how to use things such as a vegetable chopping board let alone any electronic gadgets in the kitchen. 'We do have to teach them how to use the toilet and some even don't know how to light a gas stove.' This happened with P who did not know how to use a pressure cooker and severely burnt herself.

A former senior judge while sharing her experience of domestic workers complained that when domestic workers learn the skills and find out that the employer depends on them, they try to exploit them. Once they realize that they have become indispensable to the employer, they take advantage of the situation because the employer would be reluctant to look for a new person and train him from scratch. In her words, 'I try to ignore these little things because we need their services and because of a long service tenure. We become used to them and prefer not to go for another domestic because now after spending eight to ten years, my driver and my maid know my routine, my needs/requirements and my habits'.

EMOTIONAL ASPECTS OF EMPLOYER-EMPLOYEE RELATIONS

Cock, in her book on the deprivation of South African domestics, notes that 'despite all claims of warmth, familiarity and closeness the relationship of employer and the domestic worker is one of formality and distance'.[7] Rollins in her study has given the name 'maternalism' to such an attitude.[8] During interviews with employers this notion of maternalism was very visible: the way many employers continuously suggested that their domestic workers were part of the family. They emphasized that they treated them as family members because they lived with them in the same house or daily spent time there doing household chores. Many of the workers had been with them for quite sometime and therefore employers knew about their family life. Secondly, domestic workers were always in need of employers' help, ranging from illness of a family member to other day-to-day survival matters.

However, domestic workers when interviewed pointed out that despite the employers' claims for treating them as family members, at the end of the day they still remained outsiders. While carrying out their responsibilities, they were several times reminded by their employers of their low-class status by being treated in such a way that would not be expected towards a family member, such as being given old, used, and torn clothes or leftover food.

Despite the strained nature of the relationship, there are also cases/examples where employers have come forward in a genuine manner to help the domestic workers. R mentioned that her employers give her one-way fare daily. In Ramadan, they give her *zakat* (obligatory charity) and buy clothes for her children. In case of illness they also provide extra help and never deduct money from her salary. As they treat her respectfully and take care of her needs, she too serves them wholeheartedly. Another domestic worker who works for a gynaecologist said that her employer has given her son a job in her private clinic. A few government officials in Hayatabad have helped domestic workers' families by employing male members such as sons, husbands, or brothers of the domestic workers as gardeners, peons, and guards at government departments. Another woman who works for a private bank has helped her domestic worker by contributing towards her daughter's dowry and paying for some of her wedding day expenses.

SURVEILLANCE AND CONTROL

During group discussions and individual interviews, almost every woman domestic worker mentioned that her actions and movements were under the employer's constant check. The live-in workers suffered more in this respect because they stayed with the employer twenty-four hours a day. Live-in workers have to give up their privacy and freedom of movement. They are under scrutiny all the time, whether working or not working in the house, i.e. even during non-working hours. The control of the employers over their lives is clearly visible in many aspects of their existence. It is the employers who decide and organize the employee's working hours according to their own lifestyle and convenience, totally ignoring that the domestic worker too is a human being who needs proper rest and some privacy.

Another aspect of control pointed out by the domestic workers was that in many households they were answerable to all members of the family and work not under one boss but several bosses at the same time.

They are expected to work as robots fulfilling the needs and demands of all family members. If one asks for breakfast, the other would demand clothes to be ironed at the same time. The domestic worker is expected to obey all commands and if a single task is delayed, then she has to quietly listen to derogatory remarks such as 'lazy, moron, idiot and without any common sense.'

Employers always mistrust workers and often blame them for theft even if a small thing from the house goes missing. The domestic workers also pointed out that it is very common among employers to keep groceries and other food under lock and key in the kitchen. K mentioned that one of her employers used to hold her purse and keys all the time, making it obvious that she had valuables in it. Z said that she noticed that whenever she swept the rooms, her employer stood by and made sure that all cupboards were locked. Both K and Z declare that such an attitude was humiliating and made them feel as if they were suspected of being thieves and having no self-respect. Both domestic workers pitied their employers saying that despite having all the luxuries of life they made their own lives tense, unhappy, and miserable by constantly being suspicious instead of building up a relationship based on trust with their domestic workers. '*In ko pata hai kay hamari zarroorat to buht kam hein aur hum ko in ki paisay sey matlab nahi par in ko har waqat apni paisaiy ka gham hota hai....Hum ghareeb zaroor hein magar chor nahi*' (Despite knowing that our needs are limited and we are not interested in their fortunes, the rich people are always afraid of losing their wealth. We are poor but that does not mean that we are thieves). M commented that, '*Allah nei in ko itna paisa diya hai magar kuch to itney kanjoos hotien hein kay bacha hua khana bhi freezer mein dal detin hein mahinno taq aur kisi garib bhookey ko nahi dete chahey wow din bhar ka bhooka kue na ho*' (God has given them so much wealth but still some of them are so miserly and greedy to the extent of saving even leftover food in their freezers for months but would not give to the poor who might be hungry all day long.)

Although domestic workers do not resent the affluent position of their employers, yet they complained about the unjust distribution of resources and lack of basic facilities such as good schools, health centres etc. Women like K and Z said that their struggle is to upgrade their social and economic class status, which they could achieve by giving education to their children. They also expressed their dissatisfaction with the job arrangements, which provided them with neither proper wages nor any respect for the work they do.

WOMEN VS. WOMEN: CLASS HIERARCHIES IN THE EMPLOYER/EMPLOYEE RELATIONS

The relationship of upper- and middle-class women employers and their working class domestic workers demonstrates that privileged class women exploit their employees due to the differences in class status. This exploitative attitude is depicted in the indifference of privileged women who simply turn a blind eye towards a system that creates class hierarchies and reinforces patriarchy. Privileged women escape some of the consequences of patriarchy by using the labour of women from a working class. In the majority of households in Pakistan, the division of labour by gender-specified roles exists and men do not involve themselves in household work. By hiring female domestic workers, women from the upper- and middle-classes solve the problem of their 'double burden of work and full responsibility for household chores', without challenging the patriarchal idea that 'house work is only women's work' and shift the burden to other women.[9]

Hiring domestic workers gives relief to women employers from their gender responsibilities by transferring their burden to other women who are lower in class and social status. Due to the unequal power relations employers purchase the services of domestic worker for low wages and by using their services, the employer gets free time to pursue other activities, including both productive tasks that could be remunerative and other pleasurable activities. Being in a position to use the services of domestic worker is in itself a source of enhanced class position for the employer in Pakistani society. Rollins notes that by delegating household functions to the domestic worker, not only does the woman employer escape some of the limitations of patriarchal culture, but by doing so she also serves to reinforce the sexual stereotyping of housework.[10]

A lawyer by profession and woman activist admitted that domestic workers' input is valuable as it gives the employers a chance to use their time for something else. She said,

> [With] the sort of lifestyles we lead with large/joint families, our entertainment is on a large scale, for instance on all occasions whether it is the birth of a child, a marriage ceremony, or a death, we are the people who want to have lots of people around us and we want to do things impromptu. That sort of essential element of social structure in our society is possible only because of the help provided by domestic helpers who are integral to our way of life and enable us to continue with such life styles. We can be hospitable because all the drudgery is done for us by someone else, i.e. the domestic worker.

Hiring of domestic workers also represents the reinforcement and replication of gender and class inequalities, for instance women domestic workers are discriminated against in terms of wages and working conditions. A male cook gets more salary compared to a woman domestic worker doing the same work. Similarly, male servants whether cooks, cleaners, or *chowkidars* (guards) would not do any extra work where as a woman though hired for one particular job would be asked to undertake additional chores.

Employing domestic workers also involves a social prestige. Among many other things employing more than one domestic worker has become a status symbol. The more domestic workers one has, the higher is the social status. Another indication of class differences between the employer and employee appears in the form in which food is given to domestic workers in different households and how their living space is separated.[11] Women domestic workers in their interviews openly resented the way they are given food by their employers. They are allowed to eat only after the employers have had their meal. In many households, they are given food in discarded crockery and are made to sit on the kitchen floor or eat in the corner of the courtyard. Similarly, as discussed earlier, giving domestic workers leftovers is a very common trend. Many employers only give a bit of freshly cooked food and the rest is leftover food. Others do not even bother to give fresh food. One woman domestic worker laughed out and said '*mein to kabhi khawb mein bhi nahi soch sakti keh begum sahib nei mujhi maiz par khana diya ho*' (I can't even dream of sitting and eating on the same table with my employer).

These instances reflect the difference between rhetoric and reality as Islam emphasizes dignity of labour and prohibits discrimination on the basis of class. However, in practice Muslims completely ignore these principles as women domestic workers are forced to believe that they belong to the lowest social category, their work is not valued, nor given due respect and consideration. Their low status in society makes them powerless, there is hardly any regard for their services, and employers do not treat them respectfully. They are considered as inferiors and that is also one of the reasons why their work has not brought any significant change in their status in the society. Our claim of being an Islamic country is dismantled as we fail to respect the labour of domestic workers.

The inequality of class status is also visible in the way these workers are addressed. There are specific names/titles by which domestic workers are always addressed such as *maasi*, *mai*, *Ayah*, *babbo*, *jamadarni*. (These names are like calling a cleaner 'cleaner' or a bin man 'bin man' and not calling them by their own names). Use of such phrases in day-to-day language reflects class-based tendencies of society by which people are still defined and judged by their economic status. These names also obscure the truth that all domestic workers are real workers who ought to have real rights, deserve respect and dignity and are entitled to legal protection.

During interviews domestic workers mentioned that the use of such phrases is a constant reminder to them of their low status as if they are inferior human beings. Considering domestics 'as stupid with no signs of intelligence or one who takes ages to learn a simple thing or those without common sense' are some of the comments made by almost all the employers who, either consciously or unconsciously, have a superiority complex that whoever is behind them, in respect of education, employment, financial situation or even caste, is inferior. This complex of feeling superior also reflects the class-conscious nature of Pakistani society.

Similarly the manner in which domestic workers address their employers, for instance not by their first names but by their titles such as *begum sahib*, *madam*, or *baray saab*, *sahibji*, or *khanji* reflect class hierarchies and widens the gap between the employees and the employers.

Another aspect of the class dynamics appears in the form of employers' expectations of the domestic workers to be submissive and always docile. Such compliance and subordination could be in the form of communication between the two: the way employers remind domestic workers of their inferior position because of their poor economic status, their illiteracy, and low caste. One Christian domestic worker pointed out that, '*Hum log buht parth bhi jain magar log humein humariay peshey sey he pukarien gai aur kahein gai keh is ka bap dada to jamdaar tha*' (Even if we become highly educated we will still be known as sweepers, sweeping being the profession of our forefathers). Similarly, saying to her all the time that she is *jahil* (ignorant) or *bewaqoof* (stupid) in not knowing anything about urban lifestyle, is a way of keeping the domestic worker submissive and under control.

The social stratification between the employer and employee based on stark differences in their economic status also contributes to the powerlessness of the domestic workers. It reflects that Pakistan is a class-based society where people are still defined/judged by their economic status. One domestic worker said, '*izzat usi ki hai jis kay paas paisa hai...gharib ki na koi izzat hai aur na koi zindagi...sari umar jutey khati aur taniey suntey guzar jati hai*' (Respect comes with money...if you do not have money you are not respected. A poor person spends all his life at other peoples' behest and gets the blame for everything).

REASONS FOR JOINING DOMESTIC SERVICE

Women enter into domestic service for varied reasons such as poverty, illiteracy, lack of resources, and unemployment of male family members that leave women with no choice except to engage in this occupation. Women also enter this low-skilled and low-paid economic activity because the male breadwinner is unemployed or sick or has died, and as a result, the burden of providing for the family's basic needs falls on her shoulders.

With a single earning hand, their lives are miserable because it is difficult even to get two square meals a day. Women start working with the hope of being able to provide for some of their children's basic needs and to add to the earnings of male members of the family. Despite these efforts, few are able to send their children to school. The reason is that despite being a financial supporter a woman hardly has a say in decision-making. In most cases, money brought home by a woman is spent according to the wishes of the male head of the family. In cases where male members do not earn, or are seasonal workers who do not have a fixed income, the entire burden of the household is on the woman who is supposed to fulfil her duties at home as well as to provide for daily needs by earning a living.

The case of Katchi Memons from Bhit Islands is one such example where men depend exclusively on fishing when the sea is calm. When rough weather and high tides make fishing impossible, they idle away their time with friends and relatives, doing nothing on the pretext that fishing has been their occupation for generations and they do not know any other skilled work. There are also cases where the husbands or other male members are drug addicts. J started working because her husband is a drug addict and spends whatever little he earns on buying his drugs and does not contribute towards family responsibilities. As a result, J has to bear all the burden of running the household.

A number of young girls and their mothers also get involved in domestic service in order to acquire accommodation for their families. The upper-class households in Hayatabad, Peshawar and Defence Colony, Karachi usually have one- or two-room quarters either at the back of the house or a separate small room with a small toilet and a little open space for cooking which is provided in return for domestic services. Employers use the services of domestic workers in lieu of the accommodation provided. In some instances, domestic workers are even asked to perform separate household tasks for the electricity they use in their quarters or rooms. On the one hand, this situation suggests how women domestic workers are exploited by their employers but on the other hand it also suggests that domestic workers use their services as a strategy to get living accommodation for their families and save rent.

WOMEN'S EXPERIENCES OF FORMAL AND INFORMAL MECHANISMS OF JUSTICE

As domestic work includes traditional female roles including cooking, cleaning, washing dishes, etc. It is not recognised as a 'job' and domestic workers are not acknowledged as 'workers' in the conventional sense of the term. Domestic workers are not covered by labour laws of the country. There is no law to regulate the relationship of employer and the domestic worker in Pakistan, thus a domestic worker does not exist as a person in law, and as a result, they have no legal rights to protect them in the workplace. In theory, they can bring a civil/criminal action but due to their low socio-economic status, and belonging to the underprivileged class, they do not engage with the law or with the state on a daily basis in their lives, nor can they anticipate an easy access to justice.

To assess how far the law could be an effective tool for empowering women domestic workers, they were asked about their experiences of formal and informal mechanisms of the law in the country, how they perceive the legal system in the country and what has been their experience of approaching informal and formal legal mechanisms in the country? They were also asked that if their services were to be regulated and given legal protection, would they use the law as recourse for their protection?

Women clearly expressed their distrust for informal dispute resolution mechanisms such as *jirga*s and *panchayat*s. They considered *panchayat*s and *jirga*s as biased against women and male-dominated forums. It was noted that some women had approached the alternative dispute resolution forum but some had lost their faith in its effectiveness as in the cases of R, ZN, and SH. They cited a number of incidents where family disputes and property issues were referred to these alternate dispute forums (*jirgah*s and *panchayat*s). However, in none of the cases have women been able to get justice, whether it is a matter of claiming maintenance from an ex-husband or receiving a share from the property of deceased husband or a case of child custody. R, a widow failed to get her deceased husband's share of inheritance from her in-laws. She took up the matter with the local *panchayat* but no compromise was reached between the parties because the other party was more resourceful. The *panchayat* did not pursue the matter fairly and her plea was unheard. The *panchayat* also challenged her by saying that if she had the courage she could take the matter up to the formal court on her own. Unfortunately, her parents did not have the resources to pursue the matter further in court so she had no other recourse but to give up the case. ZN in her interview said, '*jab zulm karney walaiy insaf ki kursi par beith jain to insaf nahi milta*' (How can you get justice if the judge himself is the perpetrator?).

When women were asked about their views on the possibility of being protected by the law, it was found that women in Karachi and Peshawar were aware of the fact that workers in other jobs such as factories or public institutions are protected by the law. They also knew of labour unions which support workers against any exploitation by the employers. This could be because their male family members are factory workers. When asked whether they would like their jobs to be regulated by the formal law, the majority of them responded in the affirmative. However, they expressed their deep concern on the possibility of using the law. This concern and reluctance to approach the courts was not because they did not have trust in the formal legal system but, due to their own vulnerable position in the society, they considered it extremely difficult to access justice through courts.

As discussed in Chapter 3, rights enshrined in the constitution of Pakistan and supported by specific labour legislation do not protect workers across the board. This is particularly so in the case of women agricultural workers, home-based workers, and women domestic workers who are excluded from the legislation. The question that arises here is why are these rights unavailable to this section of society? Despite considering courts as a better option for access to justice, in comparison to informal dispute resolution mechanisms, women still do not see these rights as entitlements. Is this because of the class hierarchies in the society or has this to do with their socio-economic position, as litigation itself is a costly process? Firstly, women are conscious of the fact that there are class hierarchies in society where employers are in a more powerful position than employees and can easily flout the law by using their influence and contacts. Secondly, due to their vulnerable socio-economic position, approaching the courts is an uphill task for them. Illiteracy, lack of awareness and poverty are major hindrances as in some cases they do not have the slightest idea about the formal legal system in the country.

Due to ignorance and illiteracy, legal procedures are beyond their comprehension. Under such circumstances, it is not easy for a woman to approach the courts on her own. Thirdly, respondents also mentioned the need for some form of organizational support, because they are conscious of the fact that being illiterate and poor they are dependent on others to facilitate access to justice for them. Fourthly, taking legal action is not an easy decision for any woman in Pakistan. The social culture of the country inhibits women from approaching courts to redress their grievances, as such an act is perceived as going against the male ego. His position as head of the family is jeopardized if a woman goes out of the family to seek justice.[12]

A woman generally does not have the economic means to approach the courts if she is seeking redress against male members of her family who have complete control over all the finances. In civil cases of inheritance, for instance, redress is sought against a close relative, e.g., a brother or an uncle, on whom a woman may be economically dependent. In such cases, if a woman seeks justice in court, there is always a fear of losing support from the family; besides she would be ruining her reputation without which it would be hard to survive in a conservative and patriarchal society like Pakistan. Moreover, due to the fear of social stigma women are generally reluctant to discuss distressing aspects of their lives and jobs in public. Finally, the formal legal system is an expensive process and involves court fees and lawyers' fees which are beyond the means of women domestic workers as well as other marginalized groups. Women therefore strongly felt that they are in need of some support structures that could help them in obtaining legal aid as well as in organizing them on a more formal level.

HARASSMENT IN THE WORKPLACE

Women domestic workers face abuse in the workplace by employers, co-workers and even children.[13] Living and working in the homes of their employers have made domestic workers prone to abuse. Many participants referred to experiences ranging from verbal abuse, to physical/sexual abuse by employers, their children when they do not get what they want and even co-workers who do not miss any opportunity to harass women domestics by passing verbal comments as well as physical touching. K during the discussions said '*Gharibi key hatoan aur bachoan ka pet bharney key liye yeh sab bardashat karna parta hai* (Due to poverty and to feed children one has to face all this). During the interviews, it was noticed that women were not open in discussing this issue in group discussions and kept repeating that '*achey aur burey log her jaga par hotien hein, mard hamey tang kartey hein mager aurat khud mazboot ho to koi kuch nahi bagar sakta*' (Good and bad people are everywhere, men do tease us but if a woman herself is of a strong character no one can harm her). Harassment in the workplace is a serious issue but in a conservative society such as Pakistan it is very difficult for women to talk openly about it.

Women did not openly share their personal experiences but mentioned some incidents of abuse by using examples or referring it to other women without disclosing their names and identities. One of them said that her previous employer's son had sexually abused her co-worker. Another interviewee said that her employer used to live in a joint family and the family used to employ at least two to three women domestics including young girls. Her employer's aged father-in-law never missed a chance of physically touching the young maids. When cross-questioned about her own experience of working in such an environment she said that the employer's father-in-law never had the courage to tease her because compared to the young innocent girls she was mature and strong enough to keep her distance from him. However, when individual interviews were taken, there was contact with a migrant Punjabi worker in Karachi who was raped by the cook in her employer's house when the employer was away. She reported the incident to her employer on her return but did not report the matter to police. The only action taken was that the cook was removed from his job. Besides, a woman domestic worker told me that her daughter was raped in her own house when she was away at work (see detailed case study).

S mentioned that she worked for a famous local female singer whose husband was of 'loose' character. Once when the singer was not at home he made an attempt to rape S, but she managed to escape because the doorbell rang. After that incident she left the job because she felt insecure working for that couple.

As pointed out by some workers harassment is not limited to the workplace as they also become targets of physical and verbal abuse when they come out of their homes. Bus drivers, passengers and men standing on the roadside do not miss a chance of either touching or pinching a woman or passing a vulgar comment on her character.[14] These are just a few examples of harassment that these downtrodden women domestic workers come across while going to work.

Another important issue related to harassment is domestic violence that women domestic workers suffer from at the hands of their own male family members. One domestic worker in Karachi mentioned that she was badly beaten by her husband many times. Initially she used to remain quiet and bear the beating but now she was sick and tired of the situation and whenever the husband tries to beat her up, she starts shouting and resists by holding back his hand. She felt that since she has started resisting the husband too has become conscious of his behaviour and does not beat her as often as before.

PERCEPTION OF SELF AS A WOMAN AND AS A WORKER

This section examines how women domestic workers perceive themselves as workers, what are the perceptions of society about women in domestic service and how do these perceptions affect women's domestic workers' struggle towards empowerment?

During interviews, women were asked such questions as how they evaluated their own work contribution as compared to their male counterparts? Has their work given them any satisfaction and did they feel entitled to any privileges because of their work participation? Was there a positive impact of their work on their status in the family and in society? These questions provided some basic insights about women's perceptions of their own work, helped to initiate the discussion around the issue of 'woman's agency' and highlighted the extent to which these women domestic workers struggle and resist against exploitative conditions in the workplace.

In the discussions women mentioned that they gained confidence due to their work and coming out of their homes provided them an opportunity to understand the world. While sharing her experiences S recalled how dependent she was on male family members for every little thing while living in a small village before coming to Karachi. After moving to Karachi and working for different households over the years, she has gained confidence to carry out her daily chores whether it is paying the utility bills, visiting a doctor in case of illness or buying groceries from the market.

Women domestic workers are also conscious of the fact that they are providing support to their husbands or male members of the family and work to provide a better living for their children. N takes pride in her self because she considers her salary as an addition to what her husband is earning and it is her economic contribution that enabled them to complete their children's schooling. They are also able to save some money for constructing a small house in Christian Colony. Moreover, she told me that while working with foreign couples she has learnt a little bit of English and can communicate with them, which for her is an achievement, as she has never had a chance to go to school.

Women domestic workers also perceive themselves as hard working and honest. They want to spend their lives with dignity and are very conscious of their self-respect. J and P are above sixty years but still work as part-time domestics. They do not want to become a burden on their children because they feel that their children have their own family responsibilities.

As far as perceptions of society about domestic workers are concerned, women domestic workers find it distressing that their work is undervalued. Although they work similar hours as other informal sector workers, in return they do not receive their due respect and appreciation for the work they perform. The undervaluation of their work affects their self-respect at times but they still feel that performing jobs in other households and earning a living has made them realize that they are not just a burden on their families rather, they are a big support to them.

Improved self-perception of women domestic workers also suggests that the confidence they have gained will help them in accessing justice and in the effective implementation of a legislative framework for protection.

DECISION-MAKING POWER

As discussed in Chapter 4 the issue of decision-making is closely linked with women's positions in families. The same trend was found amongst women in domestic service. Y, a widow, wanted to move to Karachi city from Bhit Islands with her children because she thought that this would save her time and money spent daily on travelling by boats. Her brother and father were not willing to let her go on the pretext that they could fulfil their duty of protecting her better in their house. They were also not willing to move with her to the city and desert the island where they were born and brought up, as they perceived their *marna jeena* (life and death) as attached to this place. In cases where women have reached the age of being considered an elder in the family, i.e. a mother-in-law or a grandmother, their opinion is taken into consideration. Similarly, widows and divorcees (in case there are no male members in the family or as long as their sons are young,) make decisions themselves. But when the sons grow up they want their mothers to stay at home and make it an issue of *izzat* or honour and do not want their mothers to go out of the house and work. P, who started working after the death of her husband thirty years ago, continues to do the laundry for her employers with whom she has worked for twenty-five years. She performs this work without telling her three sons who now want her to stay at home. P still wants to earn a living to avoid dependence on her sons as well as to contribute to their meagre incomes, which is not sufficient to support a family of eight to ten people.

Although it is a good idea for children to look after their parents in their old age, unemployment or low paid work makes it very difficult to financially support their parents. In most cases sons are not in a position of even providing for their own families. Also some of them have large families to support. BB is working because her son earns only Rs 2000 a month and has three children. She works to support her son and every month she pays the rent for a one-bedroom quarter where she lives with them.

Among the young women workers a mixed trend was observed as far as control over their earnings is concerned. Women like UZ and K who are in the age group of 25 to 45 complained that their husbands kept a check on their earnings. Every month their husbands' took their salaries and spent it as they wished. However, K had found a way out for herself after eight years of work. Now she does not disclose her actual earnings to her husband and saves Rs 50 to Rs 100 for a 'rainy' day. M's case is different from the other two workers as her husband allows her to keep her salary and he also contributes on a monthly basis: in this way she runs the household herself. Those households are comparatively better off where women are able to keep their salaries or manage to save a small amount. M has been able to buy some second-hand electric appliances such as a washing machine, TV, fridge and VCR by paying in monthly instalments or in the form of committees.[15]

Although economic empowerment can bring some change in a woman's life, it does not automatically lead to women domestic workers' social empowerment. The rise in women's employment shows that it is now acceptable to some extent in society or by their families that women can go out and work. They can leave the house in the morning, come back in the evening, and bring in money at the end of the month. Men do want women to share the burden of contributing to household expenses because of the economic needs and pressures on them. However, it is still not acceptable that women can be totally independent or be assertive in decision-making. Women's participation in gainful employment does not indicate male generosity or an attitudinal change. The permission for women to work outside the house is the result of a calculated decision by the men to relieve themselves of economic pressures and it has not resulted in enhancing women's status or her decision-making power as a family member in every case. This suggests that women's decision-making power, in terms of engaging with formal law, depends on factors such as her age and position in the family.

RESPONSIBILITIES AT HOME AND ATTITUDES OF HUSBANDS AND OTHER FAMILY MEMBERS

Increased participation of women in waged labour has been a rising phenomenon yet this has not brought a significant change as far as their personal domestic responsibilities are concerned. Due to existing gender hierarchies in society, it has always been difficult for women to ask men to share domestic responsibilities. A woman is now under double burden of work as she is expected to do all household chores when she returns back from work. In comparison, when a man comes home from work he wants to rest, expects food to be ready and served to him irrespective of the fact that the woman too has been working all day outside and is tired. After a rest, the man goes out in the evening and spends time with his friends or neighbours whereas the woman after coming home is engaged in the second labour of doing the house chores and looking after her children. In cases where there is a joint family the burden is transferred to other women in the family. RS who travels daily by boat from Baba Bhit Island to Karachi, lives in a joint family but for support at home, she is dependent on the mood swings of her mother-in-law. If she is in a good mood, she will do the house chores in RS's absence. Otherwise, when RS comes home from work she is expected to do the cooking and other duties. Her husband is a seasonal worker, is at home most of the time, but never bothers to help: not even looking after the children who spend their day in the streets when their mother is not around.

Another distressing aspect of the husband/wife relationship pointed out by many domestic workers is the lack of trust and suspicion by husbands concerning their wives' character. K mentioned in her interview that whenever she wears clean clothes her husband starts suspecting her and asking why and for whom has she dressed up nicely. Similarly, he makes it a point to have sexual intercourse on that particular night just to confirm that she has not slept with anyone else. This degrading attitude causes frustration among women and makes them feel that they are second-rate creatures born to satisfy their husbands' lust.

Exploitation by male relatives and other kin is another issue brought forward by the women domestic workers in their discussions. Women consider themselves the last to benefit from their earnings. The concept of family in Pakistan is much more complex and elaborate than in the West. As such, the range of relations is much wider and more demanding. These women actually support a network of dependants including husband and children, and other female members of the family. At the same time quite often, they are expected to offer gifts to their relatives. Women relatives also do not hesitate to take away clothes or shoes given to the worker by the employer on the pretext that the worker would get another from the employer. In some cases, male members are very demanding: for instance asking them to buy items such as a wristwatch or a small cassette player. In cases where husbands, brothers, or sons are addicts, they fritter away the hard-earned money of these women domestic workers on buying drugs.

CHILD CARE AND EDUCATION

An unfortunate aspect of domestic service reported in studies on migrant domestic workers is that women who serve as nannies and take care of others' children do so at the cost of their own kids.[16] The same has been the case of women domestic workers and their siblings in Pakistan. When women are away at work, their children roam about in the streets all day. It is ironic that children of nannies are denied the same care that their mothers are giving to their employer's children. Children are often left alone at home, especially among the migrant community from Punjab who, unlike the extended family system in villages, do not have an elderly person at home to take care of them. In the four ghettos where women domestic workers were interviewed, children were seen playing on garbage heaps or swimming in stagnant ponds where cows also bathed. Their living conditions reflected the poor infrastructure and failure of the government's institutions to provide these residents with the basic amenities of life.

Very few children in this social class go to school. The respondents told me that private schools in the area charge fees that are beyond their means and the problem with government-run schools is that the teachers are not committed to their profession. Most of the time, the teacher is on leave, classes are not held regularly and as a result, the children become disinterested in their studies. Private education is expensive and beyond their means, while the situation in government schools is pathetic because of non-availability of staff and poor infrastructure of schools. Women domestic workers also complained that it is very difficult for them to buy books and other school stationary and the uniform because of daily price hikes. A and N are the two domestic workers who are being helped by their employers with payment for children's school fees but others do not receive any support for their children's education.

The security of children is a major problem especially in the case of young girls who are left alone at home when their mothers go to work. The case of thirteen-year old F who was raped by a neighbour when her mother R was away at work is one such example. Although R succeeded in filing a case against the accused with the help of her employer, and the accused is now in jail, the damage done to the young girl remains irreparable as she is still traumatized by the horrifying experience.

It was also noticed that the majority of the women interviewed had at least four to five children. They said that their husbands were against family planning because they considered children as their only asset. Preferring a son to daughter is another reason for producing more children. However, men in these communities do not realize that without providing a reasonable living standard and education, children would not prove to be an asset. They also forget that it is also unfair to the children if parents are unable to provide a proper upbringing.

EXPERIENCES OF CHRISTIAN AND HINDU WOMEN DOMESTIC WORKERS

The issue of diverse or multiple identities is relevant in the case of women domestic workers in Pakistan who are not simply a class of women workers: their experiences vary according to their ethnic and religious backgrounds. These variations affect relations with employers as well as within their own families, as was evident in my interviews with Christian and Hindu women in Peshawar and Karachi.

While interviewing these women, it was noticed that they were a bit reluctant in disclosing their identity for fear of losing their jobs on the basis of their religion. Christian and Hindu workers complained that some employers separate their utensils, for fear of pollution by non-Muslim hands and workers are made to sit and eat outside the kitchen. They feel degraded at this treatment as if they are not human beings. Some workers also complained that their relations with the employer were not based on trust. Hindu workers mentioned that although the trend is changing now and people are becoming more liberal, still some Muslim employers would not allow a Hindu worker to cook or perform any other job in the kitchen. She said they do not want to work in such households where people treat them as if they are untouchables.

Another complaint by women from both Hindu and Christian communities is that the majority of the employers do not care about their festivals and such occasions as Christmas, Holi, and Easter. Muslim workers get money or clothes on occasions such as Eid but on non-Muslim festivals most of the employers were not bothered to even greet them, let alone give gifts.

Domestic work is also an inter-generational activity, like many other sectors of informal employment such as brick kiln workers or home-based workers.[17] However, this pattern of inter-generational activity appears to be changing among the Christian domestic workers. There is an upward mobility among them as their daughters are gaining education and entering other employment sectors such as teaching, nursing, or factory workers.

A positive trend found among Christian and Hindu women is that they are more conscious of the importance of education and learning skills than their Muslim counterparts. They make every effort to send their children to school. N has been working since she got married. She realises that because she is not educated she has no other choice but to work as a domestic worker. She does not want her children to suffer like her and is making every effort to educate them. She bears all the expenses of their education by working in other households. It is because of her own efforts that her daughter is now studying in a college and her son goes to school in the morning and works as an apprentice in a workshop in the evening.

CASE STUDIES

KA (ROLE AS A WIFE)

KA comes from Sargodha, which is in Southern Punjab. When she was sixteen years old, her father gave her in marriage to a person who worked as a watchman/guard in a factory in Karachi. During the first few years of marriage, she was happy and had spent a comparatively good life but then her husband lost his job when the factory was closed down. Her husband could not find a suitable job for almost one year. Due to her husband's unemployment and for the sake of her five children, she started working in private homes as a part-time domestic worker. For the last four years, she has been working in different households. Although her husband has now found a job and is earning three thousand rupees monthly, yet she continues to work because she thinks that survival on a single person's salary nowadays is not possible. She also mentioned that her husband keeps a full check on her earnings suspecting that she might send money to her parents as they are very poor and her brother is also not earning much and has his own family to look after. She complained that despite her hard work and financial support that she is giving her husband she still has no control over her earnings.

Her three sons go to school but her daughters remain at home and do the housework in her absence. She wants to send her daughters to school but due to financial constraints and the need to have someone to look after the younger daughter and the house in her absence, she only sends her sons to school. She does not want her sons to suffer like her husband. She realises that because of her husband's illiteracy he cannot earn a good living so she wants her sons to be educated. Realizing that her daughters too might suffer in future like their mother but with no other help available at home, she has to depend on her elder daughter. Although she is keen to educate both her daughters, she also complained that the state-run school is not close to her house and the private school which is near the house is too expensive. It is therefore not possible for her to send them to school.

KA works in two houses daily where she does the cleaning and dishwashing, and earns Rs 700 from each house. For another house, she does the laundry every other day and earns an extra Rs 600 monthly, bringing her monthly earnings to Rs 2000. From her salary, she manages to pay the school fees for her sons and some other needs, whereas her husband's salary goes to the *kiraya* (rent) (which is Rs 1500 for a one-room accommodation) and some basic groceries.

Her day starts at 5.30 in the morning when she gets up, prepares tea and *roti*, helps her sons to get ready for school, cleans the house and sets off to work at 8 o'clock and gets back around 2 to 3 pm. Her daughter helps with household chores.

Discussing her relationship with her employers, KA said that during the last three years she dropped one job because that employer was paying only 400 rupees for doing the laundry, whereas the going rate was Rs 600-800 depending on the workload. She said that she had to wash clothes, linen, and once even a carpet for which no extra money was paid.

Therefore, when she managed to find another job she stopped working there. When asked whether she informed her employer beforehand that she would no longer be working for them, she told me that she informed her employer through a co-worker that she has left the job because of the low salary given to her.

This clearly suggests that in the absence of any formal agreement/contract and a proper wage structure the employer is at liberty to throw out a worker. Similarly, the worker can also leave the job without any notice if she gets a better option.

SH (VICTIM OF A PATRIARCHAL SOCIETY/ WOMAN'S EXPERIENCE OF THE JUSTICE SYSTEM)

SH is fifty-five years old, separated from her husband and lives with her three children. She started working as a domestic worker when she was a young girl. Her mother died when she was fourteen and her father was a drug addict and unskilled labourer who spent his earnings on drugs. Being the eldest amongst six children, she had to support the family. Her first employer was the village landlord and her duties at work included looking after a three-year-old boy and washing his clothes daily. She was not paid any money for her services: instead, her family was given a sack of wheat twice a year, and at the end of each day, she was given some leftover food to carry home for her younger brother and three sisters. When she used to go to work there was no one at home to look after her younger brother and sisters as her father was not bothered about the children and her grandmother was too old and bed-ridden to do the job. Whatever was given to her to eat during the day at work she used to keep for her siblings. On her request, and knowing her family situation, her employer found a job with another family for her other sister who was a year younger than her.

SH was only sixteen years old when her father married her off. At the time of her marriage she found out that her father had received Rs 5000 from her husband. On her marriage, the landlord's family gave her five hundred rupees and some clothes. After her marriage, she came to Karachi with her husband who used to work in a factory. In the initial few years, she did not work but later when the children were born, her husband's income proved insufficient for them and she had to take up a job as a domestic worker to support the family.

Five years ago her brother and sisters also came to Karachi and they started living in Hijrat Colony. Her brother wanted to marry a girl but the girl's parents refused to accept the proposal. Upon the parent's refusal the girl ran away with SH's brother and both went into hiding. The girl's parents registered a case of kidnapping against SH and her brother. She was arrested along with her younger brother as her name was also mentioned in the First Information Report (FIR) lodged by the girl's parents. She remained in prison for one year until her brother was caught. When she was put into prison she was four months pregnant and she gave birth to her son in prison. The husband refused to help her get out of prison and deserted her. SH had not committed any offence and her only fault was that she was the sister of the actual culprit. Her name had been given by the other party to pressurize her absconding brother. In this family feud, she suffered at the hands of her brother and also lost her husband who due to the pressure from his own family did not come to her rescue and deserted her. She thinks that in this male-dominated society men consider women inferior. They use women as a cheap commodity so often that they do not mind saying that women are at their disposal and can be used for any purpose whenever, wherever and however they want and that woman can be exploited by men according to their wishes.

SH also mentioned that her experience in prison and in the courts was an eye-opener for her. She expressed her confidence in the judiciary saying that although the procedures were long and time-consuming, at the end of the day one got justice. She complained that the only distressing part of the story was that her family and society, despite knowing very well that she was innocent, suspected her and did not give her due respect. She resented that her children also suffered undeservedly as they became the target of sarcastic remarks by society. SH was released from prison after a year when her brother was caught. To support her children she started to work again as a domestic worker.

K (FINDING HER OWN WAY)

K lived in a small village in Punjab and came to Karachi with her husband and two children ten years ago. Her other two children were born in Karachi. The gap between each child is no more than a year and a half. Her eldest daughter is now twelve. Her husband used to work along with her father-in-law for a landlord and in return for their labour they were given two sacks of wheat a year. As they were living in extreme poverty, the husband and wife decided to move to Karachi in search of jobs. The husband started working as a waged labourer with a construction company but for almost six months, she could not find any work. A relative who worked as a domestic worker had to go back to the village and requested her employer to employ K for work in her absence. Through this arrangement, K got her first job as a domestic. She worked in that house for three months. For one week, she worked alongside her relative to understand the type of work she was supposed to do and also to familiarize herself with the area and how to commute daily from her house. Although her relative was getting six hundred rupees for the work, she was given only four hundred rupees on the pretext that she had no previous experience. This three-month job proved to be a training period, in which she learnt some Urdu, got some idea about people's life-styles in the city and this gave her the courage to look for another job on the return of her relative. In two weeks time she managed to find a part-time job in the same neighbourhood. Since then she has been working in different households and now earns about Rs 2500 per month.

K has struggled hard coming from a poor, remote rural area. She has learnt to cope with the stressful and complicated urban lifestyle. She has learnt the language, mastered a new job, how to cook new dishes, and she keeps herself neat and clean. She also does small jobs for her employers and in this way gets favours. She sends her children to school on her own by paying their fees and schoolbooks because her husband does not give her any money and spends his own earnings on drugs, which he started taking a few years back in the company of his friends. This habit has also affected his job because he does not get up early in the morning and often spends the whole day lying in bed at home, where as K hardly takes a day off. With experience, she had found a way out to secure her old job and at the same time benefit from temporarily working at the farm (when she goes back to the village for a month or two). She has made an alternative arrangement for her employers by providing them with another worker who serves them in her absence when she is away for a month or two. She has been doing this for quite sometime. Now she thinks that she can earn more by staying in Karachi instead of going to the village as most of her family members have now moved to Karachi. As such, she no longer has a reason to return to the village.

K walks about three to four kilometres daily to avoid spending money on bus fares. When she comes home she does her household chores including bringing water from the hand-pump installed at a distance from her home. Every month she tries to save Rs 50 or Rs 100. With her savings, she has been able to buy a second-hand television and a washing machine.

SU (HARD WORK AND CONTINUOUS STRUGGLE)

SU, like many other women from Bhit Island travels daily by boat to Kemari and from there she boards the bus for the Defence Society where she works for two households. She spends twenty to twenty five rupees daily on travelling. Sometimes one of her employers gives her the fare but most of the time she pays it herself. Her husband is a fisherman who works for a Seth Naqua who owns many launches and fishing equipment. Using the seth's boats he goes into the open sea to fishing however he has to pay for the petrol, fishing equipment and the boat rental when the fish is sold. Thus, he is left with barely eighty to a hundred rupees per trip depending on the quantity of fish they catch. Sometimes when the tide is high, they are unable to go fishing for several weeks. Due to her husband's unsteady income, SU decided to work as a domestic worker. In the beginning, her husband was not in favour of her going out for work but then due to their poor financial condition he gave her permission to work.

SU has four children and lives with her in-laws. Her day starts very early in the morning. She prepares breakfast, cleans the house and then leaves for work at 7.30 in the morning. She comes home around 5 to 6 in the evening and then she prepares dinner. Her mother-in-law helps her only sometimes as it is considered the responsibility of the daughter-in-law to perform household chores. Her husband also does not share in the household chores. Now he does realise how hard she works for the sake of family and sometimes does value her for instance she has been able to convince him to send their eldest son to school. However SU in general like many other women from Bhit Island complained that their men have developed a habit of not doing any work other than fishing. These men have made an excuse for themselves that the only job they can do is fishing because this has been their occupation for generations and that is the only skill they possess. They do not want to struggle and work hard by finding work in Karachi. They never bother to go and search for a job because the *ghar ka kharcha pani* (household expenses) are being taken care of by their wives, mothers and sisters.

When SU started working two years ago, the *malikin* (employer) used to pay her only Rs 1500 for cooking, cleaning and shopping. She used to work from nine to five. Her employer was very strict and used to ridicule SH by using abusive language when she committed any minor mistake. Once while washing the dishes she broke a glass and twenty rupees were deducted from her salary. SU worked in that house for three months but when she found another job with a better salary, she left. Before leaving she demanded an increase in her salary but the employer straight away refused saying, '*Tum aurat ho aur tum ko mein itni tankhwah nahi dey sakti....yeh to mard khansama key rate hein...aurtoon kay nahi*' (you are a woman and you can't get this much salary these are the rates for male cooks and not for women domestic workers).

SU is now very conscious of being exploited by her employers. She is well aware that domestics are not paid fairly for work they do and that their working hours are also not fixed. She thinks that due to their lower status in society and their poverty they are in a very weak position. Realizing her low status and helplessness SU thinks that it is better to leave the job and search for another. There are always exceptions and SU is happy with her new employers because they are much better in their dealings with servants. They sometimes give her the bus fare. Once they also gave her extra money when her daughter was ill and unlike other employers did not deduct it from her salary when she could not come to work for four days.

SU also pointed out that she does not have any chances of progress without formal training. She thinks that if women domestic workers are trained as cooks this may improve their job opportunities otherwise they would always be exploited and their work would always be underestimated as work done by untrained women. She feels strongly that, as these women are illiterate and poor they need support from organisations or individuals who could support these women as negotiators between domestic workers and employers. She also said that '*Agar humarey ialaqaiy ka councillor hum sey vote mangta hai to phir usay humara khyal bhi rakhna chahiey*' (If our area councillors expect us to vote for them then they should take up the responsibility to look after our interests and support us).

R (VULNERABILITY OF CHILDREN DUE TO LACK OF PROPER SUPPORT SYSTEMS)

This is the case of a woman who moved from her own town for better prospects for her children but unfortunately, her daughter was raped when she was at work. R lived in a small village called Pindi Bhatiyan near Rawalpindi in Punjab province. Her husband married another woman and she, along with her five children, were thrown out of the house. Her youngest child was seven days old at the time. Her parents had died and her brothers were married, had their own families and she did not want to burden them. Therefore with the help of a relative who had migrated to Karachi a few years earlier she came to Karachi with her five children. For two weeks, she stayed with her relatives. Their neighbour worked as a part-time domestic worker with a family who lived in a huge house and were in need of an extra helper. R thus found her job for five hundred rupees. Her responsibilities included cleaning the verandas and laundry twice a week. She worked in that house for six months and then she found another job where she was paid eight hundred rupees for dishwashing and cleaning. She used to live in a *jhugee* (hut) with her children.

With her meagre salary, she hardly managed to provide the children with food. They used to roam the roads all day. Her fourteen years old son started working as an apprentice in a cycle shop but that also did not make much difference as he was paid only fifteen rupees daily. R then started looking for a second job, which she found in the same neighbourhood. The second job gave her some relief as she now had more money. Meanwhile due to the death of her younger brother, she had to go back to the village. When she returned to Karachi after two months, she had lost her jobs and was back to square one. However, a friend of her previous employer was in need of a domestic worker so she sent her to that woman and R got a new job. Her new employer is a banker by profession, employed in a very senior post. She is a kind-hearted person and when she came to know R's story she employed her son in the bank as a peon.

When R started working with this woman four years ago she was paid Rs 1500 per month for all the household chores, working from eight to five. Her salary was gradually increased and now she is getting Rs 3000 per month. R was now able to move from the hut to a one-room accommodation in a nearby squatter settlement. R was satisfied with this job because she could afford to send her other two children to school. A year ago, an unfortunate incident took place. Her eldest daughter, who was thirteen years old, used to stay at home and look after the house in her mother's absence. One day a young male resident of the same colony knocked at the door and asked for water. When she opened the door he pushed her, came in, locked her in the room and raped her. When R came home in the evening the daughter was in a terrible state. When the mother cross-questioned her, she told her about the incident. R was shocked by the incident and did not know what to do, as she did not want to take the matter to police. She went to see the father of the man and complained but he refused to accept the charges. The next day when she came to work, she informed her employer about the incident. The employer told her to go to the police station and file a complaint. When she went to the police station the officer on duty first refused to file an FIR, told her to forget about the incident, and started accusing R and her daughter of immoral conduct. R came back to her employer, who then immediately contacted a local NGO 'War Against Rape' and requested them to take up the matter. Later on with the NGOs intervention, the FIR was lodged but the other party bribed the police heavily and when the statements were being recorded, the police twisted all the statements in such a way that the mother and daughter were accused of 'loose' character and blackmailing the father and son for the sake of money. The medical report showed that the girl was not raped.

This incident is an example of the corrupt police system in Pakistan and how the poor and powerless are exploited and their voices remain unheard. However, when the matter was taken up in court, the judge was not convinced by the police statements and ordered the arrest of the father and son. A year has passed and the case is still in court. After the incident R, due to threats from the accused and his family, left that settlement and moved to another area. Her two children who were attending school also suffered because there is no government school where she is living now. This incident has once again affected her badly. R is demoralized and feels that all her struggles have been in vain. She came to Karachi for a better future for her children but this incident has once again ruined their lives. She is extremely worried for her daughter who is badly traumatized by the incident.

R's case suggests that when mothers are at work the children are exposed to all sorts of dangers. It also explains the helplessness of women who do not have financial means and other backup and consequently are mistreated by the police. Although she had the support of an NGO, yet it is extremely difficult for her to pursue the case because of the financial costs involved. At least twice a month she has to visit the lawyer or go to court for the hearing and every visit costs her twenty five to fifty rupees.

AZ AND BJ (DOMESTIC WORK AS AN INTER-GENERATIONAL ACTIVITY)

This is an interesting case, which demonstrates that domestic work has become an inter-generational activity in Pakistan. AZ is the eldest grandchild of BJ. BJ started working as a domestic worker forty years ago as a young widow. She had three sons and two daughters. She sent all three sons to school but only one son was able to reach college and to graduate. After that, he got a clerical job in one of the government departments. B J's sons now do not want their mother to work and fear that '*kali maalat khalaq ba khabaray kai chai sta ghaza parado kauroon no kai kar kai*' (Co-villagers and relatives would ridicule them saying that their mother still works in other households).

However, BJ still works because she does not want to be a burden on her sons and she wants to help her eldest son's family. Now that she has grown old and cannot work alone, AZ therefore comes along with her grandmother to work. AZ and BJ now work as part-time workers and do the laundry for one employer. AZ's paternal aunt (BJ's daughter) also sometimes comes when BJ is not well and works as her replacement with AZ. In this way, this is the third generation of workers. AZ's mother has never worked because in AZ's words '*meri ma to bachey paida karney ki machine hai who ghar ka kam karti hai yah bachey sambhalti hai*' (My mother has been a child-making machine because every year she gives birth to a child. She has never been to any of the bungalows and she only looks after the house and her children).

A few years ago, AZ's father used to work as a waiter in a restaurant. Later he joined an extreme religious group. As most of his time was spent in *tabligh* (proselytizing) in far-flung areas in the country, he lost his job and started neglecting his household responsibilities and children. One day when he returned from *tabligh* he found out that his wife had left for her parent's house along with the children in protest that he did not take care of them. This became an issue of *ghairat* and *paighore* (pride and honour) for him and he went after his wife to her parent's village. In the heat of the moment, he killed two of his children who were playing in the fields outside their grandparents' house. On hearing the gunshots people came out and he was caught red-handed and handed over to the police. His wife filed a case against him and he was sentenced to life imprisonment but after two years, AZ's mother was pressurized by her in-laws to withdraw the case and forgive her husband. Being illiterate and dependent on her in-laws, she had to bow down to their demand. Now AZ's father is out of prison but due to his mental condition he has become a burden on AZ and her grandmother.

Due to her family circumstances, AZ has lost faith in the institution of marriage. She has decided never to get married because she feels illiterate wives become only what she calls 'child-producing machines.' She deeply regrets that she could not go to school because of her father's irresponsible attitude and her mother's inability to earn: being illiterate and poor she too could not do anything for her children. AZ says that sometimes she quarrels with her mother because she thinks that her mother should have learnt a lesson from her own experiences and should have sent AZ and her sister to school or at least to the vocational centre to learn stitching. When asked why she thinks that going to school would have brought some improvement in her position, she said, '*Agar mein school ya centre jati to mein yah teacher ban jati ya kaprey si kar paisey kamati*' (Had I been to school or to the centre, I could be a teacher in the primary school or could have made a living by stitching clothes).

Now AZ wants to work in more households so that she can earn some extra money but she is not allowed to work in other households by her uncles. She got permission to work with her current employer only because her grandmother had served this family for the past thirty-five years and her uncles trust them. Sometimes when needed AZ also stays for a night or two, for instance when there are houseguests in the employer's home. For this extra work, she is sometimes paid fifty or hundred rupees. AZ gives her salary to her mother for the household expenses. She also tries to save some money which she receives in the form of charity given by her employer or on festive occasions such as Eid.

CONCLUSION

Fieldwork analysis has helped in uncovering a form of women's work that has been deliberately ignored and remained hidden in the private sphere for a very long time. It has provided a deep insight into the nature of the work undertaken by women domestic workers' nature of work, working conditions and their own perceptions about themselves as workers.

The data from the field has also been useful in understanding the law in its social context by listening to women domestic workers' experiences of both formal and informal law. It clearly suggests that women consider formal state law as a better mode of gaining access to justice as compared to informal customary mechanisms such as *jirgas* and *panchayat*. However, due to lack of support structures and their precarious socio-economic status they are not in a position to use the legal system. For an effective implementation of laws, it is pertinent to look for some other means of support so that access to justice can be made possible for women.

Employer-employee relations are not straightforward contractual relations. It is a relationship based on power in which one party is much stronger and more influential than the other. The power relationship is reflected both in the direct abuse which these women face and also in the degrading and demeaning status attached to this type of work. As a result, it is not only men but also privileged women who exploit their workers, and therefore it is pertinent to address the inequalities that exist in the form of class status. Discussions with employers and domestic workers exposed the complicated nature of domestic labour. These discussions suggest that domestic labour is a class issue. It is a power relationship where the employer wants to exert full control over the domestic worker, as there is always a surplus labour force available, so throwing out a domestic is not a big issue. At the same time lack of reciprocal sympathy for employers by the employees is the natural result of the difference between the haves and have-nots and the wide class difference. Knowing that the employers have money and resources make the employees feel that any loss would not make much difference in the employer's life.

Domestic work has not brought any significant change in the living standard of the workers because whatever they earn is so low that they hardly manage to fulfil the basic requirements of life. There is a lot of disparity in the way the poor classes in Pakistani society live as compared to the middle or upper classes. These workers not only live on very low wages but also have no benefits from the state or employers in the form of housing subsidy, free health care, or free education for children.

The fieldwork also suggests that the absence of any safety networks and lack of basic facilities of life, such as health and education, add to the problems of domestic workers. In this regard the state and the local government system has a crucial role to play in improving and providing basic facilities or improving their basic living conditions, which would take away some pressure from the domestic workers. At the same time at a community and at individual level it is the responsibility of the better off people to provide support to domestic workers.

NOTES

1. Domestic Servants Service,' Registration Number 0577 12 C, Tauheed Commercial Area, Defence, Phase 5, Karachi.
2. Cf., chapter 2 on literature review indicates that in both developed and developing countries, the majority of women are engaged as domestic workers in other households.
3. The equivalent of 1000 rupees is less than £10 which means that the average income of a household worker in Pakistan is not more than £10 to £15 per month and for the part-time workers who receive 500 rupees it comes to less than £5. With such low income it is extremely difficult to even feed the families when the price of a 5kg flour bag is between 150-200 rupees.
4. Dasgupta, A. (1984), *Domestic Workers: Profile of Women Dwelling in the Slums of South Delhi*, New Delhi: People's Institute for Development and Training, p. 9.
5. This case study represents domestic work as an intergenerational activity. It is discussed in detail at the end of this chapter.
6. Ragurham, P. (1993), *Coping Strategies of Domestic Workers: A Study of Three Settlements in Delhi Metropolitan Region*, India, New Castle Upon Tyne: PhD thesis.
7. Cock, J., supra note 74, ch. 2, p. 146.
8. Rollins, J., supra note 11, ch. 2, p. 20.
9. See discussion/literature review in chapter 2 on migrant workers.
10. Rollins, J., supra note 11, ch. 2, p. 158.
11. This treatment of domestic workers also resonates with Victorian England where servants and masters ate separately. Similarly, separate living quarters for domestic workers in Pakistan remind one of the Victorian times where the layout and structure of the houses made two separate lifestyles possible.
12. Although statistics suggest that the divorce rate has risen over the last twenty years. Now women are approaching courts to seek dissolution of a marriage but at the same time there is rapid increase in cases of honour killing, *karo kari* and other customary practices.
13. The two recent incidents of sexual abuse in the case of domestic bonded labour discussed in the Literature Review chapter provide an example of harassment at the workplace.
14. Cf., see chapter 4, section on 'Women's Mobility'.
15. It is a method of saving, common among women, who pool their money together every month. In this way, a substantial sum is generated and given to every member in turn.
16. Hochschild, A.R., supra note 30, ch. 2, p. 21.
17. Young girls instead of going to school join their mothers in performing their duty as helpers, which conditions them by apprenticeship throughout their childhood into a career of household service. This deprives them not only of their right to obtain an education but also of the joys that are the rights of that age level. The justification given for girls' labour is that it prepares them for their future roles of mothers and wives. This justification is ironic and mocks reality because actually the girl-child is used for supporting the family income and in this way she shares the economic burden with her parents.

6

Towards an Integrated Approach: Non-Legal and Legal Strategies for the Protection of Women Domestic Workers in Pakistan

INTRODUCTION

The data analysed here discredits the misconception that women domestic workers are inarticulate, ignorant, and always passive victims of abuse. Indeed, they are productive, hardworking, sensible individuals who have the ability and strength to cope with tough situations from a very young age. It further strengthens the theoretical concept of woman's agency and therefore to consider women domestic workers as passive victims of violence and abuse is erroneous. Despite the presence of negative factors (such as gender and class differences to name a few), they have the capability to resist and to struggle, provided they have due support. The chapter begins with a discussion on women's personal struggle and the various strategies adopted by them to cope with their own situations. It also looks into the possibility of networking and organizational support and analyses the possibilities whether domestic service can be organized as a service industry. The chapter further explores the role of local government in providing protection to women domestic workers. Finally, it provides an outline for a legislative framework so that the status of domestic workers could be enhanced by achieving a balance between decent employment standards and the requirements of the employers.

FINDING THEIR OWN WAY

Cohen in her study discusses the external, internal and cognitive strategies used by women domestic workers in Canada.[1] The use of the same strategies was also seen amongst Pakistani women domestic workers. The data from the field demonstrates that women in domestic service make an effort by adopting different ways to cope with their isolation, problems with employers and difficulties at the work place. The data also suggests that if given support these workers are capable of bringing some positive changes in their lives.

The external strategy used by women domestic workers to overcome their isolation (especially those who work as live-in workers away from their homes) is to keep linkages with their own communities and families. Women domestic workers who leave their families behind in villages visit them on occasions like *Eid* and some times after every four to six months by taking few days off from work. Migrant workers also try to keep in touch with the family by making arrangements to phone them twice a month.[2] It was also noted that migrant communities, Hindu and Christian communities are also supportive of each other and there is a sense of solidarity among the women domestic workers which is displayed in two ways: (i) they help each other in finding jobs and they also try to support each other in difficult times by sharing each other's problems. For instance when a worker loses a job, other co-workers inform her if there is a job available in some other household and (ii) when they find out that a co-worker has been exploited and abused by an employer, they will not accept that job even if the employer is willing to pay above the usual rate. However, this is a casual way of looking for jobs and it does not solve the problem of getting secure jobs. Therefore, the need for the formal organizational structure still remains.

Women domestic workers have, despite their vulnerability and in the absence of any formal legal protective structures, found ways of protecting themselves against abusive employers. They have devised their own internal strategies from their experiences at work. Women domestic workers have learnt that they should be careful while selecting an employer. They try to get jobs in nuclear families and avoid extensive joint family households.[3] Similarly, they prefer working with professional women because they are not at home during most of the day and the domestic worker is at liberty to perform her tasks without constant surveillance. However, sometimes they have to take a job even if they are unable to find a suitable employer because they cannot afford to take the risk of being unemployed for a long time.

In daily life, the household is a political arena where 'personal becomes political'. An example of this could be seen when the domestic worker, by adopting a variety of strategies, challenged the power structure, i.e. the superior and dominant status of the employer. In group discussions some domestic workers openly advised their co-workers by sharing their way of tackling the unreasonable attitude of their employers. One of them suggested that the best way to avoid workload is to mess up your duties or stop performing one of the tasks assigned with the same diligence and care. The internal strategy she adopted was to wash clothes carelessly and to continuously complain about the heavy workload. As a result, her employer hired another woman for doing the laundry without reducing her salary because the employer already knew that she was paying her less and because of the satisfactory care her child was receiving. Women domestic workers from Karachi also mentioned their refusal to work for extremely low wages and demand for increased wages when there is another job available to them. These efforts to resist and subvert the control and exploitative treatment of the employers reveals that women are not merely passive victims, rather agents of change, who do challenge the stereotypical attitudes of employers in their own way.

Women domestic workers from minority groups in particular try to negotiate with their employers within their own means and positions. They may not be successful in every case but still have succeeded in restraining the exploitative treatment of the employers. For instance, Hindu and Christian workers' refusal to work in those households where they are discriminated against on the basis of their religious beliefs suggests that the negotiating power of these workers cannot be underestimated.

Daytime workers and part-time workers have greater autonomy as compared to their fellow domestics who work as live-in workers, whether they work with either single or multiple employers. They do not have the same intensity of dependence and subordination as live-in workers who are at the disposal of their employers twenty-four hours a day. The silence or patience on the part of domestic workers should not be taken as their weakness or total submission to unfair and unjust treatment. Women domestic workers resent and resist this unjust treatment in their own ways. Despite hardships, women domestic workers have sought out ways of reducing their dependency on employers. Their refusal to accept rotten food or leaving a job because they feel insulted when searched every day by the employer's guard (as discussed in the previous section) indicates their resistance to degrading treatment.

Domestic workers have also adopted what Cohen calls 'cognitive strategy' which is in the form of a desire for alleviating their existing status. They want to learn other skills such as stitching clothes or working in a factory. They also strongly feel that educating their children would help improve their social status. Women domestic workers also think that they have more peace of mind as compared to their employers who, despite all comforts, either suffer from depression or are unable to enjoy their lives. In the words of a worker, '*Hum to roti kay tukray kha kar chain ki neend so jatein hein magar sahib log sab kuch honey kai bawajood neend ki golian laitey hein*' (Although we may have few pieces of bread to eat at night but at least we have a peaceful sleep but our employers despite all comforts still have to take sedatives to go to sleep). This comment indicates the coping strategies of women domestic workers and their perception that, at least in some way, they are in a better position than their employers.

An issue emerging from the fieldwork is that women domestic workers in Pakistan have accepted the challenges posed by their extreme poverty, patriarchal structures of society, class and gender differences and of migration and dislocation (in the case of women domestic workers who have moved from interior parts of Pakistan to cities).[4] Due to their economic needs they have accepted the challenge to come out of their homes and make use of whatever skills they have to earn a living for their family. Coming out of their homes actually challenges the traditional view that a woman must remain within the four walls of the home. This has an impact on redefining their roles as providers for the family. Migration or dislocation has given them the courage to face and struggle for survival in an entirely different environment in which class disparities are apparent and a constant source of discrimination and humiliation. It has given them consciousness of social injustices that exist in the society and the motivation to strategize against them.

BUILDING COALITIONS: NETWORKING FOR CHANGE

Despite devising their own strategies as discussed in the previous section, the power of the domestic workers to resist exploitative treatment is curtailed because they have no support to fall back on. Collective action and more concerted efforts are therefore needed along with the coping strategies adopted by women domestic workers. Migration of families from impoverished parts of the country to urban areas constantly creates new entrants into domestic service. Availability of surplus labour is a factor that keeps the worker away from countervailing their employers. Workers are not in a position to take any action in their individual capacity due to the fear of losing their jobs. Similarly, employers too are not keen on improving relations with, or changing working conditions for workers because of the availability of surplus labour force. However, despite these constraints women domestic workers voiced the need for some kind of organizational support for improving their work situation. They have the potential to strategize and if given support can work towards the betterment of their work situations.

In order to organize women domestic workers it is pertinent to look at the role of the women's movement in protecting their rights in Pakistan. The women's movement has so far focused on issues such as rape, domestic violence, and honour killings. The passage of the Women's Protection Bill, after strong resistance for many years by the religious sections of society, is an example of the efforts of the women's movement in Pakistan.[5] Punishments like stoning to death and lashes meted out to women by the lower courts were averted due to strong protests by the women's movement. Activists managed to mobilize public opinion against those discriminatory decisions and as a result these punishments were never imposed.[6]

Despite its successes, the women's movement has failed on certain fronts: it has neglected, or could not, draw the attention of women activists in Pakistan towards issues such as exploitative working conditions, wages, maternity rights, childcare for working women, harassment in the workplace, organizing women's participation in trade unions and pressuring the government to include agricultural workers and domestic workers within the ambit of labour legislation. In this context, the criticism made against the women's movement in Pakistan, as being elitist and dominated by upper and middle class women, comes to mind. It raises questions as to whether silence on the part of the movement regarding domestic workers' problems is due to a conflict of interest between employers and employees. In other words since most members of the women's movement are themselves employers it is not in their interest to espouse the cause of women domestic workers. If the women's movement in Pakistan is committed to the cause of empowering Pakistani women then a concerted effort is needed on its part to improve the situation of women domestic workers. It could play a catalyst role in raising awareness among women domestic workers, employers and the general public as a whole, as well as pressurize the state to bring changes in the labour laws of the country. It needs to identify like-minded people at policy making level in government as well as among legislators and labour lawyers who could work with the government and help in drafting appropriate policy and legislation in this area.

Unfortunately, in Pakistan there is not much support given to domestic workers by women's associations, religious groups, and other kinds of NGO support/advocacy bodies. Within the trade union movement too, attention is not being paid to the need to organize and support unprotected, domestic workers. In their interviews women workers expressed the need for support from other organizations as well as wanting to form local associations and organizations so that they could take the initiative and streamline efforts of women domestic workers in the right direction. Such associations could better identify problems faced by these women, and any local setup would be easily accessible to women domestic workers.

Another possibility of organizing support could be in the form of trade unions. Although women's representation is low in trade unions, it could be improved by setting up a women's desk or a cell for women inside the general trade union. This desk or cell could urge trade union leadership to address and raise workplace issues of women domestic workers through mass campaigns. Networking with other organizations is also vital. There are women organizations and unions in other employment sectors including unions of industrial workers and women in fisheries. Therefore, setting up such bodies for women in domestic service would not be something exceptional. Many problems faced by women domestic workers are similar to problems faced by women working in the other informal employment sectors. Working together as a pressure group with these organizations could therefore be a more effective strategy for women in domestic service. The Pakistan Institute of Labour, Education and Research (hereinafter referred as PILER) is a pioneer organization that has played a key role in raising a voice for workers in Pakistan. This organization has also taken the initiative of forming community-based labour organizations and women's groups in some sectors of the informal economy. These include 'All Karachi Labour and Hosiery Garments Labour Association', 'Working Women Forum' and 'Fisher Folk Forum', which could help the domestic workers and workers in other informal sectors to take a collective action to solve their problems. They could also play the role of a bridge in linking women in domestic service to the trade unions, and their interaction with trade unions could provide a base for a larger organization of domestic workers.

Presently there is one small women domestic workers association formed by a local NGO 'Lawyers for Human Rights and Legal Aid' (hereinafter referred as LHRLA) in Karachi and a 'Centre for Rehabilitation of Child Domestic Workers' (IPEC) in Islamabad which, was launched by the Ministry of Women Development in collaboration with ILO-IPEC in 2002.[7] However, these have not been vocal on the issue which suggests that a commitment to the cause of women in domestic service is also needed, otherwise mere formation of organizations will not bring any change in their situation.

Several associations and centres for domestic workers all over the country are needed who are committed to the cause of women in domestic service. Such associations could assist workers in obtaining jobs, solving disputes between the employer and domestic worker, run awareness campaigns, and provide training and support to the workers in different work situations. These organizations could also have a separate recruiting unit to help find jobs and a mechanism where prospective employers and domestic workers could register themselves. A formal contract authorized by the labour department could be signed before starting a job and specifically lay down terms and conditions of employment mentioning working hours, paid holiday, wages and job responsibilities. To keep a record of regular wage payments, a register signed or thumb stamped by both the employer and employee could be maintained. This strategy would help in binding the employer to give wages on time and on a regular basis. It could also stop them from making unreasonable deductions from salaries. However, the need remains to pursue these initiatives and keep them working and alive for the cause of women in domestic service.

Women domestic workers organizations in Pakistan could also benefit from the experiences and various strategies adopted by organizations working at the international level for instance 'INTERCEDE' in Canada, 'KALAYAAN' in the UK, 'Break the Chain Campaign for Domestic Workers Rights' in the US to name a few. Learning from the experiences of organizations in South Asia is also important. The National Women Domestic Workers Movement in India (NDWM) which has played an important role in organizing domestic workers in fifteen major parts of India is a case in point.[8] The NDWM has a sister organization in Bangalore, Karnataka (KDWM) with over five hundred thousand members from all over India and 10,000 members in Mumbai. The organization is trying to pressurize the government through protest rallies and meetings to guarantee their rights. In 1998, the Maharashtra government tabled the Domestic Workers' Bill, which is still pending. The organization is also pressing government to recognize them as labourers so that they receive basic rights under labour laws of the country. The NDWM and KDWM are two examples which suggest that organizing domestic workers in Pakistan is also possible where the socio-economic position, conditions and nature of work is more or less similar to India.

Apart from organizations/associations, the need for employment agencies can also not be overlooked. In a megacity like Karachi there is only one employment exchange for domestic workers. These agencies can help both the employers and employees in finding suitable jobs. However, the agencies must keep their fee structure to reasonable levels as both employers and domestics avoid registering with agencies due to the fee charged. It is also important to remember that the role of agencies is controversial because there have been cases in some countries where agencies trap women and charge them huge amounts of fees in lieu of jobs. But if agencies are registered with the government and a strict check is kept on their performance only then can they play a positive role in finding jobs for women domestic workers.

Organizing through 'women collectives', though an idealistic solution, still carries weight. Makeshift cooking and child-care arrangements would give women an opportunity to use their spare time in developing their skills or in earning more income. There are already some communal systems in vogue among these communities such as pooling their money in the form of monthly 'committees' or helping women to find jobs through relatives, community members and neighbours. Therefore, suggestions such as a collective kitchen, childcare and laundries would not be some thing totally alien to their culture. As most of the domestic workers live in the same localities, therefore, they can organize collectively to do their daily household chores by distributing it amongst themselves. This would also help women in taking decisions and enhancing their organizational skills.

DOMESTIC WORK AS A SERVICE INDUSTRY

An important question that arises here is whether today's domestic worker's job situation can be improved and developed into a career of multiple jobs? Can domestic work in other households be organized as a formal service industry?

Firstly to organize it as a separate sector in the service industry, it is important to recognize domestic work as a form of productive labour. Women domestic workers are producers, contributing towards society through their services. To gain recognition as a service industry, the domestic worker should be included in the definition of a 'worker' in all legislation pertaining to employment. This would secure a stronger position for them and ensure protection through various legislative provisions, social security, maternity benefits, working hours, etc.

As domestic work is so rarely recognized as 'work', promoting the training and professional recognition of domestic workers would be a great boost to their status. Becoming professionalized is another step in this regard, as it would further lead to a formal job structure and give respect to them as workers. Training or skill enhancement would increase their chances of better salaries. Raising workers' skills and status would also improve their bargaining position with employers. It is also pertinent that women in domestic service must be offered some informal basic literacy courses in which they can at least learn to read and write. These courses or informal schools could be run in their communities/residential areas where women could come and attend in the evenings or on a day-off.

Singh in her study of domestic workers in Delhi suggests that 'proper and need-based kind of worker's education and training programmes' will enhance workers work efficiency and the quality of services.[9] This could be in the form of a cooking and childcare training, a basic hygiene course, and use of electric appliances. In South Africa a massive training project named as 'The Domestic Workers Skills Development Project' has been launched and financed by the Department of Labour's National Skills Fund to the tune of Rs 120 million, the project aims to train twenty seven thousand domestic workers around the country over the next three years. Trainees will receive formal recognition for their skills.[10]

Chances of upward mobility are slim among women domestic workers without providing any training and basic literacy. Many of them aspire to have better jobs but are at the same time aware of their limitations and realize that if the same state of affairs continues, their chances for advancement are slim. This suggests the need for some kind of skill development training and basic literacy skills. There are organizations in Pakistan that are providing basic literacy skills at an informal level to poor children who do not have access to schools as well as working towards improving the state of schools from the general maintenance level to curriculum development and teacher training. The Idara-i-Taleem-o-Agahi or 'Centre for Education and Consciousness Public Trust' in Lahore is one such example that is providing exemplary services in the education sector. It's 'Adopt a School' and 'School Improvement Network Pakistan' (SINP) programmes have helped in both public and private sector education in improving the school system in Pakistan. Such organizations can extend their programmes to include the children of women in domestic service and can offer some basic literacy courses for these women as well.

For upward mobility of women in domestic service, the possibility of extending small loans to them can be looked at, which might help them in learning some other skills such as sewing or any other home-based activity that can be done along side their jobs as domestic workers. The Orangi Pilot Project is one such example which is known for its community development work and income generating programmes for the urban poor in Orangi town, Karachi.[11] Apart from its activities of providing low cost housing, health, family planning and education, it has also helped women *zari* workers by providing loans under its 'Banking with the Poor' project in collaboration with one of the leading banks in Pakistan.[12] The bank provided a loan through the cooperative society to fifty-four families of *zari* workers to make joint purchases of raw materials and arranging for marketing of the finished products thereby eliminating the intermediaries. Another very successful example is the Grameen Bank of Bangladesh which aims at empowering women in the forms of extending loans to establish their own small scale businesses. Involvement in such projects could be a source of upward mobility and can be an alternative job in particular when women in domestic service are unemployed. If women have an additional source of income, at least they would be in a position to meet basic needs of the family even when they are out of job.

By providing training and upgrading the profession, employers will also benefit because they would get better childcare and better domestic services. With well-trained domestic workers they will not have to worry about the safety of their children. Similarly, if trained workers are available employers will not have to change their domestic workers every now and then. With improved working conditions, domestic workers would also prefer to stay with one employer instead of frequently changing jobs. Moreover, training courses would also provide an opportunity to bring previously isolated workers together, and to organize themselves, either in their own or by joining a trade union.

AWARENESS-RAISING

Raising awareness among women in domestic service could be another non-legal strategy, which could help in implementation of any legislative provisions. Raising consciousness among vulnerable groups such as women domestic workers through training programmes, holding community meetings and discussion groups/support groups would also be helpful in organising this sector. An awareness of their own rights could lead to collective action because otherwise a domestic worker works within the closed environment of a private home where interaction with other co-workers is limited. Through such programmes they would become aware of the legal protection available to them. They could access information regarding health-care, safe working conditions and awareness/strategies for dealing with other social problems such as violence and sexual harassment. The organization that takes responsibility of organizing domestic workers could arrange for providing free legal aid and information on related issues.

This process of raising consciousness should not be limited to domestic workers as it is equally pertinent to make employers aware of the rights of domestic workers. A change in the thinking and attitude of employers is essential for improving the status of domestic workers.

The media can be a useful tool for raising consciousness and bringing issues of domestic workers to light and newspaper articles, radio and television talk shows and theatre can also be a useful. The women domestic workers organizations could regularly invite journalists to their seminars and group discussions so that the issue is continuously reported in the press.

A public acknowledgement of paid domestic work is also necessary to achieve social reform. In Latin America and in California, USA 30 March has been declared as 'Domestic Worker Appreciation Day'. Any such declaration could be a step forward in recognition of the services of domestic workers and in acknowledging that domestic workers must be protected and included in the definition of a 'worker'.[13] Another way of public acknowledgement could be that a diverse range of people such as journalists and activists should raise their voices on the issue of domestic workers. Only then it would not be perceived as merely a western agenda of 'human rights'. Diversity of concerned voices will present the issue from various perspectives.

Last but not least, what is required foremost is to raise the esteem in which domestic workers are held throughout society and everywhere in the world. This implies stronger awareness campaigns targeted at all sections of civil society including government officials as well as legislators.

ROLE OF THE STATE VIS-À-VIS LOCAL GOVERNMENT

In the present day world the political role of the state is now dominated by democratization, free and fair elections, good governance, and the protection of human rights. The state also has a role in providing primary education, health care, housing, water, and sanitation. The state cannot be absolved from its responsibilities of providing these basic facilities to its citizens. Women domestic workers from all the four squatter settlements interviewed complained that they cannot afford to send their children to private schools, and state schools are either non-functional or not worth sending their children to. They have no money to buy schoolbooks and uniforms. Similarly, in most localities there are no health centres/hospitals and if there is, as in Baba Aileen, the doctors practice at the hospital for only two hours in the morning and after that patients have to visit his private clinic in the afternoon where he charges a fee for his services. Housing, water, and sanitation provisions in these areas are in an extremely poor condition.

Lack of basic civic amenities, healthcare and education systems further aggravates the miseries of women in domestic service. In countries such as the United Kingdom, local domestic workers at least have access to basic amenities of life. Free education to children, free healthcare and housing are provided by the state. It raises the concern whether the public in Pakistan has still not recovered from the colonial mindset that views government as rulers and not as service-providers. Is there a need to change the ethos of governance, so that those in government should consider themselves as service providers and not the ruling elite who cannot be challenged for their mismanagement? Improving the infrastructure by providing civic amenities, school and health-care system is the responsibility of the government. By improving the general living conditions of these workers and by providing a simple decent living standard, some of their main problems could be solved and it would be taking a burden off their shoulders.

A unique institutionalized approach for welfare system has been laid down in Islam through *Zakat, ushr* and *sadaqat.*[14] Pakistan is among one of the few Muslim states to operate an official *zakat* system.[15] *Zakat* is collected through banks and the Government of Pakistan has established a Central *Zakat* Council to oversee the collection and disbursement of *zakat* at federal, provincial, district and local levels. The *zakat* funds thus collected from the public could easily be utilized for the welfare of domestic workers. Labour welfare facilities such as unemployment allowance, financial assistance to disabled or disadvantaged workers, educational and health provisions for workers and their children can be financed from the *zakat* funds. Proper use of these resources can help in improving the situation of domestic workers in Pakistan.

The state could also play its role with the involvement of local government, which could be regarded as an instrument of democratic decentralization. The policy of devolution of power and authority to local governments (generally referred to as decentralization) is increasingly adopted and applied in many countries as one of the objectives of 'good governance'.[16] It is considered as a measure for democratization, peoples' empowerment and poverty reduction.

In Pakistan, the local government set-up was reinstalled in 2000. For the first time in the history of Pakistan, 40,000 women local councillors were elected to local bodies. A local government set-up is more responsive to the local needs of the community.[17] Local councillors can also be contacted easily. They can also provide more services than central government as they have more local knowledge of the social and economic position of the community and have a hold and a say in the community.

Local government is a possible avenue to be considered in improving the status of women domestic workers. Bearing in mind the limitations of women domestic workers, this local government platform could be an easily accessible way out for domestic workers before approaching the formal court structure. Local councillors could they act as mediators between employers and domestic workers, in case of any dispute, as it is easier to access them. A complaint cell could be set-up at the local council level which also should have provision for providing legal aid in serious matters where an issue cannot be resolved by mediation and needs to be taken up to the courts. Local councillors could come forward to listen to the complaints of a large section of their constituency otherwise they might lose their vote bank and would not be in a position to win elections. The more councillors get involved in serving the people it might also bring a change in the attitudes of those who do not either allow women to vote or participate in the election process seriously. However, there is a need to strengthen the institution of local government and the women councillors need to be given authority and respect, so that when they act as mediators their views would be heard and accepted by the parties involved. They should not be stopped from intervening on the pretext that it is an issue which involves the privacy of a household.

A council of domestic workers could also be formed at every district council level which includes members from the workers, employers, and local councillors. The council could work in collaboration with the provincial labour departments that could oversee matters and provide guidance. Local government could also be given the task of registering domestic workers. It is an important measure that must be done by involving local government institutions. Councillors could be given the responsibility of registering domestic workers in their area. Registration of these workers by local councils will help in maintaining a record of the number of workers in each area.

The institution of local government may not work wonders for domestic workers but it could be a beginning, a step forward on a long road. However, handing over adjudicating powers to the local councils may have adverse repercussions as this could lead to the establishment of a parallel judicial system, whereas past experience has shown that it has never worked in favour of women. To what extent a local councillor could act as a mediator is yet to be determined, as well as how they could be an effective source to which domestic workers could turn to for redress of their complaints. It will have to be seen whether councillors could play an impartial role by taking decisions against the powerful in the community.

TOWARDS A LEGAL POLICY FRAMEWORK[18]

As discussed above, domestic workers in Pakistan are not covered under labour laws of the country.[19] The foremost task would be to include domestic workers in the definition of the 'Worker' in all employment related laws.[20] There are no contractual arrangements between the employer and the employee. In the absence of any written contractual arrangements, their jobs remain insecure as they can be thrown out without any prior notification. As part of a legal framework for domestic workers, an employment contract, with all terms and conditions clearly mentioned, could be signed between the employer and employee.[21] Both parties could also have the right to terminate the contract and a one-month notice given for termination of the contract. In case of a gross mistake committed by the employee, or under any such circumstances in which the stay of the employee is harmful for the employer, the employer could substitute period of notice by paying to the employee the corresponding amount, in which case, the employee must leave the accommodation within twenty-four hours. The compensation/substitute could be half of the monthly salary multiplied by number of years of service. If she has worked for less than a year and for more than three months, then one-month salary could be paid in the absence of a termination notice. Similarly, if being mistreated or injured by the employer, the employee could also terminate the contract and be given compensation.

The legislative cover could include minimum wages for domestics and specify working conditions such as hours of work, overtime pay, salary increases, deductions, annual and sick leave. The wages women domestic workers receive must not be below the minimum wage standard. Women who perform part-time domestic jobs must not receive less than Rs 500 per task. They should also receive double pay on Sundays or public holidays and an annual increase of 8 per cent. Domestic workers should be entitled to severance pay of one week for each year of service. All employers could be required to register their employees for the Old Age Benefit Scheme. A contribution of 1 per cent at least by both employers and domestic workers towards the fund must be made. Another possibility of determining minimum wage could be on the basis of areas where domestic work is performed. The well-off areas can have a higher minimum wage rate compared to middle-income groups and working class areas.

Legislation should also regulate working hours. Live-in workers domestic workers could work no more than forty-five hours a week. They should not work more than nine hours a day if they work a five-day week or more than eight hours a day if they work for more than five days a week. Domestics could work not more than fifteen hours per week overtime, and not more than three hours on any one day. There could also be a provision for eight to nine hours rest-time at night. They could also be given an hour's lunch break and half an hour tea break in the evening. Live-in staff could be entitled to a twenty-four-hour weekly rest period or, in other words, a full one-day off every week. They could also be provided with a reasonable accommodation and sufficient healthy food. Rest periods, holiday and sickness leave provisions could also be extended to domestic workers who do not live in the house of the employer.

Employers whose domestics live on the property may deduct 5 per cent of their salary for accommodation, subject to the condition that accommodation complies with minimum standards laid down in the legislation. A one-month paid sickness leave could also be given to employees who have served the employer for a period of twelve months. In case of less than one-year employment a one day leave for seventeen days of work. Employer must ensure that the employee receives all necessary medical care. If at the end of this leave the employee cannot return to work or gets sick again, the employee should be given the chance to provide a substitute in her place until she is in a position to resume her job, otherwise the employer has the right to terminate the contract without indemnity to the employee. In case of maternity, an employee who has served for more than a year must be entitled to one month paid maternity leave as well as four months' unpaid maternity leave. An employee must be entitled to a five-day-per-year family responsibility leave.

Framing a law in itself will not be sufficient, as the mechanisms of implementation and protection to women domestic workers need to be considered. In Pakistan, there are separate labour tribunals for deciding labour disputes. However, these tribunals are already overburdened by the caseload. One possibility to avoid delays could be in the form of setting up a separate tribunal for domestic workers. These tribunals could be setup at the district and divisional level and work under the supervision of every provincial High Court. During the past two years, the Supreme Court of Pakistan has started taking *suo moto* actions through which it has intervened in areas where there has been gross violation of human rights as well as violation of laws made in the social sector.[22] The Supreme Court on the basis of *suo moto* action can directly take up any case where there is a violation of domestic workers rights. Certain codes of practice or guidelines could also be laid down by the courts. These may not have the same force as legislation but may be strengthened if issued by courts and adopted as statements of good practice.

It is also important to examine the various routes through which a complaint can be lodged. The aggrieved party could either file a suit itself with the support of the workers' association or local council. The possibility of setting up of an Ombudsman's office can also be considered. Although the Ombudsmen offices in different countries across the world look into complaints mostly about government departments and its agencies, it is yet to be seen whether the same offices could be used for complaints against employers in the private sector and vice versa.[23] A suitable procedure for lodging complaints could be adopted. Is an individual complaint a better way out or would a class/representative action procedure be a good strategy for handling cases especially those where discriminatory practice exists against a particular group or affecting a large group of people.

Finally, before formulating a legal framework it is important to initiate a consultative process involving activists, government officials, legislators, domestic workers, and employers. It would also be beneficial to take the opinion of the members of Tripartite Labour Conference who are negotiating with the government on the new labour policy and are also involved in the process of codification of labour laws in the country.

Coordination among policy makers, legislators, non-governmental organizations, and researchers is also vital. Legislators and policy makers could bear in mind the rural/urban settings in which the domestic workers work. There is a huge difference in the work environment and the terms and conditions of domestic work in urban and rural areas as in the later case domestic workers work in lieu of kind rather than cash for their services. In rural areas, domestic work is also often closely linked with debt bondage where women and children are forced to work without getting a single penny in return for debts taken by the family. The data from the field clearly shows that wages are decided not only based on the nature of work performed but also depend on the area/vicinity where the domestic worker is employed. Those working in posh areas are expected to get more for the same kind of job as compared to those who work in a middle class locality.

CONCLUSION

As discussed in earlier chapters, women domestic workers earn below the minimum wage level and live at a sub-subsistence level. Any attempt to change their poverty situation and poor working conditions in today's economy is an uphill task because the social and economic fabric of the country is biased and favours the rich. Any change in the present structure would be possible by recognising and validating the 'worker role' and by organising women workers and enhancing their collective strength.

This chapter has looked into various possibilities of organizing and providing legal protection to women domestic workers in Pakistan. It has analysed the various ways that could help in improving their working conditions. Concerted effort on part of the state and its institutions, women's movement, NGOs, human rights activists, employers and domestic workers themselves is needed to make that change possible and to project a stronger voice for the rights of domestic workers. New strategies have to be devised and new avenues explored for providing support and protection to these workers. One such avenue that has been explored is the institution of local government but pros and cons of the local government setup must be borne in mind before assigning the task to it.

A legislative framework is also needed so that domestic workers get recognition as 'workers' under labour law and can claim their rights. However, legislation alone is not going to work unless other support systems are put in place as only then access to justice for women domestic workers in Pakistan would be possible. In light of discussions on domestic workers in Chapter 4 and data from the field in Chapter 6, there is considerable optimism that an organized 'voice' and legal policy responses, will be able to change the terms on which women domestic workers are employed and improve their living and work conditions.

NOTES

1. Cohen, R., supra note 65, ch. 2, p. 197.
2. As the families cannot afford to have a telephone line at home they prearrange a time and either go to the telephone exchange or go to a well-off neighbour or house of the village head who has a telephone. It was also interesting to note that women domestic workers were aware of telephone calling cards and were using it.
3. Cf., see chapter 5.
4. The term 'dislocation' has been used by Parrenas, R.S., supra note 2, ch. 2.
5. Women's Protection Act 2006.
6. The case of Zafran Bibi is a clear example of the harm caused by the Hudood Ordinance. This woman was charged with adultery and sentenced to death by stoning by the local court, as she was unable to provide four male witnesses. Due to immense pressure from the women activist groups, the Federal Shariat Court overturned the sentence on technical grounds but the law that led to her conviction still remains in effect and continues to be a major source of abuse against women. Such types of cases reflect the attitude of the lower judiciary which often is biased and discriminatory against women. The danger involved in this sort of approach is that due to the presence of restrictive and misinterpreted interpretations of Islam, women are denied most of their rights even those guaranteed by Islam itself—let alone the ones guaranteed by the Constitution.
7. The LHRLA carried out a survey on domestic workers in Karachi that has been discussed in chapter 2. It also organized a two-day 'National Consultation on Domestic Workers Rights' in September 2003 in which it submitted a proposal for drafting legislation for domestic workers.
8. 'National Women Domestic Movement' in India and 'Association for Women Domestic Workers' in Bangladesh are working for the cause of women domestic workers in their respective countries. The NDWM now has 100,000 members and has opened counselling centres for abused workers and helps domestic workers find work with a list of employers.
9. Singh, A. N. (2001), *Women Domestic Workers: Socio- Economic Life*, New Delhi: Shipra Publications, p. 125.
10. The training is being overseen by the Services Sector Education and Training Authority (Seta), which has set up a discrete chamber for domestic services, based in Port Elizabeth in the Eastern Cape.
11. http://www.urckarachi.org/orangi.htm.
12. *Zari* work is fancy hand-made embroidery with fine glittery thread of gold or silver.
13. Sotelo, P.H., supra note 22, ch. 2, pp. 241-2.
14. *Zakat* means obligatory charitable wealth tax, *Ushr* is tax on agricultural produce, *Sadaq*at is non-obligatory charity.
15. The government of Pakistan's *Zakat* and *Ushr* Ordinance (1980) mandates that 2.5 per cent of the value of all declared, fixed assets for those possessing *Nisaab* (assets) are to

be automatically deducted at source by the state as *Zakat* at the beginning of the Islamic holy month of Ramadan.

16. Many developing countries in South Asia and in West Africa have adopted the decentralization of power through local government setup. For detailed accounts on different local governments, see Crook, R. and Manor J. (1998), *Democracy and Decentralisation in South Asia and West Africa: Participation, Accountability, and Performance*, Cambridge, New York: Cambridge University Press; Sharma, K.C. (1995), 'Critical Issues in Local Government Management and Development Related to Central-local Government Relations in Botswana: Lessons of Relevance for Restructuring of Local Government in Post-apartheid South Africa,' in Reddy, P.S. (ed.), *Perspectives on Local Government Management and Development in Africa*, Pinetown: Kohler Carton and Print; Aril, S. (2000), 'Democratic Local Government and Responsiveness: Lessons from Zimbabwe and Tanzania,' in Tukumbi, Lumumba Kasongo (ed.), *Dynamics and Policy Implications of Global Reforms at the End of Second Millennium*, Leiden: Brill; Geldenhuys, A.J. (1996), 'Analysing Democracy for Local Government,' in Bekker, K. (ed.), *Citizen Participation in Local Government*, Pretoria: J.L. van Schaik; Ikhide, S. (1999), 'Local Government Finance and Accountability: A Case Study of Selected Local Government Areas in Nigeria,' in Olowu, D. et al. (eds.), *Governance and Democratisation in West Africa*, Dakar, Senegal: CODESRIA.
17. Report on The State of Women in Urban Local Government, Pakistan. Available at: http://www.unescap.org/huset/women/reports/pakistan.pdf.
18. This section draws upon information from domestic workers laws adopted by countries such as Argentina's 'Decree Law No. 326/56 on Domestic Workers' and South Africa's 'The Domestic Workers Act.'
19. The proposed drafts of the 'Wages Act 2003', 'Draft Labour Protection Policy 2005' and the 'Condition of Employment Act 2003' have excluded agriculture and domestic workers from its definition of the worker under the codification of labour laws programme. The Finance Act 2006 which amends several labour acts relating to workmen's compensation, industrial and commercial employment, companies profits, minimum wages for unskilled workers, workers' welfare fund, and employees' old-age benefits also does not include domestic workers. For further details see [Part I] *The Gazette Of Pakistan*, Extra, 1 July 2006, 183.
20. The term 'domestic worker' could include nannies, housemaids, child carers/governesses, helpers/handy people, laundresses, drivers, cooks, and gardeners working in a private home (either with a single person or a family).
21. The contract could include; the full name and address of the employer, the name and occupation of the domestic worker, or a brief description of the work for which he/she is employed, the place of work, and where he/she is required or permitted to work, date of employment, the domestic worker's ordinary hours of work and days of work, the domestic worker's wage or rate and method of payment, the rate of pay for overtime work, any other cash payments he/she is entitled to, any payment in kind he/she is entitled to and the value of payment in kind, how frequently wages will be paid, any deductions to be made from wages, the leave he/she is entitled to, the period of notice required to terminate employment, or if employment is for a specified period, the date when employment is to be terminated.
22. The Supreme Court of Pakistan has taken *suo moto* action on a number of social issues. A ban on serving meals at weddings is imposed under the Marriage Ordinance; however, there have been blatant violations of this law. Another important case is of tribal practice of *vani* and *swara* in which the federal government has been asked to amend Section 310 of the Pakistan Penal Code or the Family Act, 1964, to provide for

dissolution of marriages of women given in *vani* or *sawara*. All these cases suggest that the judiciary is playing a proactive role in upholding the rights of individuals and in having existing laws implemented. For reports on these cases visit www.dawn.com/National; 25 April 2006.htm

23. For information on Ombudsman offices in various regions of the world, visit http://www.law.ualberta.ca/centres/ioi/eng/eng_home.html.

Conclusion

This study has shown that lives of women domestic workers in Pakistan depict the picture of those trapped in a circle of poverty and deprived of basic facilities of life. Their basic human needs remain unfulfilled due to lack of attention and indifferent attitude of the state, civil society and individual employers. By its nature being an 'invisible' form of work the total number of those working as domestic workers, remains largely unknown in Pakistan.

The main recommendation of this study is that as an important initial step towards empowering this category of women a countrywide survey should be undertaken by the government. Any strategy for improving the situation of women domestic workers is dependent on this information.

The study highlights the fact that women domestic workers both in developed as well as in developing countries suffer discrimination in terms of low wages, long working hours, harassment in the workplace and double burdens of work. Above all, as domestic service is performed in the privacy of a home they face numerous difficulties in the absence of any legal protection and support structures. In most of the countries across the North-South divide they are marginalized, remain invisible, and are not included in labour statistics and the labour framework. Due to the lack of any legal coverage they remain at the mercy of their employers. This feeling of constant insecurity adversely affects their living conditions and their capabilities.

Despite all hardships and being in a vulnerable situation these women continue to struggle hard for themselves and for their families. Though unorganized in the formal sense, they resist the oppressive system in their own way. Although such a struggle may not appear very sustainable and the process of change could be very slow and arduous, it has created some space and tolerance for the work done by women. Many women interviewed in Peshawar stated, that (irrespective of the fact that they are pushed into this world of work due to extreme poverty), there is now a wider acceptance of women going out of the house to earn a living for the sake of their children and to support their husbands. This indicates a change in women's role from housewives to earners but with the proviso that legitimacy for their work is rarely given when a woman seeks to improve her quality of life.

The data from the fieldwork also suggests that the work of these women gives them a sense of achievement and pride as they are able to contribute towards the family income and improving their living conditions. Women domestic workers have the potential to strategize and organize themselves but they need the support of local expertise and organizations to help them in their initial organization. From thereon they could further link up with other local, regional, and later on even international organizations.

Networking has the potential for advancing the interests of women domestic workers, as bringing any revolutionary change in their lives is not possible, yet with combined effort and support a gradual but steady change in their day-to-day lives is possible. The need to hire domestic workers has increased with more women involved in carrying out economic activities outside their homes and no sharing of household chores by male members of the family. Not only in terms of division of labour but also due to the poor socio-economic conditions of a large section of the population, domestic service is likely to continue. Therefore, there is a strong need to strategize so that working conditions for these women domestic workers may be improved.

The present study further explored the limits of the law as an effective process and mechanism for empowerment of women domestic workers. Due to the presence and strong influence of the informal laws/plural legal norms, any effort to empower women through black letter law will remain ineffective and would have little acceptability and ownership amongst the people. It is therefore suggested that an engagement with the formal law would be effective only by adopting a broader framework. In the words of Davies:

> What is common to all the post-positivist approaches to legal change…is an emphasis on fundamental transformations in the meanings of law, and a view that mere evolution in doctrine is insufficient if the goal is to achieve significant change in social relationships and values. That does not mean that law reform is always meaningless—clearly it is frequently of great significance—but that it needs to be framed by a broader context of legal and social transition.[1]

This study has shown that black letter law alone cannot provide enough protection to these workers because, the employers in comparison to women in domestic service, are in a privileged position and can easily flout the law. It is already seen in the case of other informal workers that, despite the protection provided by the labour laws, employers have violated, changed, and misused the law for their own vested interest. Legislation or court's guidelines and directives of policy makers would only be effective when a multi-pronged strategy is adopted.

Women respondents in their interviews expressed their approval of the court system as compared to any other informal mechanism but they are a bit wary of approaching the courts due to the fact that these being located in the 'public sector,' cannot be easily accessed by women. Without having any idea of how the court system works, and in the absence of legal aid, it is extremely difficult for them to approach the formal legal system.

A further recommendation of the study is to give recognition to domestic work as real work like any other form of employment and to treat domestic workers as real workers under the labour code. The blurring of the line between 'worker' and 'part of the family' leaves much room for abuse and exploitation of women domestic workers. It is therefore proposed to include domestic workers in the definition of a 'worker', and like other countries such as Argentina and South Africa, to regulate the working conditions of domestic workers and a separate legislative code could be framed.

The original contribution of this study has been the attempt to provide a deeper insight into the lived realities of women domestic workers in Pakistan. It has raised the question of the efficacy of black letter law as a tool for empowerment and has attempted to explore different strategies for improving women domestic workers' situations. Besides, it has highlighted the issue of women domestic workers in Pakistan as the literature reviewed itself explains the dearth of research studies and surveys on domestic workers in the country. The government and civil society members could use this study to pressurise policy makers to include domestic workers under the labour legislation, as well as to look into the means of making access to justice possible for them.

Though a ground breaking study, it still has its limitations. It is only the first step in the direction of addressing the complex situation of women domestic workers in Pakistan and there is still room for further research in this area. There are wide variations among this category of workers for instance women domestic workers in rural areas, bonded domestic labour, and child domestic labour. These categories are not fully explored in this study. The issue of class hierarchy is addressed to a certain extent but due to its ideological underpinnings it needs to be further explored. Regulating a form of work carried out in the privacy of home also requires a deeper analysis into mechanisms for scrutiny and surveillance. Further in-depth studies and surveys could be carried out to address the above mentioned shortcomings of the study. This would in turn help in listening to hitherto unheard voices of women domestic workers in Pakistan.

NOTE

1. Davies, M. (2003), 'Legal Theory and Law Reform,' *Alternative Law Journal*, Vol. 28, p. 170.

Appendix 1
Objective of the Study

Researcher's Role: Interaction between the Researcher and Researched

In the present study I had multiple roles as a researcher. My role in group discussions was of moderator/facilitator, a listener for individual interviews as well as some of them viewed from my position of an employer. As a moderator/facilitator I was only raising questions and issues, which were then discussed in the form of group interaction It has been mentioned in many case studies carried out with diverse groups that there is always a power dynamic that operates between the researcher and the researched. While collecting data from the field I also felt the same power dynamics working in the case of women domestic workers and myself as an employer. My own position as a person who has been using the services of women domestic workers in the past was in sharp contrast to my present role of researching their lives. I had to adopt a conscious approach of looking at the issue of domestic workers from a different angle by keeping my own personal biases aside. The distance women domestic workers cover everyday on foot in the scorching heat of summer or on chilly winter mornings made me realize the unsympathetic attitude of the employer who scolds the worker for not arriving on time for work.

I noticed that since I had lived in Peshawar, women domestic workers in that city were initially careful in discussing their relations with employers due to the fear that their opinions may be disclosed to their employers. To check my sincerity and commitment to the cause of women domestic workers I was assessed by them in various ways. In the initial group meetings I could see women whispering amongst themselves regarding the purpose of my research, how was it going to benefit them and whether I was doing this research at the behest of government or some other agency. To overcome this barrier I used different strategies. I explained the purpose of the research study as discussed in the section on ethical issues. I also assured them that their identities would not be disclosed. On every visit I also consciously kept my appearance very modest so that they would not be under the fear of talking to a 'Begum Sahib'.[1]

Domestic workers are always expected to sit on the floor and are not allowed to sit in a chair next to their employers. To make them sit on the floor is a constant reminder from the employer that a domestic worker belongs to a lower category and cannot be at par with their employers in any respect. I made it a point to sit with them on the floor so that they could feel relaxed in my presence and overcome any inhibitions or feeling of class difference between us. However, I feel that there was one positive aspect of my privileged position of coming from a different class background, as it provided an edge to me in the sense that men (male relations of woman domestic workers) from the community did not resist/object to my presence. They were in a weak position because of their low socio-economic position to challenge my presence in their homes or to stop their women from participating in the discussions. Another important factor that could be a reason for non-resistance from the communities I approached was that for many of them it was the first time in their lives that someone had approached them to listen to their voices. In all four research sites I found that women in every community were very keen to talk to me and discuss their problems. Women were thankful and time and again expressed their gratitude as it was the first time that some one had taken interest in what they do and what their problems and needs are. From their response it was clear that they wanted to raise their concerns. I could see that they were desperate about their situation and were looking for a way out. This experience also gave them some hope for the future and has in return helped me in gaining their confidence and build up a relationship based on trust.

Research Settings and Characteristics of Samples

This study was carried out in two phases, from May to June 2003 and then from March to June 2004. The first phase was exploratory in nature and it was utilized for the purpose of identifying research settings and initiating contacts with prospective respondents. This phase was also used for testing my sample research questions with a small group of women domestic workers and helped me in reformulating and revising some of the questions in the second phase of interviews.

The empirical data was collected in two urban settings.[2] As it was not possible to cover women domestic workers working in all the four provinces in Pakistan, I chose two cities and some particular communities within each city to represent the religious and ethnic diversity among women domestic workers. I started my empirical research in Karachi which is a cosmopolitan city located in southern Pakistan and is home to many domestic workers who migrate to this city from the interior parts of the country.[3] It was therefore easy to contact women domestic workers belonging to different ethnic groups. The city's population has grown at an enormous rate and at present it comprises fourteen million people.[4]

Karachi as a city is governed by the City District Government of Karachi (CDGK) and has an elected city council that looks after the working of the CDGK.[5] It is the chief financial, commercial and manufacturing centre where people from other parts of the country migrate in search of job opportunities. Adjacent to all upper and middle class residential areas are urban squatter settlements where migrant workers and poor residents of the city live. The proximity of these slums to the residential areas facilitates women working as domestic workers in nearby areas.

In Karachi, I interviewed women domestic workers who work in the affluent localities of Defence Housing Society and Clifton and live in a squatter settlement called Hijrat colony, which is an illegal settlement near the Clifton railway track. Clifton is a mixture of commercial offices and residential apartment buildings and private houses. In sharp contrast to modern skyscrapers and expansively designed and decorated bungalows (with all sorts of amenities for comfortable and luxurious life styles), Hijrat Colony presents the picture of a completely neglected area with no basic amenities. The sewerage conditions are extremely poor: heaps of garbage can be seen near the railway track and rain water ponds serve as a breeding place for mosquitoes and flies. The word *hijrat* means 'migration' and as such, reflects the status of its residents. The inhabitants consist of migrants mainly from Punjab, North-West Frontier Province, some from interior Sindh, as well as some Urdu speaking people who migrated from India to Pakistan after creation of Pakistan in 1947. There are around 4000 to 5000 households in this area. Most of the residents live in rented premises. The rent of a single room quarter is Rs1000.[6] The quarter comprises a room and small *sehen* (courtyard) which serves the purposes of an open kitchen and a toilet in the corner. There is no piped water in the quarters and women have to fetch water from the hand pumps installed in the streets. There is a small market and a school close by. As it is an illegal settlement there is no government basic health unit and since it is very close to the residential side of Clifton therefore most of the domestic workers walk down to the employer's house. Those who work at a distance from their employer's house either take the local transport or they leave home early to walk to the place of work hereby saving the bus fare which ranges from Rs10 to Rs30 per day according to the distance travelled.

During this exploratory trip I also found that a number of women domestic workers come and work from a belt of small islands located in the Arabian Sea near Karachi. Bhit Islands in Karachi was the second site where I contacted two women domestic workers from that area and after interviewing them I decided to carry out my field research in one of those islands as well. Here I was able to discover some very interesting issues faced by women domestic workers coming from these islands. Bhit Islands is a belt of six small Islands inhabited by a population of more than 30,000 Kutchi Memon communities [7] Men in this community have been fishermen for generations. Fishing is their only source of income. As the men are seasonal workers and remain unemployed for the remaining period, women from these islands are forced to work as domestic workers, as being unskilled and illiterate they have no other job options. They travel daily by boat to work in Karachi There is only one secondary school and a government hospital with no facilities for emergency and laboratory tests in their area. A serious problem faced by the community is lack of water: every day they have to purchase water, which is brought from Karachi and sold for Rs5 to Rs10 per seven gallons.[8] Residents of Bhit Islands have little access to electricity and piped gas because of which the islanders have no alternative but to use kerosene oil which is a very expensive alternative for a poverty ridden community. Electric supply, wherever available, remains unreliable due to non-maintenance and load shedding. Although gas and other amenities are available in a nearby naval base in Manora, the adjacent island presents a picture of complete neglect by civic authorities. A small telephone exchange has only seventy-one extensions on Baba Island with only forty-five lines operational. If a caller uses a line, the remaining forty-four people have to wait for him to finish his conversation. However, one benefit that this community has received from the government so far is that during the regime of former Prime Minister Benazir Bhutto, the government allotted the land to the residents and enabled them to construct their own houses.

My second site was Peshawar and during the preliminary field trip, I interviewed five Pathan and five Christian women domestic workers. Peshawar is my hometown and it was more convenient to gain access to these workers due to my familiarity of the area. Peshawar is a frontier town and the meeting place of the subcontinent and Central Asia. It is the capital of North-West Frontier Province. It has an area of 1257 sq km and a population of more than 950,000. City District Peshawar consists of 25 Union Councils. These councils were the part of the then Municipal Corporation, Peshawar. The provincial metropolis is divided into three main residential areas: the old city, cantonment, and the new residential localities such as Hayatabad Township and University Town, where most of the women interviewed work as domestic workers. Peshawar has historical, military and political importance because of the Khyber Pass, which has remained a gateway for invaders of the subcontinent through the centuries.[9]

In Peshawar, Acheena Village was the first site where women domestic workers were contacted. This is a small village, part of the tribal belt, and lies on the outskirts of Hayatabad Township. The village is divided by a canal in two parts. The poor community in the village comprises of small farmers and labourers.[10] As the earnings are very low, women also go out of their homes to seek employment. The land is owned by landlords and farmers work as tenants. The produce is divided equally between the landlord, and the farmer (provided the farmer shares the costs of seed, fertilizer and irrigation with the landlord). There are five brick kilns as well where some of the men and children work, but here, unlike in the Punjab, women do not work as brick kiln workers. Compared to Hijrat Colony and Bhit Islands this village is comparatively clean and heaps of garbage are not visible, probably as most of the residents are living here for many years and it is a settled community. The village comprises of both mud and bricked houses. People in the village are happy with the local councillors as they have reopened the school, and now there are permanent staff in the school. Electricity and water is also available in every house.

The interviews taken in this area were not formal in nature and were more in the form of discussions. I asked semi-structured questions to explore major themes and issues related to domestic work in Pakistan. Findings from the preliminary field trip made me change the focus of my research from merely suggesting a legal framework to questioning the efficacy of law as a tool for empowerment for women domestic workers in Pakistan. Besides discussing issues like employment conditions, nature of work, working hours, relations with employers and harassment at workplace, I could also identify to what extent gender and class hierarchies affect domestic workers' lives in Pakistan.

The second phase was the main or principal phase in which in-depth interviews were carried out for the purposes of data collection. The choice of research sites for the main phase was made on the basis of first/exploratory phase and by taking into consideration the fact that women domestic workers in Pakistan have multiple identities therefore an attempt was made to make the sample representative of as many ethnic and religious groups as possible. However, this sample does not claim to be representative of all the segments of domestic workers in the country. Due to time and monetary constraints I could not broaden the universe of this study and had to confine it only to the two urban areas in Pakistan.

This research is primarily based on fully transcribed semi-structured group and individual interviews that have been tape-recorded and in some cases through note-taking. Group interviews were carried out in the form of two to three-hour discussion sessions, whereas individual interviews lasted for sixty to ninety minutes. Some of the individual interviews were conducted in two or three sittings. Most of the interviews were carried out in the evenings when women domestic workers were at home, while some of the interviews with live-in domestic workers were carried out on Sundays when they came to visit their family or friends.

Women domestic workers working for upper, upper-middle class and middle-class families were chosen for interviews to show the different class structures as well as the importance of these workers in the running of households in Pakistani society. It was not possible to interview all women domestic workers therefore respondents for the interviews and the choice of squatter settlements was made bearing in mind the wide variations of age, marital status, ethnic and religious backgrounds. Due to this careful selection, I interviewed Punjabi migrant workers, Katchi Memons, Hindu workers, Pathan and Christian workers. The workers included both part-time workers, live-in workers and full-time workers.

The women interviewed in Karachi were mostly migrant workers from Punjab and interior Sindh. They had all come from villages either with their husbands or with their parents a few years earlier as young children. The main reason for migrating to the city being their extreme poverty combined with no employment opportunities in the villages. Whatever they earn in villages by working for the landlord is extremely inadequate to support their families. Compared to these women, the Pathan women I interviewed in Peshawar have a more settled life as they have been living in the same area for generations, whereas some of the Christian women I interviewed had their roots in the interior cities of Punjab but they had come to Peshawar in search of jobs.

At each site, twenty to twenty-five women were interviewed as a group. From amongst them, I chose four to five women for individual interviews at each site. (The five case studies included in the study are based on and selected from these individual interviews). The table below indicates the total number of women interviewed at each site, their age groups, and marital status.

Research Sites	Total Number of Interviewees	Age Groups	Marital Status
Bhit Islands, Karachi	20	2 (18-25) yrs	Married
		8 (25-35) yrs	1 Divorcee, 3 Widows, 4 Married
		6 (35-45) yrs	Married
		4 (45-60) yrs	2 Married, 2 Widows
Hijrat Colony, Karachi	25	3 (18-25) yrs	1 Unmarried, 2 Married
		9 (25-35) yrs	Married
		8 (35-45) yrs	1 Separated, 7 Married
		5 (45-60) yrs	1 Widow, 4 Married
Christian Colony, Peshawar	22	3 (18-25) yrs	Married
		8 (25-35) yrs	7 Married, 1 Separated
		9 (35-45) yrs	2 Widows, 7 Married
		(45-60) yrs	1 Married, 1 Widow
Acheena Village, Peshawar	23	1 (18-25) yrs	1 Unmarried
		7 (25-35) yrs	7 Married
		10 (35-45)yrs	7 Married, 3 Widows
		5 (45-60) yrs	3 Widows, 2 Married

By explaining my background and the purpose of my research, I was able to develop a relationship of trust, which is a prerequisite for conducting interviews. I started with group interviews with respondents. Group interviews also helped women domestic workers in understanding issues that I wanted to address further and discussions with other co-workers gave them an insight into their own situations about which they might not have thought before.

Patton argues that group interview is

> ...a highly efficient qualitative data collection technique which provides some quality controls on data collection in that participants tend to provide checks and balances on each other that weed out false or extreme views...and it is fairly easy to assess the extent to which there is a relatively consistent, shared view...among the participants.[11]

The group discussions/interviews helped in stimulating women to make explicit their own viewpoint. It also led to an active involvement of my respondents in the construction of data about their lives.

After gaining some confidence through group interviews my respondents were more expressive in individual interviews and were able to speak and express themselves about issues that they tried to avoid in the presence of other co-workers. The individual interviews thus helped in extracting information on issues that were otherwise difficult to address due to cultural constraints. The technique of conducting individual interviews provided more space to women to express themselves openly, and it also created an emotional engagement with their own situations of which they did not seem very conscious earlier. It helped in expressing their true feelings about the nature of work, self-perception, their real needs, and relationship with employers.

A few case studies are also included in this study to provide a better understanding of the lived realities of women in domestic service. Case studies are in Strauss's words used as 'illustrative data to give a sense of reality to the account, to make the viewpoint of respondents more clear and also as evidence to the theoretical assumptions of the study.'[12] Answering structured questions or using formal interviewing technique does not always help women in narrating their lived realities in their own way. Therefore talking about their life stories is a natural way for women to express their feelings and experiences and this in turn helps the researcher to understand the uniqueness of each story. From amongst the women domestic workers interviewed I was able to identify a few women whose life stories covered some of the specific issues raised in the present study.

The multi-pronged strategy of using group interviews, individual interview sessions, and case studies helped in addressing the research question in a more effective manner. In-depth information was obtained about the complex nature of domestic service, women's experiences in the workplace which is hidden within the privacy of homes. I was also able to learn about the various strategies adopted by women domestic workers to cope with their situations. Besides, that I had informal conversations with a few male and female family members of domestic workers. The purpose of talking to them was to understand their perception of women working in other households, and it also helped me in understanding gender dynamics within the household. Another benefit of getting these alternative perspectives was that it validated some of the data presented by women domestic workers.

Interviews with the employers were also carried out in both the cities, Karachi and Peshawar. All interviews were tape-recorded except for one person who preferred that I should transcribe her interview instead of recording it. Three of the employers were generous enough to allow me to interview their employees. The employers I talked to varied from housewives to professional women belonging to various age groups, with different class positions, various levels of educational qualifications and with different family arrangements. All the married women I talked to had children between the age of two and twenty years. The occupation of their husbands ranged from businessmen to doctors, engineers, lawyers, civil servants and teachers. Some employers live in apartments in multi-storied complexes while others lived in single and double-storied houses. The size of the houses varied from two to six bedrooms, some comfortably furnished while others were luxuriously furnished and located in upper class areas. Overall, the sample covered both middle and upper class households.

In total I interviewed ten housewives and ten professional women. The professional women were all highly qualified with university degrees in sciences, arts, and humanities, working as lawyers, teachers, doctors or activists working for different non-governmental organizations as well as office assistants with bachelors degree.[13] Three of the housewives I interviewed had only completed their high school education and were married at a young age; four housewives had bachelors degrees, while the rest were university graduates.[14] Three professional women were unmarried, one was a widow, and the rest of them were married.

Among the three unmarried professional women, one was living independently while the other two were living with their widowed mothers.

NOTES

1. It is a term used for a female employer. The term is generally employed to describe the wife of a person of means. It also denotes class difference as it places them on a superior level as compared to domestic worker who is hired by them to do household chores for them.
2. Due to time and monetary constraints, it was not possible to cover domestic workers in rural areas.
3. The city is located at the north-western edge of the Indus River delta. Karachi is the main financial and commercial hub of Pakistan. Due to industrialization, the city has created employment opportunities and attracted migrant workers from other parts of the country.
4. The breakdown of Karachi's population is as follows: men form 53.7 per cent of Karachiites; 37.6 per cent of men are under the age of 15; 4.4 per cent of men are older than 50; 70.1 per cent of men are literate; 22.1 per cent of men are migrants from other places. According to the 1998 census the linguistic break-up of the city is Urdu 48.52 per cent; Punjabi 13.94 per cent; Sindhi 7.22 per cent; Pushto 11.42 per cent; Balochi 4.34 per cent; Seraiki 2.11 per cent; Others 12.4 per cent. The others include Gujarati, Brahui and Bengali. According to the census the religious break-up of the city is as follows: Muslim 96.45 per cent; Christian 2.42 per cent; Hindu 0.83 per cent; Qadiani 0.17 per cent; Others 0.13 per cent. The others include Parsis and Buddhists.
5. There are 100 districts, 360 tehsils/towns, and 6022 union councils in Pakistan. The city district of Karachi is divided into eighteen towns each with its own council and Nazim. These towns are Baldia, Bin Qasim, Gadap, Gulberg, Gulshan, Jamshed, Kemari, Korangi, Landhi, Liaquatabad, Lyari, Malir, New Karachi, North Nazimabad, Orangi, Saddar, Shah Faisal, SITE.
6. Quarter is a term used for very small cemented houses. It can also be a separate portion for servants in the employer's house.
7. The six islands are Bhit Island, Baba Island, Younasabad and Salehabad, Shamspur and Kaka village.
8. Approximately 5 pence to 10 pence/gallon.
9. The old name of the city was 'Purushapura', was the capital of the ancient Greco-Buddhist centre of Gandhara. It was named Peshawar by the Mughal emperor, Akbar. For centuries, it was the target of successive Afghan, Persian, and Mongol invaders. In the early nineteenth century it was taken by the Sikhs from whom the British captured it in 1848. It became an important outpost of British India and was a base for British military operations against Pathan tribes. During the decade-long Soviet occupation of Afghanistan (1979-89) it was the centre of relief operations for Afghan refugees and the command centre of the coalition of guerrilla groups intent on expelling the Soviet forces from Afghanistan.
10. By the term 'poor' I mean people with lower earnings, and living below the poverty line. The average monthly income of these families varies between Rs 1000 to 2000, i.e. equivalent of £10 to £20 per month.
11. Patton, M.Q. (1990), 2nd ed., *Qualitative Evaluation and Research Methods*, London: Sage, pp. 335-336.
12. Strauss, A.L. (1987), *Qualitative Analysis for Social Scientists*, Cambridge: Cambridge University Press, p. 216.
13. A bachelor's degree is awarded after completing four years of education at college level. College in Pakistan starts after matriculation which is equivalent to GCSE or O level.
14. University Graduates are those who have attained a master's degree.

Appendix 2
Pre-Empirical Work Plan

Introduction

The fieldwork would be based on a case study of women domestic workers in Pakistan. The case study aims at learning about the experiences and general conditions of these women workers whose voices have remained unheard for a long time. In the field work I would like to find out to what an extent they have used formal legal system, whether these women workers have trust in the formal legal system, how much are they aware of it and if a legal cover is provided for domestic service would they be in a position to use it? Raising these questions would contribute towards addressing the main research question, i.e. questioning the efficacy of law as a tool for empowerment for women in domestic service.

Research Techniques

For data collection I will use semi structured interviewing method which is one of the main tools for qualitative research. Bearing in mind the main research issues I would start with group interviews and would then move on the individual interviews. I would also see if I could include few case studies. For managing interviews I will keep in mind the following points:

- Establish rapport with interviewees
- Sequence and type of questions
- Good communication and listening skills
- Facilitating and moderating the flow of discussion
- Make sure that all issues are address
- Closing interview
- General observations and keeping a diary
- Taking notes as well as tape recording interviews

The interviews will be conducted in two cities, Karachi and Peshawar. Hijrat Colony and Bhit Islands are the two sites in Karachi where the empirical data would be collected. In Peshawar workers from Christian Colony and Acheena village who come to work in Defence Housing society and Clifton area will be interviewed. While selecting workers I will bear in mind their age, marital status, ethnic and religious backgrounds. I will also try to interview women in domestic service who are employed in upper as well as by middle class families. I intend to interview around 25-30 women domestic workers at each site. Selection will also be made keeping in mind that domestic workers working in households where the employers are working/professional women as well as housewives.

First of all I will briefly explain the purpose of interviewing them. There is a possibility that due to my previous position of being an employer they might hesitate to disclose their actual experiences. Therefore, in order to gain their confidence it would be necessary to build up a relationship of trust with them and a rapport so that they can openly discuss their problems, experiences, and feelings.

I will start the conversation by obtaining some basic information about their name, age, marital status, how many members of family there are etc. Although this research is based on qualitative analysis but I would keep a record of this basic information as well.

Some of the specific issues that I want to raise in my research study are as follows. These issues are divided into different sets of questions, which would be discussed with the workers in several sittings.

Working Conditions

- What type of work do you perform?
- For how many hours do you work?
- Do you get any breaks/rest time in between?
- Do you get food/tea while at work?
- Do you work on weekends?
- Do you get a monthly holiday?
- Do you get a monthly salary or a daily wage?
- Do you receive your monthly wages or daily wages on time?
- Do you get any sickness leave? Do employers deduct salary when you are unable to go to work for few days in case of sickness or an emergency?
- What are the advantages and disadvantages of live-in, full-time and part-time work?
- Why in your view male co-workers are better paid than female workers?

Employer/Employee Relation

- How is the treatment of your employers towards you?
- What are your main complaints against employers?
- Do you receive any extra help (monetary or otherwise) from employers?
- Reasons for changing employers?
- What sort of changes do you want/expect in employer's behaviour?
- Are you treated with respect at work?
- Do you feel that your employer is sympathetic towards you?
- Harassment at work place.

Views on Improving Working Conditions

- How can their work situation be improved?
- Are there any organizations that support them?
- Do they think that organizing themselves in the form of a union or association would be useful in improving their condition?
- Are they aware of any other groups of workers in the informal sector?

Legislative Framework

- Do they think that there can be any possibility of having a formal work contract and not a verbal understanding between employer and employee?
- How familiar are they with the legal system?
- In case of dispute with employers, do they feel that law can be a source of protection for them?

- Would it be possible for them to go to the courts?
- Have they ever used non-formal systems of the law such as *jirga* or *panchayat* for their problems?

Women Workers Views about Themselves and Treatment by their Families

- Do they feel that working out side home has given them some confidence?
- How has work affected their position in relation to household matters? Does economic empowerment brought any change in their roles within the family?
- Do they have a say in decision-making?
- How do male members of the family treat them? Do they get any help in household chores from male members of the family?
- Do they have to seek the permission of male members to start a job? Can they take such an initiative on their own?
- What was the reaction of extended family? Do the extended family approve of their work?
- How has their work improved their mobility, access, and control over earnings and do they manage to save their earnings?

Employers

- What are their general complaints against their employees?
- How do they feel that employees exploit them?
- Why is their a difference between the salaries of male and female workers?
- What are the reasons for the laying-off of a worker?
- Do they think that wages should be revised or could there be some formal written contracts?
- Do they provide any extra help to employees apart from their salaries?

NGOs/Activists

- Has there been any effort on the part of their NGO for supporting women domestic workers? If not what are the reasons for it?
- How can women domestic workers be organized?
- Can this employment sector be regulated?
- Why are domestic workers excluded under labour laws?
- What sort of protection can be provided under a legislative framework?
- What measures can be adopted for providing protection to women domestic workers against all sorts of exploitation?
- Any studies taken up on the issue of domestic workers in Pakistan?

Government Departments

- Information on new labour policy and codification of labour laws in Pakistan?
- Information with respect to Pakistan's position on international labour conventions?

Glossary

Begum Sahib/Malakan/Bibi	Names used to address women employers.
Bewaqoof	Stupid/Idiot.
Bibi	Landlord's wife (generally a respectful term for describing a female).
Chowkidar	Security guard.
Chila	Praying in seclusion for forty days and away from home.
Committees	Monthly savings that are pooled together by women in one kitty.
Eid	A religious festival celebrated twice a year according to the Islamic calendar. Eid ul Fitr is celebrated after the month of Ramadan and Eid al Azha after the Haj.
Ghairat/Izzat	Pride, honour, respect.
Ghar ka kharcha pani	Household expenses.
Holi	A Hindu religious festival.
Jirga	Council of elders (an informal dispute resolution mechanism).
Jamadarni	Sweeperess.
Jahil	Ignorant.
Jhugee	Hut.
Khan	Village landlord.
Kiraya	Rent.
Maasi, Mai, Ayah, Babbo	Terms used for domestic workers.
Marna Jeena	Life and death.
Nikah	Marriage contract.
Panchayat	Council of elders (an informal dispute resolution mechanism).
Paighore/tana	Sarcastic comment.
Per ki juti	Degrading and insulting comment by comparing a person to slippers.
Purdah	Segregation of females, sometimes also referred to as veil.
Roti	Bread.
Rupee	Pakistani currency.
Sahib Ji, Baray Saab, Sahib Ji, Khanji	Male employer.
Sarkari nokari	Government job.
Sehroza	Praying for three days in seclusion and away from home.
Seth/Naqua	Title used for men in the fishing business.
Swara	Customary practice of exchange marriage.
Tabligh	Propagation of thoughts, ideas, and teachings about religion.
Talaq-i-Tafwiz	Delegated *talaq*.
Vani	A customary practice in which females are given in penance of murder/rape committed by their relatives.

Zakat — The Islamic concept of tithing and alms; one of the five pillars of Islam, *zakat* is an obligation on Muslims.

Bibliography

Primary Sources

Government of Pakistan, (2006). *Labour Force Survey of Pakistan 2005-2006, Quarterly Report (Oct-Dec 2005).* Federal Bureau of Statistics, Islamabad, Pakistan.

________, *Pakistan Social and Living Standards Measurement Survey 2004-05.* Federal Bureau of Statistics, Islamabad, Pakistan.

________, *Economic Survey 2005-2006.* Ministry of Finance, Islamabad, Pakistan.

________, *Pakistan Social and Living Standards Measurement Survey, 2004-05.* Federal Bureau of Statistics, Islamabad, Pakistan.

________, *Economic Survey 2004-2005.* Ministry of Finance, Islamabad, Pakistan.

________, *Labour Protection Policy (First Draft).* Ministry of Labour, Manpower and Overseas Pakistanis, Islamabad, Pakistan.

________, (2004). *Rapid Assessment Studies of Bonded Labours in Different Sectors in Pakistan.* Ministry of Labour, Manpower, and Overseas Pakistanis, Bonded Labour Research Forum, and International Labour Organisation, Islamabad, Pakistan.

________, (2003). *Pakistan Economic Survey 2001-2002.* Finance Division, Islamabad, Printing Corporation of Pakistan Press, Islamabad, Pakistan.

________, *Pakistan Integrated Household Survey (PIHS). 2001-2002.* Federal Bureau of Statistics, Islamabad, Pakistan.

________, *Household Integrated Economic Survey (HIES). 2001-2002.* Federal Bureau of Statistics, Islamabad, Pakistan.

________, *Report on Hudood Ordinances 1979.* National Commission on the Status of Women, Islamabad, Pakistan.

________, *Inquiry Report on Status of Women Employment in Public Sector Organisations.* National Commission on the Status of Women, Islamabad, Pakistan.

________, (2002). *Second Annual Report.* National Commission on the Status of Women, Islamabad, Pakistan.

________, *Pakistan Integrated Household Survey.* Federal Bureau of Statistics, Printing Corporation of Pakistan Press, Islamabad.

________, *Pakistan Demographic Survey 2003.* Federal Bureau of Statistics, Islamabad, Pakistan.

________, *Annual Review 2001-2002 of Ten Year Perspective Development Plan 2001-2011 and Three Year Programme 2002-2005.* Planning Commission, Islamabad, Pakistan.

________, (2001). *Household Integrated Economic Survey 1998-1999.* Federal Bureau of Statistics, Islamabad, Printing Corporation of Pakistan Press.

________, (2000). *Pakistan Labour Manual.* Ministry of Labour, Manpower and Overseas, Islamabad, Printing Corporation of Pakistan Press.

________, (1999). *Integrated Household Survey 1998-1999.* Federal Bureau of Statistics, Islamabad, Pakistan.

________, (1998). *Compendium on Gender Statistics.* Federal Bureau of Statistics, Statistics Division, in Collaboration with Asian Development Bank.

———, *Labour Force Survey 1996-1997.* Federal Bureau of Statistics, Islamabad, Printing Corporation of Pakistan Press.

———, (1997). *Ninth Five-Year Plan 1998-2003. Report of the Working Group on Manpower and Employment.* Planning Commission, Islamabad, Printing Corporation of Pakistan Press.

———, *Labour Force Survey 1995-1996.* Federal Bureau of Statistics, Islamabad, Pakistan.

———, (1995). *Fourth World Women Conference, Beijing, September 1995 Pakistan National Report (Beijing Report).* Islamabad, Printing Corporation of Pakistan Press.

———, *Pakistan National Report for the Fourth World Conference on Women.* Ministry of Women Development, Islamabad, Pakistan.

Secondary Sources

Books

Abu-Lughad, L. (1993). *Writing Women's World: Bedouin Stories.* Berkeley: University of California Press.

Acharya, M. (2000). *Labour Market Development and Poverty: With Focus on Opportunities for Women in Nepal.* Kathmandu: Tauka Prasad Acharya Memorial Foundation and Friedrich-Ebert-Shiftung.

Agnes, F. (1999). *Law and Gender Inequality: The Politics of Women's Rights in India.* Delhi: Oxford University Press.

Ahmed, L. (1992). *Women and Gender in Islam: Historical Roots of a Modern Debate.* New Haven: Yale University Press.

Ali, S.S. (1995). *A Comparative Study of the United Nations Convention on the Elimination of All Forms of Discrimination against Women, Islamic Law and the Laws of Pakistan.* Peshawar: Shaheen Printing Press.

Ali, S.S. (1999). *Gender and Human Rights in Islam and International Law: Equal before Allah Unequal before Man?* London: Kluwer Law International.

Ali, S.S. and Rehman, J. (2001). *Indigenous Peoples and Ethnic Minorities of Pakistan: Constitutional and Legal Perspectives.* Great Britain: Curzon Press.

Amjad, A. (2001). *Labour Legislation and Trade Unions in Pakistan.* Karachi: Oxford University Press.

Anderson, B. (1993). *Britain's Secret Slaves: An Investigation into the Plight of Overseas Domestic Workers.* London: Anti Slavery International and Kalayaan.

Anderson, B. (2000). *Doing the Dirty Work: The Global Politics of Domestic Labour.* London: Zed Books.

Anderson, N.J.D. (1976). *Law Reform in the Muslim World.* London: Athlone Press.

Anleu Roach, L.S. (2000, reprinted 2001, 2002). *Law and Social Change.* London: Sage Publications.

Austin, J. (1832). *The Province of Jurisprudence Determined.* Cambridge: Cambridge University Press.

Bakan, A.B. and Stasiulis, A. (1997). *Not One of the Family: Foreign Domestic Workers in Canada.* Toronto: University of Toronto Press.

Bales, K. (2000). *Disposable People: New Slavery in the Global Economy.* Los Angeles: University of California Press.

Bano, Z. (1998). 'Faslain', in Z. Bano, *Zinda Dukh.* Lahore: Maqbool Academy.

Barnett, H. (1998). *Introduction to Feminist Jurisprudence.* London: Cavendish Publishing Limited.

Bartlett, K.T. and Harris, A.P. (1998). *Gender and Law: Theory, Doctrine, Commentary.* New York: Aspen Law and Business.

Basu, M. (2001). *Hindu Women and Marriage Law: From Sacrament to Contract.* New Delhi: Oxford University Press.

Bentzon, A. et al. (1998). *Pursuing Grounded Theory in Law: South-North Experiences in Developing Women's Law.* Oslo: TANO Aschehoug: Mond Books.

Boserup, E. (1989). *Women's Role in the Economic Development.* London: Earth Scan Publication Ltd.

Buechler, S.M. (1990). *Women's Movements in the United States: Woman Suffrage, Equal Rights, and Beyond.* New York: Rutgers University Press.

Campbell, T. (1996). *The Legal Theory of Ethical Positivism.* Dartmouth: Aldershot.

Chamallas, M. (1998). *Introduction to Feminist Legal Theory,* New York: Aspen Law and Business.

Chandra, S. (1999). *Enslaved Daughters: Colonialism, Law and Women's Rights.* New Delhi: Oxford University Press.

Chang, G. (2000). *Disposable Domestics: Immigrant Women Workers in the Global Economy.* Massachusetts: South End Press.

Chhachhi, A. and Pittin, R. (1995). *Confronting State, Capital and Patriarchy: Women Organising in the Process of Industrialisation.* London: MacMillan Press.

Chiba, M. (1989). *Legal Pluralism: Towards a General Theory through Japanese Legal Culture.* Tokyo: Tokyo University Press.

Chin, C.B.N. (1998). *In Service and Servitude Female Foreign Domestic Workers and the Malaysian 'Modernity' Project.* New York: Columbia University Press.

Chughtai, A. (1985). 'Ghubar i Karawan.' in *Khawateen Ka Alami Adab: A Selection of Literary Creations of the Women Writers of the World.* Islamabad: Academy of Letters.

Chunn, D.E. and Lacombe, D. (2000). (1st ed.). *Law as a Gendering Practice.* Oxford: Oxford University Press.

Cock, J. (1989). *Maids and Madams: Domestic Workers under Apartheid.* London: The Women's Press.

Coulson, N.J. (1964). *A History of Islamic Law.* Edinburgh: Edinburgh University Press.

Cox, R. (2006). *Servant Problem: Domestic Employment in Global Economy.* London: I.B. Tauris and Co. Ltd.

Dahl, T.S. (1987). *Women's Law: An Introduction to Feminist Jurisprudence.* Oslo: Norwegian University Press.

Dasgupta, A. (1984). *Domestic Workers: Profile of Women Dwelling in the Slums of South Delhi.* New Delhi: People's Institute for Development and Training.

Davidoff, L. (1995). *Worlds Between: Historical Perspectives on Gender and Class.* Cambridge: Polity Press.

Denzin, N.K. and Lincoln, Y.S. (2005). (1st ed.). *Handbook of Qualitative Research.* Thousand Oaks: Sage Publications.

Dudden, F.E. (1983). *Serving Women: Household Service in Nineteenth Century America.* Middletown, Connecticut: Wesleyan University Press.

Dworkin, R. (1986). (2nd ed.). *Law's Empire.* Cambridge, MA: Harvard University Press.

Ehrenreich, B. (2001). *Nickel and Dimed: On (not). Getting by in America.* New York: Henry Holt and Company, LLC.

Ehrenreich, B. and Hochschild A.R. (2003). (1st ed.). *Global Women: Nannies and Maids in Global Economy.* London: Granta Books.

Ehrlich, E. (1936). *Fundamental Principles of Sociology of Law.* Cambridge: Harvard University Press.

El Saddawi, N. (1980). *The Hidden Face of Eve: Women in the Arab World.* London: Zed Books.

Engineer, A.A. (2004). (2nd ed.). *The Rights of Women in Islam.* India: New Dawn Press.

Esposito, J. L. (1991). *Islam The Straight Path.* Oxford: Oxford University Press.

Esposito, J.L. (1982). (2nd ed.). *Women in Muslim Family Law.* Syracuse: Syracuse University Press.

Esterberg, K.G. (2002). *Qualitative Methods in Social Research.* Boston: McGraw Hill Company.

Evans, J. (1995). *Feminist Theory Today: An Introduction to Second Wave Feminism.* London: Sage Publications.

Faraz, A. (1957). *Tanha Tanha.* Lahore: Malik Sons Publishers.

Fineman, M. and Thomsden, M. (eds.). (1991). *At the Boundaries of Law: Feminism and Legal Theory.* New York, London: Routledge.

Fitzpatrick, P. (1992). *The Mythology of Law.* London: Routledge.

Fredman, S. (2002). *Women and the Law.* Oxford: Oxford University Press.

Fyzee, A. (1955). *Outlines of Muhammadan Law.* London: Oxford University Press.

Glaser, B.G. and Strauss, A.L. (1965). *Awareness of Dying.* Chicago: Aldine.

Glaser, B.G. and Strauss, A.L. (1967). *The Discovery of Grounded Theory: Strategies for Qualitative Research.* Chicago: Aldine.

Gregson, N. and Lowe, M. (1994). *Servicing the Middle Classes: Class, Gender and Waged Domestic Labour in Contemporary Britain.* New York: Routledge.

Griffiths, A. (1997). *In the Shadow of Marriage: Gender and Justice in an African Community.* Chicago and London: The University of Chicago Press.

Haddad, Y.Y. and Esposito, J.L. (1998). (2nd ed.). *Islam Gender and Social Change.* New York: Oxford University Press

Hafeez, S. (1981). *Metropolitan Women of Pakistan.* Karachi: Royal Book Company.

Hafeez, S. (1989). *Women in Industry.* Islamabad: Women Division, Government of Pakistan.

Hallaq, W.B. (1997). *A History of Islamic Legal Theories: An Introduction to Sunni Usul al-Fiqh.* Cambridge: Cambridge University Press.

Hart, H.L.A. (1994). (2nd ed.). *The Concept of Law.* Oxford: Clarendon Press.

Haynes, D. and Prakash, G. (1991). (1st ed.). *Contesting Power: Resistance and Every Day Social Relations in South Asia.* Delhi: Oxford University Press.

Hecht, J. (1956). *The Domestic Servant Class in Eighteenth Century England.* London: Routledge and Kegan Paul.

Hellum, A. (1999). *Women's Human Rights and Legal Pluralism in Africa: Mixed Norms and Identities in Infertility Management in Zimbabwe.* Tano Aschehoug: Mond Books.

Hirsch, S.F. (1998). *Pronouncing and Persevering: Gender and the Discourses of Disputing in an African Islamic Court.* Chicago: University of Chicago Press.

Hooker, M.B. (1975). *Legal Pluralism: An Introduction to Colonial and Neo- Colonial Laws.* Oxford: Clarendon Press.

Hoskyns, C. and Threlfall, M. (1996). *Mapping the Women's Movement: Feminist Politics and Social Transformation in the North.* New York: Verso.

Hussain, A. (1987). *The Status of Women in Islam.* Lahore: Lahore Publishing Company.

Hussain, F. (1984). *Muslim Women.* Worcester: Croom Helm.

Jahangir, A. and Jilani, H. (1990). *The Hudood Ordinances: A Divine Sanction?* Lahore: Rohtas Books.

Jayawardena, K. (1993). *Feminism and Nationalism in the Third World.* Lahore: ASR Publications.

Jhappan, R. (2002). *Women's Legal Strategies in Canada*. Toronto: University of Toronto Press.

Judith, R. (1985). *Women Using Other Women.* Philadelphia: Temple University Press.

Kandiyoti, D. (1991). *Women, Islam and the State*. London: Macmillan Press Ltd.

Kapur, R. and Cossman, B. (1998). *Subversive Sites: Feminist Engagements with Law in India.* New Delhi: Sage Publications.

Karam, A.M. (1998). *Women, Islamisms and the State: Contemporary Feminisms in Egypt.* Great Britain: MacMillan Press Ltd.

Karlekar, M. (1980). *Poverty and Women's Work: A Study of Sweeper Women in Delhi.* New Delhi: Vikas Publishing House.

Karlekar, M. (1991). *Voices from Within: Early Personal Narratives of Bengali Women.* New Delhi: Oxford University Press.

Katzman, D. M. (1978). *Seven Days a Week: Women and Domestic Service in Industrializing America.* New York: Oxford University Press.

Kelsen, H. (1945). *General Theory of Law and State.* Trans. A. Wedberg, rept. 1961. New York: Russell and Russell.

Khan, N. et al. (1995). (1st ed.). *A Celebration of Women: Essays and Abstracts from the Women Studies Conference March 1994*. Lahore: ASR Publications.

Khan, N.S. (1997). *Unveiling the Issues: Pakistani Women's Perspectives on Social, Political and Ideological Issues.* Lahore: ASR Publications.

Khan, S.R. (2000). *Fifty Years of Pakistan Economy.* Oxford: Oxford University Press.

Kumari, R. (1998). *Gender, Work and Power Relations: A Case Study of Haryana*. New Delhi: Har-Anand Publications.

Langewin, L. and Belleau, M.C. (2000). *Trafficking in Women in Canada: A Critical Analysis of the Legal Framework Governing Live-In Care-Givers and Mail Order Bride*. Quebec: Status of Women Canada.

Mac Kinnon, C. (1987). *Feminism Unmodified: Discourses on Life and Law*. Cambridge: Harvard University Press.

Marilley, S.M. (1996). *Woman Suffrage and the Origins of Liberal Feminism in the United States, 1820-1920.* Cambridge, Massachusetts: Harvard University Press.

Maynard, M. and Purvis, J. (1994). *Researching Women's Lives from a Feminist Perspective.* London: Taylor and Francis.

Mehdi, R. (1994). *The Islamization of the Law in Pakistan*. London: Curzon Press.

Mehdi, R. (2001). *Gender and Property Law in Pakistan—Resources and Discourses.* Copenhagen: DJOF Publishing.

Mernissi, F. (1993). (Mary Jo Lakelan, trans.). *The Forgotten Queens of Islam*. Oxford: Polity Press.

Merriam, S.B. (2002). *Qualitative Research in Practice: Examples for Discussion and Analysis.* San Francisco: Jossey Bass.

Mies, M. (1986). *Patriarchy and Accumulation on a World Scale, Women in the International Division of Labour*. London: Zed Books.

Minault, G. (1986). *Voices of Silence*. Delhi: Chanakya.

Mirza, J. (2002). *Between Chaddor and Market: Female Office Workers in Lahore*. Karachi: Oxford University Press.

Mitter, S. (1986). *Common Fate Common Bond—Women in the Global Economy*. London: Pluto Press Ltd.

Mohanty, C.P. (2003). *Feminism without Borders: Decolonizing Theory, Practicing Solidarity.* Durham, NC: Duke University Press.

Mohanty, C.T., Russo, A. and Torres, L. (1991). *Third World Women and the Politics of Feminism*. USA: Indiana University Press.

Mukhopadhyay, S. (1998). *In the Name of Justice: Women and Law in Society.* New Delhi: Manohar Publishers.

Mumtaz, K. and Shaheed, F. (1987). *Women of Pakistan: One Step Forward Two Steps Back.* Pakistan: Vanguard Books (Pvt.) Ltd.

Naim, A.A. (1990). *Towards An Islamic Reformation.* Syracuse: Syracuse University Press.

Nair, J. (2002). *Women and Law in Colonial India: A Social History*. Bangalore: Kali for Women and National Law School of India University Bangalore.

Narasimhan, S. (1999). *Empowering Women: An Alternative Strategy from Rural India*. New Delhi: Sage Publications.

Narayan, U. (1997). *Dis/Locating Cultures/Identities, Traditions, and Third World Feminism*. New York: Routledge.

Novarra, V. (1980). *Women's Work Men's Work: The Ambivalence of Equality.* Boston: Marion Boyars.

Palmer, P. (1989). *Housewives and Domestic Servants in the United States 1920-1945.* Philadelphia: Temple University Press.

Parrenas, R.S. (2001). *Servants of Globalization: Women, Migration and Domestic Work.* Stanford, California: Stanford University Press.

Pearl, D. and Meniski, F. (1998). (3rd ed.). *Muslim Family Law*. London: Sweet and Maxwell.

Pooya, M. (1999). *Women, Work and Islamism: Ideology and Resistance in Islam*. New York: Oxford University Press.

Raheja, G.G. and Gold, A. (1994). *Listen to the Herons' Words: Reimagining Gender and Kinship in North India*. Berkeley: University of California Press.

Raju, S. and Bagchi, D. (1993). *Women and Work in South Asia.* London: Routledge.

Raz, J. (1979). *The Authority of Law*. Oxford: Clarendon Press.

Reinharz, S. (1992). *Feminist Methods in Social Research.* New York: Oxford University Press.

Roavh Andleu, L.S. (2002). *Law and Social Change*. London, Thousand Oaks, New Delhi: Sage Publications.

Rollins, J. (1985). *Women Using Other Women.* Philadelphia: Temple University Press.

Salmon, L.M. (reprint 1972). *Domestic Service.* New York: Arno Press.

Santos, B. (2002). (2nd ed.). *Toward a New Legal Common Sense: Law, Globalisation and Emancipation.* London: ButterWorths.

Schacht, J. (1964). *An Introduction to Islamic Law.* Oxford: Clarendon Press.

Shaheed, F. and Mehdi, R. (1997). *Women's Law in Legal Education and Practice in Pakistan: North South Cooperation*. Copenhagen: New Social Science Monographs.

Siddiqui, A.H. (1989). *The Life of Muhammad.* Lahore: Islamic Publications Limited.

Silvera, M. (1989). *Silenced: Talks with Working Class Caribbean Women About their Lives and Struggles as Domestic Workers in Canada*. Toronto: Sister Vision Black Women and Women of Colour Press.

Singh, A.N. (2001). *Women Domestic Workers: Socio-Economic Life.* New Delhi: Shipra Publications.

Smart, C. (1989). *Feminism and the Power of Law*. London: Routledge.

Sotelo, P.H. (2001). *Domestica: Immigrant Workers Cleaning and Caring in the Shadows of Affluence*. Berkeley, Los Angeles, and London: University of California Press.

Sutherland, D. (1981). *Americans and their Servants: Domestic Service in the United States from 1800 to 1920.* London: Louisiana State University Press.

Tabassum, Wajida. (1976). *Utran*. Lahore: Mehmood Publishers.

Taylor, B., Rush, S. and Munro, R.J. (1999). *Feminist Jurisprudence, Women and the Law: Critical Essays, Research Agenda, and Bibliography*. Colo: F.B. Rothman.

Walby, S. (1986). *Patriarchy at Work*. Cambridge: Polity Press.

Walby, S. (1999). Theorising Patriarchy. Oxford: Basil Blackwell.

Weis, A. (1992). *Walls Within Walls: Life Histories of Working Women in the Old City of Lahore*. Oxford: Westview Press.

Weiss, B. (1998). *The Spirit of Islamic Law*. London: University of Georgia Press.

Weiss, M.A. and Gilani, S.Z. (eds). (2001). *Power and Civil Society in Pakistan*. Karachi: Oxford University Press.

Wichterich, C. (2000). *The Globalised Woman: Reports from a Future of Inequality*. New York: Zed Books Ltd.

Widge, A. (1995). *Women in the Informal Sector: Multi Disadvantages of Domestic Workers*. New Delhi: Indian Social Institute.

WLUML. (1994). *Women's Law Initiatives in the Muslim World*. Lahore: Pakistan.

Yamani, M. (ed.). (1996). *Feminism in Islam: Legal and Literary Perspectives*. United Kingdom: Ithaca Press.

Yasin, M. and Banuri, T. (2004). *The Dispensation of Justice in Pakistan*. SDPI and Oxford University Press.

Yilmaz, I. (2005). *Muslim Laws, Politics and Society in Modern Nation States: Dynamic Legal Pluralisms in England, Turkey and Pakistan*. United Kingdom: Ashgate.

Chapters in Books

Afshar, H. (1996). 'Islam and Feminism: An Analysis of Political Strategies.' In Yamani, M. (ed.), *Islam and Feminism: Legal and Literary Perspectives*. London: Ithaca Press.

Agnes, F. (1998). 'Violence against Women: A Review of Recent Enactments.' In Mukhopadhyay, S. (ed.), *In the Name of Justice: Women and Law in Society*. Delhi: Manohar.

Ali, K. and Parveen, F. (1995). 'Research in Action: Organising Women Factory Workers in Pakistan.' In Chhachhi, A. et al. (eds.), *Confronting State, Capital and Patriarchy: Women Organising in the Process of Industrialisation*. London: MacMillan Press.

Ali, S.S. (2000). 'Law, Islam and the Women's Movement in Pakistan.' In Rai, S.M. (ed.), *Gender and Democratisation: International Perspectives*. London: Routledge.

Ali, S.S. (2007). 'Where is the Toilet? Getting Down to Basics of Women's Human Rights.' In Hellum, A., Ali, S.S., Stewart, J. and Tsanga, A. (eds.), *Human Rights, Plural Legalities and Gendered Realities: Paths are Made by Walking*. Harare: Weaver Books.

Ali, S.S. and Arif, K. (1998). 'Parallel Judicial Systems in Pakistan and Its Consequences for Human Rights.' In Shaheed, F. et al. (eds.), *Shaping Women's Lives: Law, Practices and Strategies in Pakistan*. Lahore: Shirkat Gah, Women Resource Centre.

Ali, S.S. and Shahid, A. (2006). 'Women, Law and Empowerment: Securing Equal Rights for Women in the Workplace: A Case-Study of Women and Employment in Pakistan.' In Crick, P. (ed.), *Our Freedoms: A Decades Reflection on the Advancement of Human Rights*. London: International Bar Association.

Ali, S.S. (1997). 'A Critical Review of Family Laws in Pakistan: A Woman's Perspective.' In Shaheed, F. and Mehdi, R. (eds.), *Women's Law in Legal Education and Practice in Pakistan: North South Cooperation*. Copenhagen: New Social Science Monographs.

Ali, S.S. (1998). 'Misogynistic Trends in Islamic Jurisprudence: A Feminist Perspective.' In Naheed, K. (ed.), *Women, Myth and Realities*. Lahore: Hawwah Associates.

Ali, S.S. (2000). 'Using Law for Women in Pakistan.' In Stewart, A. (ed.), *Gender Law and Social Justice*. London: Black Stone Press Ltd.

Arat Koc, S. (1997). 'From Mothers of the Nation to Migrant Workers'. In Bakan, A.B. and Stasiulis, A. (eds.), *Not One of the Family Foreign Domestic Workers in Canada*. Toronto: University of Toronto Press.

Charmaz, K. (2000). 'Grounded theory: Objectivist and Constructivist Methods'. In Denzin, N.K. and Lincoln, Y.S. (eds.), *Hand Book of Qualitative Research*. Thousand Oaks: Sage Publications.

Colen, S. (1986). 'With Respect and Feelings: Voices of West Indian Child Care and Domestic Workers in New York.' In Cole, J. (ed.), *All American Women: Lines That Divide, Ties That Bind*. New York: Free Press.

Colen, S. (1995). 'Like a Mother to Them: Stratified Reproduction and West Indian Childcare Workers and Employers in New York.' In Ginsberg, F. and Rayna, R. (eds.), *Conceiving the New World Order: The Global Politics of Reproduction*. Berkeley: UC Press.

Fanow, M. and Cook, J.A. (1990). 'Knowledge and Women's Interest: Issues of Epistemology and Methodology in Feminist Social Research.' In Nielsen, J.M. (ed.), *Feminist Research Methods: Exemplary Readings in Social Sciences*. London: West View Press.

Gardner, K. (1998). 'Women and Islamic Revivalism in Bangladeshi Community.' In Jeffery, P. and Basu, A. (eds.), *Appropriating Gender: Women's Activism and Politicized Religion in South Asia*. London: Routledge.

Hassan, R. (1991). 'Muslim Women and Post-Patriarchal Islam.' In Cooey, P.M., Eakin, W.R., and McDaniel, B.J. (eds.), *After Patriarchy Feminist Transformations of the World Religions*. New York: Orbis Books.

Hassan, R. (1990). 'An Islamic Perspective.' In Belcher, J. (ed.), *Women, Religion and Sexuality*. Geneva: WCC Publications.

Hosseini, Z.M. (1998). 'Stretching the Limits: A Feminist Reading of the Shari'a in Post-Khomeini in Iran.' In Yamani, M. (ed.), *Feminism and Islam: Legal and Literary Perspectives*. London: ITHICA Press.

Iqbal, M. (1930). 'The Principle of Movement in the Structure of Islam.' In Iqbal, M. *The Reconstruction of Religious Thought in Islam*. Lahore: Kapur Art Printing Works.

Jalal, A. (1991). 'The Convenience of Subservience: Women and the State of Pakistan'. In Kandiyoti, D. (ed.), *Women Islam and State*. London: Mac Millan Press.

Jilani, H. (1998). 'Law as an Instrument of Social Control.' In Khan, N.S. et al. (eds.), *Locating the Self: Perspectives on Women and Multiple Identities*. Lahore: ASR Publications.

Kandiyoti, D. (1996). 'Islam and Patriarchy: A Comparative Perspective.' In Kiddie, N. and Brown, B. (eds.), *Women in Middle Eastern Histories: Emerging Perspectives*. New York: I.B. Tauris.

Kapur, R. (2006). 'Revisioning the Role of Law in Women's Human Rights Struggles.' In Garcia, M.S. and Cali, B. (eds.), *The Legalization of Human Rights Multidisciplinary Human Rights and Human Rights Law*. New York: Routledge.

Karmi, G. (1996). 'Women, Islam and Patriarchalism.' In Yamani, M. (eds.), *Feminism and Islam: Legal and Literacy Perspectives*. New York: New York University Press.

Kazi, S. (2000). 'Gender Inequalities and Development in Pakistan.' In Khan, S.R. (ed.), *Fifty Years of Pakistan's Economy*. Karachi: Oxford University Press.

Mohanty, C. (1991). 'Under Western Eyes: Feminist Scholarship and Colonial Discourses.' In Mohanty, C. et al. (eds.), *Third World Women and the Politics of Feminism*. Indiana: Indiana University Press.

Mumtaz, K. and Shaheed, F. (1998). 'Gauging the Economic Participation Rate of Women in Pakistan.' In Naheed, K. (ed.), *Women Myth and Realities*. Lahore: Hawwah Associates.

Ong, A. (1995). 'State Verses Islam: Malay Families, Women's Bodies and the Body Politic in Malaysia.' In Ong, A. and Peletz, M.G. (eds.), *Bewitching Women, Pious Men: Gender and Politics in South East Asia.* London, California: University of California Press.

Papanek, H. (1982). (1st ed.). 'Purdah in Pakistan: Seclusion and Modern Occupations for Women.' In Papanek, H. and Gail, M. (eds.), *Separate Worlds: Studies of Purdah in South Asia.* Delhi: Chankya Publications.

Patel, R. (2000). 'Perceptions, Norms and Women's Property Rights in India: A Discussion of Legal Pluralism.' In Stewart, A. (ed.), *Gender, Law and Social Justice.* London: Blackstone Press limited.

Pospisil, L. (1978). 'The Structure of Society and Its Multiple Legal Systems.' In Gulliver, P.H. (ed.), *Cross Examinations: Essays in Memory of Max Gluckman.* Leiden: EJ Brill.

Rahman, F. (1983). 'Status of Women in Quran.' In Nashat, G. (ed.), *Women and Revolution in Iran.* Boulder: Westview Press.

Romero, M. (1988). 'Days Work in the Suburbs: The Work Experience of Chicana Private House Keepers.' In Stratham, A., Miller, E., and Mauksch, H. (eds.), *The Worth of Women's Work: A Qualitative Synthesis.* Albany: State University of New York Press.

Rouse, S. (1994). 'Gender Struggles, the State, Religion and Society.' In Bhasin, K. et al. (eds.), *Against All Odds: Essays on Women, Religion and Development from India and Pakistan.* Delhi: ISIS and Kali for Women.

Saigol, R. (1995). 'Domestic Knowledge Systems and Patriarchy.' In Khan, N. et al. *Unveiling the Issues: Pakistani Women's Perspectives on Social, Political and Ideological Issues.* Lahore: ASR Publications.

Shaheed, F. (1997). 'The Interface of Culture, Customs and Law: Implications for Women and Activism.' In Shaheed, F. and Mehdi, R. (eds.), *Women's Law in Legal Education and Practice in Pakistan: North South Cooperation.* Copenhagen: New Social Science Monograph.

Shaheed, F. (1998). 'The Other Side of the Discourse: Women's Experiences of Identity, Religion and Activism in Pakistan.' In Jeffery, P. and Basu, A. (eds.). *Appropriating Gender Women's Activism and Politicised Religion in South Asia.* New York: Routledge.

Smith, M.G. (1969). 'Some Developments in the Analytic Framework of Pluralism.' In Kuper, L. and Smith, M.G. (eds.), *Pluralism in Africa.* Berkeley: University of California Press.

Weiss, A.M. (2001). 'Gendered Power Relations: Perpetuation and Renegotiation.' In Weiss, A.M. and Gilani, Z.H. (eds.), *Power and Civil Society in Pakistan.* Karachi: Oxford University Press.

Woodman, G.R. (1997). 'Progress Through Complexity: Options for the Subjects of Legal Pluralism.' In Mehdi, R. and Shaheed, F. (eds.), *Women's Law and Practice in Legal Education in Pakistan.* Copenhagen-Denmark: New Social Science Monograph.

Zarempka, J. (2003). 'America's Dirty Work: Migrant Maids and Modern-Day Slavery.' In Ehrenreich, B. and Hochschild, A.R. (eds.), *Global Women: Nannies and Maids in Global Economy.* Great Britain: Granta Books.

Zia, S. (1995). 'Women and Law.' In Saeed, N. et al. (eds.), *Unveiling the Issues: Pakistani Women's Perspectives on Social, Political and Ideological Issues.* Lahore: ASR Publications.

Zia, S. (1997). 'Some Experiences of the Women's Movement: Strategies for Success.' In Zia, S., Shaheed, F., Warraich, S.A., Balchin, C. and Gazdar, A. (eds.), *Shaping Women's Lives, Law, Practices and Strategies in Pakistan,* Pakistan: Shirkat Gah, Women Resource Centre.

Journal Articles

Al-Hibri, A. (1994). 'A Study of Islamic History: Or How do We get into This Mess?' *Women Studies International Forum.* Vol. 5.

Ali, A., Ali, S.S. and Rehman, F. (1990). 'Sociological Difficulties in the Implementation of Legislation Pertaining to Women in Pakistan.' *Journal of Law and Society.* Vol. 8, No. 16, Faculty of Law, University Peshawar.

Ali, S.S. (1993). 'Are Women Also Human? Women's Rights and Human Rights in Tribal Areas: A Case Study of Provincially Administered Tribal Areas of Pakistan.' *Journal of Law and Society.* Vol. 12, No. 20, Faculty of Law, University of Peshawar.

Ali, S.S. (1997-1998). 'Women's Human Rights in Islam: Towards a Theoretical Framework.' In Eugren Cotran, and Chibbli Millat. *Year Book of Islamic and Middle Eastern Law.* Vol. 4, The Hague. London. Boston: Kluwer Law International.

Ashraf, J. and Ashraf, B. (Winter 2000). 'Ethnicity and Earnings: An Analysis of Data for Karachi.' *The Pakistan Development Review.* Vol. 39, No. 4.

Aubert, V. (1966). 'Some Social Functions of Legislation.' *Acta Sociologica*. Vol. 10.

Bottomley, A. (2004). 'A Shock of a Thought: An Encounter of the Third Kind with Legal Feminism.' *Feminist Legal Studies.* Vol. 12, No. 1.

Boyd, S. and Sheehy, E. (1986). 'Feminist Perspectives on Law: Canadian Theory and Practice.' *Canadian Journal of Women and Law.*

Cain, P. (1991). 'Feminist Legal Scholarship.' *Iowa Law Review.* Vol. 9, No. 20.

Caldwell, P.M. (1991). 'A Hair Piece: Perspectives on the Intersection of Race and Gender.' Duke Law Journal. Vol. 41.

Cohen, R. (1991). 'Women of Colour in White Households: Coping Strategies of Live-in Domestic Workers.' *Qualitative Sociology.* Vol. 14, No. 2.

Conhagan, J. (2000). 'Theorizing Feminist Project in Law.' *Journal of Law and Society.* Vol. 27, No. 3.

Coser, L. (1973). 'Servants: The Obsolescence of an Occupational Role.' *Social Forces.* Vol. 52, No. 1.

Davies, M. (2003). 'Legal Theory and Law Reform.' *Alternative Law Journal.* Vol. 28.

Falkmoore, S. (1973). 'Law and Social Change: The Semi Autonomous Field as an Appropriate Subject of Study.' *Law and Society Review.* Vol. 7.

Gaitskell, D., Kimbie, J., Maconachie, M. and Unterhalter, E. (1984). 'Class, Race and Gender Domestic Workers in South Africa.' *Review of African Political Economy.* Vol. 27, No. 28.

Galanter, M. (1981). 'Justice in Many Rooms: Private Ordering and Indigenous Law.' *Journal of Legal Pluralism and Unofficial Law.* Vol. 19.

Green House, C. and Strijbosch, F. (1998). 'Legal Pluralism in Industrialized Societies.' *Journal of Legal Pluralism*. Vol. 33.

Griffiths, A. (2001). 'Review Essay. Remaking Law: Gender, Ethnography and Legal Discourse.' *Law and Society Review.* Vol. 35.

Griffiths, J. (1986). 'What Is Legal Pluralism?' *Journal of Legal Pluralism and Unofficial Law.* Vol. 25.

Guha, R. (1987). 'Chandra's Death.' *Subaltern Studies.* Vol. 5.

Hallaq, W.B. (1995). 'Ijtihad.' *The Oxford Encyclopaedia of the Modern Islamic World.* Vol. 2.

Harris, A. (1991). 'Race and Essentialism in Feminist Legal Theory.' *Stanford Law Review*. Vol. 42.

Irfan, M. (Winter 2000). 'Poverty in South Asia.' *The Pakistan Development Review* Vol. 39, No. 4.

Jureidini, R. and Moukarbel, N. (July 2004). 'Female Sri Lankan Domestic Workers in Lebanon: A Case of 'Contract Slavery'.' *Journal of Ethnic and Migrant Studies*. Vol. 30, No 4.

Kakakhel, M.N. (1982). 'The Role of Ideology in Constitutional Development in Pakistan.' *Journal of Law and Society*. Vol. 1, No. 1

Kapur, R. (2004). 'The Tragedy of Victimization Rhetoric: Resurrecting the 'Native' Subject in International/Post-Colonial Feminist Legal Politics.' *Harvard Human Rights Journal*. Vol. 15.

Khattak, S. (2003). 'Women, Work and Empowerment.' In SDPI (ed.). *Sustainable Development and Southern Realities: Past and Future in South Asia*. Islamabad: City Press.

Kozel, M. and Alderman, H. (1990). 'Factors Determining Working Participation and Labour Supply Decisions in Pakistan.' *The Pakistan Development Review*. Vol. 29, No. 1.

Lessard, H. (2001). 'Review of Law as a Gendering Practice.' UBC *Law Review*. Vol. 35.

Lim, L.L. and Oishi, N. (1996). 'International Labour Migration of Asian Women: Distinctive Characteristics and Policy Concerns.' *Asian Women in Migration, Special Issue of Asian and Pacific Migration Journal*. Vol. 5, No. 1.

Littleton, C.A. (1989). 'Book Review: Feminist Jurisprudence: The Difference Method Makes.' *Stanford Law Review*. Vol. 41.

Macklin, A. (1992). 'Foreign Domestic Worker: Surrogate Housewife or Mail Order Servant?' *Mc Gill Law Journal*. Vol. 37.

Manji, A.S. (1999). 'Imagining Women's 'Legal World': Towards a Feminist Theory of Legal Pluralism in Africa' *Comparative Perspectives on Gender, Law and Development in Social and Legal Studies*. Vol. 8, No. 4.

Merry, S.A. (1988). 'Legal Pluralism.' *Law and Society Review*. Vol. 5, No. 22.

Mehdi, R. (1990). 'The Offence of Rape in the Islamic Law of Pakistan.' *International Journal of Society and Law*. Vol. 18, No. 19.

Mullally, S. (1995). 'Separate Spheres: Protective Legislation for Women in Pakistan.' *Asian Year Book of International Law. Vol.* 4.

Nafine, N. (March 2002). 'In Praise of Legal Feminism.' in *The Journal of the Law and Society of Legal Scholars*. Vol. 22, No. 1.

Naffine, N. (2004). 'Shocking Thoughts: A Reply to Anne Bottomley.' *Feminist Legal Studies*. Vol. 12, No. 1.

Ostrander, S.A. (Jan 1987). 'Book Review: Women Using Other Women.' *Contemporary Sociology*. Vol. 16, No. 1.

Parveen, F. and Ali, K. (1993). 'Research in Action: Organising Women Factory Workers in Pakistan.' *AlMushir*. Vol. 35, No. 1.

Qayum, S. and Ray, R. (2003). 'Grappling with Modernity.' *Ethnography*. Vol. 4.

Taran, P.A. (2000). 'Status and Prospects for the UN Convention on Migrants' Rights.' *European Journal of Migration and Law*. Vol. 2, No. 85.

Sadasivam, B.(1997). 'The Impact of Structural Adjustment on Women: A Governance and Human Rights Agenda.' *Human Rights Quarterly*. Vol. 19, No. 3.

Satterwaite, M.L. (2005). 'Crossing Borders Claiming Rights: Using Human Rights Law to Empower Women Migrant Workers.' *Yale Human Rights and Development Law Journal*. Vol. 8, No. 1.

Shah, N.M. (1986). 'Changes in Women's Role in Pakistan: Are the Volume and Pace Adequate?' *Pakistan Development Review*. Vol. 25, No. 3.

Shaheed, F. (1994). 'Controlled or Autonomous: Identity and the Experience of the Network, Women Living Under Muslim Laws.' *Signs*. Vol. 19, No. 4.

Siddiqui, R., Hamid, S. and Siddiqui, R. (2000). 'Analysis of Non-Conventional Indicators of Gender Relations: Evidence from Pakistan.' *The Pakistan Development Review*. Vol. 39, No. 4.

Silvey, R. (2004). 'Trans-national Migration and the Gender Politics of Scale: Indonesian Domestic Workers in Saudi Arabia.' *Singapore Journal of Tropical Geography*. Vol. 25, No. 2.

Smart, C. (1992). 'The Woman of Legal Discourse.' *Social and Legal Studies*. Vol. 1.

Smart, C. (1995). 'Feminist Jurisprudence.' in *Law, Crime and Sexuality*. Vol. 162.

Wright, C. (1996). 'Wong: Foreign Domestic Workers in Singapore.' *Asian and Pacific Migration Journal*. Vol. 5, No. 1.

Weiss, B. (1978). 'Interpretation in Islamic Law: The Theory of Ijtihad.' *American Journal of Comparative Law*. Vol. 26, No. 2.

Wrigley, J. (Summer 1991). 'Feminists and Domestic Workers.' *Feminist Studies*. Vol. 17, No. 2.

Zaidi, S.A. (January-June 2000). 'The Nature of Social and Economic Change in Pakistan.' *Pakistan Perspectives*. Vol. 5, No. 1.

Thesis/Research Studies/Reports/Conference Papers

Ahmed, N. (1990). 'Women Home Based Piece Rate Workers: A Study of the Informal Sector of Pakistan: Problems and Policies.' The Informal Sector Study Number 3. Fredrich Eburt Stifung, Islamabad.

Ahmed, N., Qaisrani, S. and Tahir, M. (1998). 'Social Protection for Women Workers in the Informal Home-based Sector in the Leather and Textile Industries.' Islamabad: Aurat Publication and Information Service Foundation.

Ali, S.S. and Khattak, S. (1993). 'Domestic Servants and the Need for Legislation: The Case of the North West Frontier Province.' In Report on *The British Council Workshop on Women and Employment Legislation in Pakistan 11th-13th February 1993*. Islamabad: The British Council and Ministry of Women Development.

Anderson, B. and Phizaklea, A. (1997). 'Migrant Domestic Workers: A European Perspective.' Study supported by Equal Opportunities Unit, DGV and Leicester University.

Arvidsson, M. (2002). 'Ijtihad Reformation of Islamic law in the 21st Century: The Case of Sudan.' Master's Thesis. Faculty of Law, University of Lund.

Asia Foundation. (2001). 'Improving Access to Justice under the Local Government Plan: Small Scale Technical Assistance.' Islamabad: Asia Foundation.

Aurat Foundation. (2001). 'Citizens' Campaign for Women's Representation in Local Government.' Islamabad: Aurat Publications and Information Service Foundation.

Aurat Foundation. (2003). 'Leadership Development for Effective Women Councillors.' Islamabad: Aurat Publications and Information Service Foundation.

Bari, F. (2002). 'Women's Representation in Legislatures: The Way Forward.' Islamabad: Ministry of Women and Development.

Bilal, G. (2004). 'Women Parliamentarians: Swimming Against the Tide.' Islamabad: Friedrich Naumann Stiftung.

British Council in Collaboration with the Ministry of Women Development. (1994). Report on 'The British Council Workshop on Women and Employment Legislation in Pakistan 11-13 February 1993.' Islamabad.

Chew, L. (2003). 'Discussion Paper for Programme Consultation Meeting on the Protection of Domestic Workers against the Threat of Forced Labour and Trafficking.' Prepared for

Anti-Slavery International in cooperation with the ILO's Special Action Programme to Combat Forced Labour.

Chhachhi, A. et al. (1997). 'Mediating Macro and the Micro: Industrial Restructuring and Women Workers Lives.' Paper presented at the seminar on 'Policies and Strategies for Working Women in the Context of Industrial Restructuring.' 22-25 Sept 1997. Jamia Hamdard University. New Delhi.

Chigateri, S. (2004). 'Uncovering Injustice: Towards a Dalit Feminist Politics in Bangalore.' PhD Thesis. Department of Sociology, University of Warwick.

Ebery, M. and Preston, B. (1976). 'Domestic Service in Late Victorian and Edwardian England 1871-1914'. *Reading Geographical Papers*, Reading University, Department of Geography.

Human Rights Watch (2005). 'Maid to Order: Ending Abuse against Migrant Domestic Workers in Singapore.' New York: Human Rights Watch.

Imran, I. (2003). 'Legal Injustices: The Zina Hudood Ordinance of Pakistan and its Implications for Women.' Master's Thesis. Department of Women Studies, Simon Fraser University, British Columbia, Canada.

Interagency Gender and Development Group in Pakistan. (1998). 'Women's Rights in Pakistan—Next Steps Forward.' Report on Human Rights Day Seminar. Islamabad. Pakistan.

Khan, N.S. (1986). 'Women's Involvement in the Industrial Sector in Punjab-Status and Prospectus.' Lahore: ASR Publications.

Khan, N.S. (1989). 'Setting the Record Straight-Women Workers in Pakistan.' Lahore: ASR Publications.

Khan, S. (1997). 'An Assessment of Changes in the Employment Situation of Pakistani Women in the Informal Sector.' In Sabur, G. (ed.), *The Informal Sector of Pakistan: Problems and Policies.* Islamabad: Friedrich Ebert Stiftung.

Khan, S.R. and Aftab, S. (1995). 'Structural Adjustment, Labour and the Poor in Pakistan.' Pakistan: Sustainable Development Policy Institute.

Khattak, S. and Sayeed, A. (2000). 'Subcontracted Women Workers in the World Economy: The Case of Pakistan.' Islamabad: Sustainable Development Policy Institute.

Khattak, S. and Sayeed, A. (2001). 'Women's Work and Empowerment Issues in an Era of Economic Liberation.' Karachi: PILER.

Khattak, S.G. and Sayeed, A. (2000). 'Subcontracted Women Workers in the World Economy: The Case of Pakistan.' Islamabad: Sustainable Development Policy Institute.

Lawyers for Human Rights and Legal Aid (LHRLA). (2003). 'Report on National Consultation on Domestic Workers Rights.' 2-3 Sept 2003, Karachi: Pakistan, organised by LHRLA.

Legislative Watch. (2001). 'Possible Election Modalities.' No. 15-16. Islamabad: Aurat Foundation.

Legislative Watch. (2001). 'History of Women's Reserved Seats in Legislatures in Pakistan.' Islamabad: Aurat Foundation.

Mahbub ul Haq Human Development Centre. (2001). 'Human Development in South Asia 2000: The Gender Question.' Islamabad: Oxford University Press.

Mahbub ul Haq Human Development Centre. (2004). 'Human Development in South Asia 2003: The Employment Challenge.' Islamabad: Oxford University Press.

Mangi, M.H. (2003). 'Child Domestic Workers Legislation and Policies: National Consultation on Domestic Worker's Rights.' Karachi: LHRLA.

Mirza, N. (2000). 'Women's Participation in Local Government Elections 2000-2001.' Islamabad: Aurat Publication and Information Service Foundation.

Mullaly, S. (1994). 'Women and Employment Legislation in Pakistan: A Review.' Report presented to the British Council.

Parveen, F. (1996). 'Report on Cloth Code Campaign.' Karachi: Pakistan Institute of Labour, Education, and Research.

Peterson, H. 'On Women and Legal Reforms.' EUI Working Paper Law No. 94/8 European University Institute, Florence.

PILDAD. (2002). 'Women Representation in Parliament: Strengthening National and Provincial Legislative Governance in Pakistan.' A Project of Pakistan Legislative Strengthening Consortium (PLSC).

Raghuram, P. (1993). Coping Strategies of Domestic Workers: A Study of Three Settlements in Delhi Metropolitan Region, India. PhD Thesis. Department of Geography, New Castle Upon Tyne.

Ramirez-Machado, J.M. (2000). 'Domestic Work, Conditions of Work and Employment: a Legal Perspective.' Unpublished draft manuscript. Geneva: International Labour Organization, Conditions of Work Branch.

Reyes, S.L. (2002). 'Quotas for Women for Legislative Seats at the Local Level in Pakistan.' International IDEA, 2002, Women in Parliament, Stockholm. http://www.idea.int. This is an English translation of Socorro Reyes, Wan Azizah, 'Kuota Kursi Legislatif Tingkat Lokal bagi Kaum Perempuan di Pakistan,' in International IDEA, Perempuan di Parlemen: Bukan Sekedar Jumlah, Stockholm: International IDEA.

Sanjek, R. and Colen, S. (1990). 'At Work in Homes: Household Workers in World Perspective.' *American Ethnological Society Monograph Series.* No. 3.

Sattar, Z. and Kazi, S. (1997). 'Women's Autonomy, Livelihood and Fertility: A Case of Rural Punjab.' Islamabad: Pakistan Institute of Development Economics.

Sayeed A. and Ali, K. (1999). 'Labour Policies and Institutions: A Framework for Social Dialogue.' Karachi: PILER.

Shaheed, F. (2001). 'Constructing Identities: Culture, Women's Agency and the Muslim World.' Women Living under Muslim Laws Dossier 23-24.

Shahid, A. and Arif, K. (2001-2002). 'Women's Labour Legislation in NWFP: A Case Study of Women Industrial Workers in Peshawar District.' Research Project, Faculty of Law, University of Peshawar.

Sverdrup, T. (1990). 'Employees in Private Homes.' Working Papers in Women's Law (No. 33), Institute of Women's Law, University of Oslo, Norway.

Taj, F. (2004). *Policing in Purdah: Women and Women Police Station in Peshawar, NWFP.* M.Phil Thesis. Center for Women's and Gender Research, University of Bergen Norway.

UNDP. (2003). 'Human Development Report 2003'. New York: Oxford University Press.

WLUML Report. (1995). 'Women's Law Initiatives in the Muslim World.' *Discussions from the International Meeting, Towards Beijing: Women, Law and Status in the Muslim World.* Lahore: WLUML.

Web Sources

Ali, S.S. '(Re)Claiming Our Histories: A Reflection on Women, Islam and Human Rights in Contemporary Muslim Communities.' Paper for Human Rights Day, 10 December 2003. Islamabad. Organized by INGAD. http://sachet.org.pk/home/gender_columns/webcolumn_26.asp

Alvi, H. 'Women in a Changing Society.' www.ourworld.compuserve.com/homepages/sangat/pakwomen.htm

Asian Development Bank Country Briefing Paper '*Women in Pakistan: A. Situational Analysis of Women in Pakistan*.' www.adb.org

Asian Development Bank (July 2002). 'Poverty in Pakistan: Issues, Causes, and Institutional Responses'. http://www.adb.org/documents/reports/poverty_pak/default.asp

Badran, M. 'Islamic Feminism: What's in a Name?' Al-Ahram Weekly Online. 17-23 Jan 2002. Issue Num 569. http://weekly.ahram.org.eg/2002/569/cu1.htm

Blackett, A. 'Making Domestic Work Visible: The Case for Specific Regulation.' ILO's Focus Programme on Social Dialogue, Labour Law and Labour Administration. Geneva: International Labour Organisation. http://www.ilo.org/public/english/dialogue/ifpdial/publ/infocus/domestic/html

Cox, R. 'The Servant Problem: A Return to Victorian Values'. http://www.socialistworker.co.uk/article.php?article_id=8423

Feeney, G. and Alam, I. 'Fertility, Population, Growth and Accuracy of Census Enumeration in Pakistan: 1961-1998.' http://www.gfeeney.com/pubs/2003-pakistan-fertility-2/2003-pakistan-fertility-2.pdf

Glenn, D. 'Who Owns Islamic Law?'. http://www.chronicle.com

Hasan, A. (2003). 'The Changing Nature of the Informal Sector in Karachi Due to Global Restructuring and Liberalization.' *The Journal*. http://www.nipa-khi.edu.pk/journal1.asp

Human Rights Commission of Pakistan. (2004). 'The State of Human Rights in Pakistan.' http://www.hrcp-web.org/ar_2004.cfm

Jhabvala, R. and Sinha, S. 'Liberalization and the Woman Worker.' Self Employed Women Association, Ahmad Abad, India. http://www.sewa.org/globalisation/pdf/Liberlization and Women Worker.pdf

Ladner, C. 'Westerner Feminists: Vanguards or Suppressors of Third World Women? www.wlu.ca/~wwwpolsc/facpages/abrown/CRP1Cladner.htm

Law and Justice Commission of Pakistan Annual Report 2002.' Government of Pakistan, Law and Justice Commission, Islamabad. www.lcpj.gov.uk/reports/annualreport-2002(final).htm

Ministry of Labour, Manpower and Overseas Pakistanis, Government of Pakistan. 'Labour Protection Policy 2005 (First Draft).' http://www.pakistan.gov.pk/divisions/labour-division/media/LPPolicyDraft020205.pdf

Naqvi, Z.F. and Shehnaz, L. 'How Do Women Decide to Work in Pakistan.' www.pide.org.pk/pdf/psde 18AGM/How Do Women Decide To Work In Pakistan.pdf

Piper, N. and Iredale, R. (2003). 'Identification of the Obstacles to the Signing and Ratification of the UN Convention on the Protection of the Rights of All Migrant Workers and Members of their Families.' http://www.unesco.org/most/apmrn_unconv.htm

Saigol, R. 'Structural Adjustment Programmes and their Effect on Women Workers—Collusion of Patriarchy and Capitalism.' Paper presented at Regional Conference on 'Impact of Economic Globalization on Women's Work & Empowerment Issues. 22-23 November 2006. Best Western Hotel, Islamabad. http://wmt.actionaid.org/wmt/pakistan/images/regionalconfernercedoc.pdf

Satterwaite, M.L. (2005). 'Crossing Borders Claiming Rights: Using Human Rights Law to Empower Women Migrant Workers.' *Yale Human Rights and Development Law Journal*. Vol. 8, No. 1. www.westlaw.uk

Siddique, R. and Hamid, S. 'Gender and Adjustment Policies: Evidence from Pakistan.' http://www.idrc.ca/en/ev-58038-201-1-DO_TOPIC.html

Miscellaneous

Cowasjee, A. 'Blackened Man, Blackened Woman.' Pakistan. 9 March 2003. *The Dawn.*

ILO. 'Women Face Hostile Conditions at Workplaces in Asia.' Pakistan. 3 October 2001. *The Dawn.*

Kannangara, A. 'Domestic Workers' Desk Opened.' Sri Lanka. 10 August 2001. *Daily News.*

Khan, O.A. 'When Women Speak Out in Pakistan.' Pakistan. 22 October 1999. *The News.*

Mahmood, N. 'Labour Reforms Top Priority of Government, says Minister.' Pakistan. 19 February 2002. *The News.*

Index